The *Art* of Stating the *Obvious*

REG HENRY

Copyright © 2026 by Reg Henry.

All rights reserved. No part of this publication may be reproduced, distributed, or transmitted in any form or by any electronic or mechanical means, including information storage and retrieval systems, without a prior written permission from the publisher, except by reviewers, who may quote brief passages in a review, and certain other noncommercial uses permitted by the copyright law.

Library of Congress Control Number: 2025920287

ISBN: 979-8-89228-804-0   (Paperback)
ISBN: 979-8-90252-091-7   (Hardcover)
ISBN: 979-8-89228-805-7   (eBook)

Printed in the United States of America

Contents

Chapter 1

In the End

"The great question is whether life is a comedy or a tragedy. If you have just lost a loved one, you will certainly not see the joke, but that all our efforts seem for nothing is a joke on a cosmic scale. And what do we instinctively say when tragedy strikes? 'Are you kidding me?' That is the right question." Duffer's speech at the Mulgabimbi Post Hotel, 1971.

In the modern way of things, the word got around that Robert "Duffer" O'Grady had died. Someone emailed someone else, or they texted, and somebody put the bad news on social media. He had been a character like no other. In fact, his stated profession was Pub Philosopher, a description that baffled government tax officials in three countries.

A memorial was planned. The number of people who actually thought he was a great and funny man had dwindled since he had mysteriously gone silent, but the remnant remained faithful to his memory. The Celebration of Life was to be held in the saloon where he once held court in Monterey, California. The man who wouldn't be caught dead at a social event was now having one put on to mark his passing.

Who had arranged this event was unknown, probably his flamboyant partner, Kitty. All his fans knew was that Duffer had died, apparently in some sort of fishing accident up north. The source of the news was as unclear as the circumstances of his death. The meager facts made the announcement all the more stunning, coming like a roll of thunder out of a clear sky, or a politician telling an unfavorable truth about himself. Even people who thought he had died already were taken aback.

"So he's dead then. Who would have thought it?"

"Well, he was overweight, he smoked and drank a lot, and liked bacon. And for lunch he'd eat french fry sandwiches."

"Yes, that's true, but a guy like that, he seemed larger than life. He spoke eternal truths. You'd think he would live for an eternity. He was a real wise guy, not in the sense that he was a smart ass, but someone who made humorous remarks that really were wise."

A pause would follow for contemplation.

"All I know is that he will be missed."

"Missed, yes." Then another pause while the speakers silently figured out when they had last seen him, even thought about him. Was it a year ago, two years ago? When exactly had Duffer gone away to find himself?

"So when is the Celebration of Life?"

"Next Saturday. You going?"

"Dunno. I'll see what's up. I'm not much for funerals. I like to celebrate people when they are alive."

This is the standard excuse of people who don't want to go to the trouble of going to a funeral, who want to rationalize their laziness, who don't understand that funerals or celebrations of life are not solely about the dead person, but as much about the people left behind by the loss, the survivors who have to reaffirm their humanity and make peace with their grief.

When next Saturday came around, about fifty people put aside whatever reservations they may have had about life, death, and appropriately timed celebrations and gathered in the Pink Otter Cocktail Lounge in New Monterey, California, a former tiki bar not far from Cannery Row, to pay tribute to this man who had made his name telling funny stories in pubs and clubs when he wasn't being an assistant college professor or toiling in some of his other unlikely occupations, bank teller, soldier, farm laborer, and postman. Some even wore the prosthetic beer bellies that were once the signature artifact identifying fans of the great man when he was briefly considered great.

It was a relatively large gathering, given that Duffer O'Grady had perhaps exhausted his Andy Warhol allotment of ten minutes of fame. Some of them even looked sad, but not everyone.

There was a big older guy wearing a hoodie who was surveying the scene with a little smile. He seemed a mysterious presence, maybe even sinister. When he first arrived in the bar, Kitty put her hand to her mouth, an unwitting gesture of anxiety that went unnoticed by others.

She had her reasons to be concerned. She knew why Duffer had stopped his performances. It wasn't to find himself; it was to protect her and her son. While Duffer had his fans, he also had his enemies, as anybody who boldly speaks out does. And who was this who had come to a funeral-like event in a hoodie? This was funky California, but still it was strange.

Despite the fair attendance, it turned out that there was a lack of competent witnesses who could coherently explain what anybody should celebrate at this Celebration of Life.

Worse yet, nobody seemed to be in charge, so the people just milled about, enjoying a little too much the exotic cocktails that the

Pink Otter Cocktail Lounge specialized in. Although Kitty was there, dressed in black, as she had been known to do anyway, nobody expected her to lead the proceedings in her grief. She was a performance artist, a mother, and an inventor, but today she seemed determined only to be a widow.

Finally, Joanna Bishop, the lady who owned and ran the bar, shouted out in her best sergeant major voice, "Listen up, people, we need to raise a glass to Duffer, who touched us all in different ways." Joanna was a close friend of Duffer's and Kitty's from the moment when they came to California, and she had agreed to let her bar be a venue for his speaking performances on Sunday afternoons. It turned out to be the perfect place for him. The bar's patrons were a colorful collection of eccentrics, weirdos, poseurs, and oddballs who did justice to the memory of the assorted characters who in times past had famously inhabited nearby Cannery Row.

The toast part of the remembrance went well. As you might expect, the members of the crowd were proficient drinkers, and there were shouts of "Here's to you, Duff," "Thanks, old man," "You touched me, Duffer, usually for a loan," "You were Aussie awesome, old boy!"

But things broke down a bit after that. The crowd fell awkwardly silent as people sorted their unfocused memories and emotions. As no one was designated to make a formal speech of remembrance, Joanna now invited people from the crowd to make impromptu remarks. "Those of you with memories of Duffer, please come up to the front and share them with us."

A few came up. "He was the funniest guy I ever saw," the first said. The crowd waited for the jokes and anecdotes to follow. "How so?" someone said at last. "I can't remember any of his lines, but he was really funny," the speaker said. And so it went on for a while, one unsatisfying testimony after another. The hooded guy, not smiling anymore, stayed silent on the fringes.

A portly man, looking very ordinary in gray office pants and a white collared shirt, took the microphone and said, "Hi, I'm Dave. What I liked about Duffer is that he didn't look like a celebrity or someone famous. He looked like an ordinary person like myself, maybe not as good-looking," he stopped to smile here, but everyone still wondered if he was being serious.

"I think that was a great advantage for him. He was that guy who sits unnoticed on the sidelines, seemingly just a spectator of life, but taking everything in and making mental notes to himself to use later in his little speeches.

"I remember him once saying, and maybe it was a joke, that he attended an Ordinary Persons Ball, and the other ordinary guests nudged each other, pointed in his direction, and said, 'Who is that ordinary-looking guy over there?'

"I think he was a different sort of VIP, a Very Inconspicuous Person. His gift was being an amazing speaker despite looking like a loser," the ordinary man said. Then he sat down, wondering if he had overdone the praise.

Then an older, gray-haired woman wearing a dowdy brown suit and carrying a handbag that seemed large enough to contain an old-fashioned phone book stepped out of the audience to make the most coherent remarks of the afternoon. Unlike all the others, she gave the impression of having known Duffer personally. Was she some sort of relative? That was anybody's guess. Her accent was hard to place. She spoke in a deep voice that fluttered to a higher pitch at times.

"Duffer didn't have any answers to life's great questions," the strange lady said. "What he did was ask the questions in a funny way so that people might think about them. Everybody, he thought, shared in the greater knowledge of the human race. We live individual lives, but our immortality lies in the sum of our shared experiences, the wisdom that grows out of them. He was a great one for living life to the full so that he could learn more from his experiences."

The drinkers looked down at their bellies and collectively had a thought, *yeah, but Duffer would have said it more amusingly.*

His friends and family back in Australia might have agreed with this observation, but they weren't in Monterey for the Celebration of Life for the simple reason that they had not yet been told that Duffer had died. His ex-wife, known to all as the "Long-Suffering Sheila," did not know, neither did his annoying brother, George, nor his sister, Margaret, who everybody called the Brains of the Operation, the one who had helped him become sort of famous. What stories they could have told. How sad.

If his best friend Wombat had been there, he would have found the event very odd. He knew, as apparently nobody else did, that Duffer himself was very conservative when it came to funeral arrangements. He wanted to be seen dead. He wanted an old-fashioned viewing with an open casket when he died, so that everybody could make peace with his passing, the better to kick-start the stages of grief, which, as Duffer understood them, were shock, tears, drinking, and sorting through the legal papers. He wanted people to become so used to the fact of his death that they would crowd around the casket, have a jolly time, and, in the time-honored way, remark, "I have never seen him look better."

Wombat knew that Duffer only started to think like this because of his stay in Pittsburgh, Pennsylvania, where he first lived when he came to America, before he moved to California. They love a good viewing in Pittsburgh, Duffer used to say, and he was impressed with the wisdom of it, being of the any-excuse-for-a-party way of thinking.

Yes, it may have been a better party if his Aussie friends and relatives had attended, but the locals in Monterey tried their hardest to have a good time and smile bravely through their tears. Some smiled more than they cried, and this led to a jarring note at the end of the afternoon. Dave, the ordinary man, the one who had briefly spoken and was by now obviously overserved, lurched up to Kitty, who was standing next to the gray-haired lady who also had spoken earlier, and said in a slurred voice, "I don't think Duffer is dead!"

"What the heck?" Kitty said angrily, and gave the ordinary jerk an atomic-grade stare that should have evaporated the man on the spot.

"I think he's faking it!" Dave said, oblivious to all social clues that this wasn't the most consoling thing to say at a funeral celebration. Then he lurched off to the exit before the now glowering gray-haired lady had the chance to slap him in the head.

Chapter 2

The News Spreads Slowly

"Did space aliens make our world and are we now their entertainment? Do they have a good laugh at our expense? No. I'd be more surprised if they had a sense of humor than if they could fly faster than the speed of light. Only suffering humanity can get the joke." Duffer at the New Age Church for Optimistic Eternal Outcomes, Sydney, 1972.

The news was slow in reaching Australia. Duffer's sister, Margaret O'Grady, was called in Melbourne by their older brother, George, in Brisbane to say that Duffer had died back in California.

"Duffer is dead? He can't be dead. I got a late Christmas card from him just a few months ago."

"I assure you that our brother Robert is dead. I got a call from a Courier-Mail reporter asking for a comment. Apparently there was an Associated Press story in America at the time."

"What happened to him?"

"It seems he went fishing off some rocks in Northern California and was lost in the ocean after a rogue wave hit him. The details were a bit vague, though it did say some sort of service was held in Monterey back in February."

"How come his family in Australia is just finding out now in April?" asked Margaret.

"I don't know. Maybe he was sort of forgotten. He had gone off the boil a bit in terms of his popularity," he paused and added a qualifier to the word popularity, "his notoriety."

"So what did you tell the Courier?"

"That Robert will be missed by his family and friends. That he had an unusual talent. A short story came out this morning, and I was quoted."

To Margaret's ear, it seemed George was rather pleased to have been quoted.

Another pause and a rustling of paper, then, George proceeded to read the story, starting with the headline, which he spoke slowly with obvious disdain.

'Duffer' Dies in USA

Controversial Brisbane-born pub philosopher and author Robert 'Duffer' O'Grady has died in the United States at the age of 64. He reportedly drowned in January when he was swept away by a freak wave while fishing in Northern California.

Starting in the 1970s, O'Grady won media attention and a rabid following by delivering so-called "suds sermons" to drinkers in the backrooms of hotels, first in Mulgabimbi, NSW, then Brisbane and Sydney. He said his jokes and stories were based on experiences as a Vietnam veteran and Post Office employee.

O'Grady took his act to England in 1973, where his fans wore false beer bellies and put on T-shirts adorned with the words "We Can't Get Enuff of Duff." He also wrote several books. Later he moved to America, where he also established a following.

According to an Associated Press report from Monterey, California, where he had retired, fans wearing prosthetic beer guts held a remembrance service in March at a local cocktail lounge.

His older brother, George O'Grady Sr., a St. Lucia resident and chief accountant for Brisbane-based Colossal Coal Pty. Ltd., said yesterday, "We will all miss Robert (Duffer). He was a man of different talents, bank teller, army private, postman, college lecturer, and sort of an entertainer."

He is also survived by his California partner, Kitty Giordano, stepson Benny, and his sister, Margaret Witherspoon O'Grady, of Melbourne. No services in Australia are planned.

"Not exactly a fulsome description of his talents. A sort of entertainer, really?"

"Well, he was sort of an entertainer. That's a fact. What else could I call him?"

"Well, you could have called him Duffer, for one thing, like everybody else did. Instead, you insisted on calling him Robert, a name his fans would be surprised to know he had."

"Dad never called him that. Besides, Duffer is a ridiculous nickname. A duffer, as you well know, is a person who is lousy at golf or else is a doddering old fella. Robert didn't play golf, and he wasn't particularly old, although he might have doddered some after a night on the booze."

"It was his nickname, for goodness sake. Australia is full of people with nicknames that often make no sense. This is a place where red-haired men are called Bluey and where tall men are called Tiny. Who knows where Duffer came from?"

"His nickname was childish and demeaning to our family," George offered as a parting shot.

"I don't know," Margaret countered. "He is the only mildly famous person ever known in the history of this family. I know it spoils it a bit that his fans walked around with fake beer guts. But demeaning? I say marketable. If he had been known as Robert, I can tell you that he would never have been known at all."

When Margaret spoke of Duffer's marketability, she knew what she was talking about. If your client is a goofy person, it helps that he or she has a goofy name in order for the public to become interested. But a goofy name is not enough. Without Margaret's efforts to promote Duffer, he would have enjoyed well-deserved obscurity on every continent, instead of being a curiosity on at least three.

The wonder of it was that Duffer became even mildly famous. He did indeed look like an ordinary person, although not every ordinary person has a friend named for a marsupial.

It was his old army mate Bill "Wombat" Berrigan who first explained to Margaret that being naturally inconspicuous was Duffer's super power. People constantly underestimated him. Only when he stood in front of a microphone did he transform into an unlikely something else, the center of attention, and all that he had noticed while not being noticed was suddenly revealed.

Still, timing was everything in his ascent to modest prominence. It wasn't until the infancy of the internet that he really got going, despite his many previous speaking gigs in pubs and clubs. In the old days of newspapers and TV sets with rabbit ears, before everybody was heads down and tails up, stooped over their iPhones, encouraging evolution to develop their thumbs into lobster claws, the market for strange characters and views was somewhat limited.

When this amazing new medium of expression and communication came along, he was ready. Like the surfer he had once been, and with the help of his sister Margaret, always the entrepreneurial one, Duffer caught the breaking wave of the World Wide Web. Margaret encouraged him to start blogging, and in the end he was also making podcasts.

Yes, she reminded herself, she was the one who had made him what he was. *Did she ever get any thanks? None, zilch, nada,* she thought, *well, OK, some, but not enough.*

"Yes, sir," she now said aloud to the wandering ghost of Duffer strolling through her memory, "if you had only listened to me more, you would have been truly famous. I said that you needed to learn the guitar if you wanted to have your message remembered. But you said you couldn't carry a tune in a suitcase. Heck, I would have bought you a guitar and a suitcase, and I would have followed you to America and been your agent there. But, no, you had to play silly buggers, leaving me no choice but to go back home."

If Margaret was being honest with herself, she might have said that the real reason she didn't go to America was that she wanted to stay in England with Colin Witherspoon, an accountant she had met in London. Colin didn't want to go to America because he didn't much care for the sort of football over there, and he thought someone would shoot him for not liking it, which he believed happened all the time in that gun-crazy nation.

Margaret eventually married Colin Witherspoon and took him back to Australia. She decided to keep her own last name and vowed to stay with him as long as nothing else about him withered. They settled in Melbourne, which was a good choice because the city is famous for having four climates in a day, in other words, it can be just like England, or at least Brisbane people think so, as they know only two sorts of climates, hot and wet and hot and dry. Colin, not one for exaggerated emotions, was quietly happy that his sort of football was available locally and that he was never shot at, although Margaret might have been tempted at times had guns been readily available.

Quiet people can be just as irritating as talkative people in their own way.

Duffer had let her know a year before that he was retiring from the pontificating business, but she was still mad about that, and she had hoped he might change his mind.

"Well, it's completely over," she said to herself in a resigned voice. "Elvis has died, and the hunk-a-hunk of burning love has died with him."

That was when the great idea came to her. The love didn't stop with Elvis's death, she was suddenly reminded, it grew and grew, and some fans refused, against all the evidence, to believe he had died. And as the love went on, so did the royalties to the dead man's relatives.

Why, all that was required for such a controversy to be brought to the boil was a cup of celebrity mixed in a bowl of mysterious circumstances. Margaret could almost taste the marketing opportunity.

Why couldn't Duffer join the post-mortem hall of enduring fame? Margaret thought. True, Duffer was not as well-known as some, but he had certainly died mysteriously, and what was unexplained could easily be filled in with an interesting narrative full of tantalizing questions thought up by herself.

But she realized that she had to know a few more details about Duffer's demise for the story to sound vaguely plausible. For an instant, she thought of calling her brother George back. She quickly decided that George would be no help, he didn't have any more information, and he wouldn't support her in any project to keep Duffer's name alive, especially by promoting the notion that Duffer might still be in the land of the living.

Then she thought of Duffer's best mate Wombat, who had not only served with him in Vietnam but also had witnessed his first efforts at public philosophizing in Australia and was later in England with him. Wombat was an enterprising bloke, he could find out what happened.

Wombat, real name William, was a cinematographer, a skill he had learned in the army. While they were all together in England, Margaret convinced Wombat to make a documentary about Duffer, who by then was becoming well known around the local pubs as a curious comedian.

Wombat started to film Duffer as he did his act. This footage was to provide a rare record of what Duffer said and how he said it, but the documentary was never completed, due largely to the fact that Duffer unexpectedly left England for America. To his lasting regret, Wombat did not follow him. He had met a Swedish girl named Malena, who was as unlikely a siren on the rocks as Colin had been a natural partner for Margaret, and they too had settled in Melbourne.

Margaret now called him on the phone. "Hello, Wombat," she said when he answered.

"Margaret, is that you?"

"Yes, and sorry to bother you with very bad news, but we have heard that Duffer died in America."

"Crikey!" Wombat said slowly and sadly. "I can't believe it."

"Well, that's the thing. The details are murky, and part of me doesn't believe it either, but I am wondering if you could look into it. I know you are busy, but maybe you could take a vacation over there sometime and get to the bottom of it."

In the background, the voice of Malena could be heard, "Who's on the phone, dahling?"

Wombat half whispered, "The Brains of the Operation!"

Although she realized something serious had happened, Malena couldn't hear much of what Margaret was saying, but she did hear her husband say, "Has the Long-Suffering Sheila been told?"

Chapter 3

The Long-Suffering Sheila

"Love is like musical chairs. You pick a partner, you sashay around your partner and then other people's partners, and then the music stops and you find your partner." A voice interjected. "No, mate, that's square dancing." Duffer went on, "As I was saying, love is like square dancing." Duffer speaking to the Mulgabimbi Bush Balladeers, 1972.

Margaret did decide later that it was only fair to call Duffer's ex-wife and tell her that he was deceased. She wouldn't be heartbroken to hear this, she wasn't known as the Long-Suffering Sheila for nothing, but she might be curious. She was there soon after Duffer first stood in front of a microphone.

Margaret still had her phone number from all those years ago. "Hello," Sheila answered, with a slight hint of a cocktail-hour slur.

"Hi, Sheila," said Margaret, not knowing whether to be perky or serious and wishing she had a glass of wine to help her decide, but it was only two o'clock in the afternoon. "It's me, Margaret O'Grady. I am calling with some bad news." She corrected herself, rethinking the definition of bad from Sheila's perspective. "Well, some news anyway. Duffer died."

"He did? That's strange. When? Where?"

"A couple of months ago. In California. They had a Celebration of Life service for him in Monterey."

"Aw, sorry, I missed it," said the un-sorry Sheila, "I could have provided a brooding silence at the celebrating part. Or I could have scrunched up paper napkins and thrown them into the urn with the ashes. What did he die of anyway?"

"The details are a bit unclear. Something about a fishing accident with a freak wave, but I wonder whether he just had a heart attack while he was fishing. As we all know, he wasn't Mr. Health and Fitness. We only just found out."

"Well, that does sound right. Sketchy in life, sketchy in death, and the important details forgotten."

"Well," Margaret said, "I thought I should tell you, and I was hoping perhaps it might bring some closure for you."

"I do thank you for calling," Sheila said, "but closure, really? Why do people always go on about closure when people die? It's curtains for the dead people, of course, but the only closure I ever enjoyed was the backdoor slamming when I left Duffer years ago. When the skunk squirts your clothes, and finally you get them clean, is that closure? When someone gets up your nose, the smell stays in your memory forever, or so I reckon. I don't owe him anything. He owed me for my support in making him sort of famous."

Sheila was a bit harsh on the concept of closure, even for someone notoriously long-suffering and not known for her delicate feelings. She was also harsh on Duffer, who was more koala-like than skunk-like.

Duffer had met his wife-to-be, who later became his wife not-to-be-anymore, at a pub in New South Wales. Of course, he did. The Long-Suffering Sheila had gone to the Mulgabimbi Post Hotel to have a drink with Nancy, a friend from the hospital where they both worked as nurses. Nancy said that she had heard that there was a bloke who made funny little speeches at the pub and he was going to be there tonight. She didn't understand that they would be attending a poetry reading.

So they took their drinks and found some vacant fold-up chairs, which were in plentiful supply in the back room. The sparse crowd was not spoiled by expensive décor. It was relatively small and dark in the room, despite the efforts of a few gallant lightbulbs hiding under frilly shades.

The Mulgabimbi Historical Society met there Monday nights, the Country Women's Association on Tuesdays, and the Western Region Cricket Umpires on Wednesdays, at least until one of their members misplaced his thick eyeglasses and tripped in the gloom over the ragged carpet. Alcoholics Anonymous had considered the room in the pub for the Thursday meetings but thought better of it. This spot was grabbed by the Mulgabimbi Bush Balladeers, otherwise known to the locals in the town as the Poetry Pud Pullers.

The Poetry Pud Pullers sort of did what the name suggests. Well, they didn't act out the vulgar part of the name, as far as it was authoritatively known, but they did write poetry and they gathered on Thursday nights to inflict their poems on each other in the name of Culture and Art.

Sometimes an addled drinker, there being no other type towards the end of the week, would poke his head into the room by mistake and make wise-arse comments. As it happened, though, the beefy local constable was a poet himself and attended the meetings. One look at him and his fist of a face and the interloper would leave at once, fearing that he would be charged with threatening iambic pentameter in a public place.

Had T.S. Eliot wandered through the bar of the Mulgabimbi Post Hotel and back into poets' corner, he would have thought his own Waste Land a darn nice place by comparison. Dylan Thomas would definitely have stayed in the bar.

The poetry heard at the pub was very sincere, penned as it was by honest, straightforward men and women with the hearts of true poets but none of the necessary ability. Most of the poems had common features, they all rhymed and they were all horrible, the haikus didn't rhyme but they were horrible, too. They had titles like "The Bullock's Last Feed" and "Mum's New Dress," the constable was quite a hit with his sonnet, "Copping It Sweet." For anyone with any literary taste to hear these poems was to be caught in a mental state somewhere between laughter and tears.

As poetry was the one thing that people never associated with Duffer, it may seem odd that he made his first performances at a poetry reading. In fact, while he was not a poet, he appreciated poetry, though his taste ran to the more traditional poets, Keats, Shelley, Byron, Wordsworth, the greats that every boy at the Brisbane Boys Academy had to learn in that era.

His father had hoped that sending Duffer to a prestigious private grammar school instead of the local state high school might give him a bit of polish so that he wouldn't grow up to be a bludger. In later years, his dad was not consoled that his son had grown up to be a slightly polished bludger who had no actual talent except babbling to characters who were similarly hopeless. Case in point, making a spectacle of himself before the Poetry Pud Pullers in Mulgabimbi, New South Wales.

The poets were glad to have him. They were glad to have anyone take an interest. They did notice that when he first came and asked politely to speak, it was like a Quaker meeting where people could speak in turn when the spirit of poetry came upon them, he did not deliver a poem that rhymed, which was quite shocking to the audience.

"Yeah, mate," he said later when he was questioned about it, "I do prose poems."

"Ah," someone said, "We have heard of them. Very good then." And they all nodded. After all, they didn't want to be the poetry police who would stop someone and take his poetic license away. Presumably the constable would do that anyway.

All they knew was that these prose poems were funny, entertaining, insightful, and easier to listen to than Mr. Briggs' thirty-minute epic on milking cows in sprung rhythm. Duffer became a regular at the end of the meeting, by which time everybody was desperate for a laugh, especially as they were poets, doomed to think deeply about this sad old world and capture it in couplets.

Sheila and Nancy came in while the last of the dreary conventional poets were declaiming, and it was all rhyme and no reason as far as the girls could tell. Sheila leaned over to Nancy and said in her best attempt at a whisper, which was really more like a hog caller's lament, "Nance, let's get the bloody hell out of here."

"Wait a sec, Sheila, the guy who makes the funny speeches is standing over there ready to come on."

And, yes, she looked over now and saw him for the first time. If a recording angel chronicles our mortal days, the one assigned to Sheila was now writing with a golden quill in the Book of Life, "This was the moment when the long sufferings of Sheila Megan Flaherty began."

There is love at first sight and then there is the sort of love that takes its time to subvert the victim's emotional defenses, like water eroding a rock with every breaking wave over a long time. This was more like what happened to Sheila. If she were a martini, she was shaken, not stirred, but the drink tasted good as it went down. On that night, the more Duffer did his little prose poem that wasn't, the more she was intrigued and entertained.

It is important to note that this was before Duffer became a physical ruin of a man. The seed of a beer gut was surely in his flat stomach and he was irrigating it one glass at a time, but it had not yet flowered into the full human belly pumpkin. He was just out of the army and a tour of Vietnam and had come down from Brisbane to stay on his Uncle Frank's property outside Mulgabimbi while he sorted out what he was going to do with the rest of his life, other than drink beer. He had previously worked in a bank, but the prospect of that seemed boring after Vietnam. For the moment, he was happy to help Uncle Frank with the farm work.

When Duffer first saw Sheila, he needed no slow dance for love to develop its all-encompassing tentacles. He was smitten.

Sheila was then in her prime. She had light brown hair, blue eyes, a cute nose, and a shapely figure, but her overall appearance did not quite live up to the sum of its attractive parts. Her manner was too blunt, the cast of her face was set too hard, and when she smiled it seemed a little forced, as if her mouth was taking a holiday from the stern business of dealing with a world of idiots. She was smart with a quick wit, but she was loud, too, and she was no-nonsense in her views and showed no restraint in expressing them.

Duffer, the supposed budding prophet of human wisdom, could not see her character for her cleavage, admittedly a common failing in the male of the species. But what did they have in common to be attracted to each other? They were both of Irish descent and were nominally Catholic, but the call of the blood seems the least likely explanation of their mutual attraction. They both liked to drink and party and talk, activities that nicely dovetailed.

But really they were as different as chalk and cheese, living proof of the theory that opposites attract. Duffer was the quiet observer with romantic notions, shy in all social situations except oddly in front of a microphone when he became a performer, and Sheila was the outgoing, voluble one who was practical-minded, unsentimental, and therefore basically unromantic.

Yet Sheila was never solely to blame for bringing the long suffering down on herself. It takes two to tango and two to stop stepping on each other's toes and stop tangoing. Duffer was irritating enough in his own way to make the marital going tough. No, her main mistake was the one common to much of the female gender throughout the ages, she thought she could train her partner to be less irritating.

It's easy to say now, of course, but they should never have married. Yet six months later, having said their vows at the local registry office, with Nancy standing as a bridesmaid, they gathered at the same pub, the Mulgabimbi Post Hotel, for their reception.

Still shocked that a lively, pretty woman actually seemed impressed by him, and before she could change her mind, Duffer had proposed the first night they met. She didn't accept immediately but decided to wait and see. After all, he was still working on his uncle's farm and he didn't look like he could ever support a family. Then he applied for a permanent job with the Post Office and marrying him seemed a more realistic proposition. Love will find a way, but a paycheck can be of assistance.

The wedding was relatively small. Sheila's mother and father were the only relatives on her side of the family who came. Various aunts and uncles made their excuses, pleading that they could not come on such short notice.

Duffer's parents came, as did his Uncle Frank, whose offer of employment on the farm had brought Duffer to Mulgabimbi in the first place. His dad seemed more pleased to see his brother-in-law Frank than his son Duffer. Margaret was also there, and George Jr. was the best man and even then insisted on calling his brother by his real name, Robert, which was a surprise to everyone not in the family. These included half a dozen army mates, a few guys from school, and, of course, the Mulgabimbi Pud Pullers. Mr. Briggs, the farmer who viewed cows as muses, offered to read a poem especially written for the occasion, but his offer was kindly refused, as they had to be out of the hall by ten p.m. and it was already seven thirty.

So began the long sufferings of Sheila. She may have gotten the first inkling of them on her honeymoon. When she returned to Mulgabimbi after a week away, she had a chat with Nancy in the lunchroom at the hospital. "How was it on the honeymoon?" Nancy naturally asked.

"Oh, yeah, well great, except on the wedding night, he was rooting away and then he suddenly stops and asks me, 'How are things on your end of the penis?' Who in the world says that?"

"None of the fellas I know," Nancy said. "So what did you say?"

"I told him to get on with it because we had to get up early in the morning to catch the plane to Hayman Island."

Chapter 4

In the Beginning

"Several options are available to become a wise person. You can climb a mountain or move to a monastery to contemplate life. Or you can live a life full of travel and adventure and contemplate everything later, which is more fun." Duffer's speech to the Mulgabimbi Rotary Club, 1972.

After his wedding, having charmed a small group with his pretend prose poems, Duffer thought he might like to try his luck entertaining the regular patrons, so he approached the pub owner and told him he was a stand-up comedian and not a poet or an entertainer of poets, descriptions he knew would certainly cause a general audience to stampede to the exits.

The pub owner was not enthusiastic because he had hired an exotic dancer for the next open date. This being Mulgabimbi, the exotic dancer was not all that racy, but the pub owner knew that the blokes would be attracted anyway because blokes can't help themselves.

However, when the exotic dancer said she couldn't do the gig because she had misplaced her python, Duffer was called in as a substitute. Sheila stayed home that night because she had a shift at the hospital.

She didn't think she would miss much. It seemed to promise just the usual scene, ordinary people at a rundown pub in an Australian country town on a Friday night. They would want a drink and perhaps a bite to eat, but their deeper need was to keep boredom at bay in the company of fellow human sufferers.

But it turned out to be a memorable night for reasons farcical and consequential. This was the moment when Duffer really started out on his mission to answer the questions that most people had never thought to ask, and this by virtue of a dancer's python going AWOL.

As the people filed in, they saw an odd, disheveled young man adjusting the microphone to his height, which was in the medium range, not towering and not stubby. His clothes, casual and wrinkled, consisted of a faded Hawaiian shirt, khaki slacks, and sandals. He looked like he might have just wandered back from the public bar, which in fact was the case.

Actually, everybody had wandered back from the bar. They lined their drinks up on the tables and many talked and smoked, smoking being the custom then, before cool became the big chill courtesy of coughing and cancer, and the music from the disco next door went thump, thump, thump.

Somebody said, "Is this the venue for the lady with the python? I'd really like to see the python."

"No," someone said, "this is tonight's entertainment."

"What entertainment?"

"That fella over there!" And the person who knew pointed in the direction of the bloke adjusting the microphone. It was Duffer, of course, but most of the crowd didn't know him yet.

He was fairly lean, but his figure looked like it had the potential for middle-aged expansion. He had some reddish tints of sunburn on his face and arms, and his hair, apparently a stranger to any comb or stylist, grew in brownish clumps, mostly at the side of his head, like mullets that had lost their way. His round face had not stood very close to a razor in recent days, and stubble covered his chin.

"G'day," he said. This came out very loud, louder even than the thump, thump, thump of the music next door, as if the Almighty had come down and was making an unlikely appearance on open mic night, so the man leaned over and adjusted the amplifier.

"G'day," he said again, and this time the drinkers, startled in mid-swig by his first introduction, settled back in their chairs a little bit, in the hope that this odd man might sing a song or maybe the exotic dancer might find her snake at the last minute. No such luck.

"My name is Duffer O'Grady and I am here to tell you how I got so smart. If you follow my six-point plan, you too can know everything there is to know about life." Of course, he wasn't being serious, but nobody knew then that the man's talent was joking when he appeared serious and sometimes serious when he was joking.

He was greeted with guffaws and wolf whistles, and deservedly so. Some people immediately got up and left, because it sounded to them like a preliminary pitch for life insurance, but curiosity kept the others seated, that and the powerful force of inertia that works on the human butt once settled in a chair. The speaker seemed strangely pleased with this reaction and smiled back at what was left of the crowd.

"Hey, Duffer," one of the drinkers yelled, "how much is this six-point plan going to cost us?"

"Not a thing, but you can buy me a beer later."

His voice was projected at the right volume after he had fiddled with the apparatus, and the more those in the audience heard it, the more puzzled they became. Their eyes saw one thing, but their ears heard another.

Duffer looked like a real Ocker, the old slang word for a stereotypical Australian with vowels proudly immune to speech therapists, but the words coming out of his mouth seemed to the crowd vaguely modulated, even educated, as if he were really an announcer for the Australian Broadcasting Commission in an ingenious disguise. They did not know that while he was currently a farm laborer, he had applied for a position as a postman, a step up on the social ladder. He could hardly wait to say to people who thought he had barely attended school, "Hey, mate, I am a man of letters."

A woman in the audience, with very red hair, which seemed about as inflamed as her temper, now yelled out, "Hey, Duffo, or whatever your name is, why don't you just shut up and let us drink in peace?"

For Duffer, a female heckler was his worst nightmare. While in principle sympathetic to the unfair plight of women in a stupid male society, he was terrified of them in practice. Besides, he could tell a man to pull his head in, but it didn't seem right to tell that to a woman, especially as women spent so much money on hairdos. Duffer was one of nature's gentlemen, but he hadn't studied the finer points of how to look like a gentleman.

His only recourse was to joke his way out of this tight spot.

"Madam," he said, "there is no such thing as drinking in peace, unless you drink by yourself, which is a bit like having sex by yourself, it sort of misses the main point.

"Drinking is meant to be a social activity. It lubricates the tonsils and gets people talking, and when they talk they argue, and when they argue they drink some more. The only peace that drinkers have is to regularly get up and go to the toilet, and perhaps they are lucky enough to get a stall for their contemplative convenience. They also have to stand up after every few rounds and buy their fellow drinkers some more drinks, and there is a heck of an argument if they don't.

"No, there's no peace for drinkers. You could take an olive branch to a bar to make the peace, but someone would grab the olives and put them in their martini. Besides, if you want to tell me to shut up, you'll have to marry me so that you have the proper authority."

The crowd could not disagree with any of this, and they laughed despite their better judgment. Even the red-haired woman laughed, but not very much and only to be seen as a good sport.

When the uproar had subsided, Duffer said, "I think it's time to go on and tell you about the Six Steps to Wisdom and Understanding. Feel free to ask questions later. I don't want to do the individual to-and-fro of the Socratic method just yet."

"What the heck is the Socratic method?" asked a questioner from the back of the room, ignoring the suggestion to move on.

"Have you heard of Socrates?"

"Can't say I have. Did he play Rugby League for Manly?"

"No. Socrates is the name of the bouncer at this establishment. You don't want to know his method of dealing with troublesome patrons, so let me go and tell you a parable."

"OK, fair enough. I like a good parable as much as the next person."

"Well, once upon a time, there was a family who were so poor they could afford only one pair of underpants among the six of them and had to share." He then proceeded to tell a story that he said he heard first in the army. But his parable really was just a joke, one so old that the pharaohs may have told it, assuming that the pharaohs wore underpants, which history teachers in our schools have not made clear, which is a great pity, because their students might pay attention for once. (Suggested class assignment: Did the pharaohs walk like Egyptians because they were itchy?)

In later years, Duffer would only tell stories that he knew from his own experience, or else stories that he had heard from his mates and believed had at least a chance of being true, but on this occasion he was just telling a joke. He may have figured that the joke was so old that none of this mob would have heard it. He was probably right about that, because every face in that dreary back room was lit up with wonder by the absurd poignancy of the story.

To the few sensitive thinkers who felt that poor people with a shortage of underpants should not be made fun of, Duffer reassuringly explained that the dad in the family had long been out of a job and was going to an important job interview, and the battling dad was the one chosen by the family to wear the underpants that day,and that with his loins properly girded, he projected great confidence, and so he got the job, allowing the family to prosper and live happily ever after, with a big house, plenty of food on the table, and each with their own pair of underpants. If there was a punchline, it was long forgotten. This was a joke that was all in the telling, and Duffer was the man for the job.

How exactly this so-called parable illustrated the Six Steps to Wisdom and Understanding was not clear. Was it that what you hear and learn in military service can be instructive? Was it that a loyal family is the foundation for human growth? Was it that confidence is the key to success? Was it about never underestimating the power of the absurd? That self-sacrifice was key? Was it love?

As it happens, many of these themes were in Duffer's philosophy, and he was just about to explain this when the door suddenly was flung open, and one of the bartenders came in holding tickets in his right hand above his head and shouting, "Last call for chook raffle tickets! Get your chook raffle tickets!"

The so-called chook raffle, chook being a slang word for chicken, is a long tradition in Aussie drinking establishments, where social enthusiasm is measured in kegs, lawn bowling clubs, football clubs, pubs, and the like. The proceeds of the raffle might go to some local worthy cause, such as the Surf Lifesavers, the Girl Guides, or perhaps, as some cynics suspected, the Benevolent Society of Retired Pub Owners.

But as far as the drinkers were concerned, the good cause was the food to be won. Things have changed over the years, as they have an annoying habit of doing.

Once in distant memory, chooks were a luxury food item, something that Mum might serve at Christmas, and winning a chook raffle had a lot of appeal to drinkers, who, if they didn't drink so much, might be able to afford one. Then chooks became ordinary fare and were in every pot, so meat raffles largely took over from the chook ones, with a tempting array of steaks, chops, and sausages on offer. Then it sometimes happened that seafood raffles were held, and it is quite possible that one day bartenders will walk past drinkers shouting, "Get your vegan raffle tickets here!" And drinkers will rush to buy a chance for a delicious offering of turnips and kale. Some of you may hope not to be alive at that hour.

But this was still the olden days. "Get your chook raffle tickets here," the bartender shouted, and thump, thump, thump went the music down the hall. Any other people's philosopher starting out in the wisdom business might have reacted angrily to this rude intrusion. Instead, Duffer said, "Hey, over here, I'll take one." This started something of a mini-stampede among the audience, who weren't going to lose their chance of a chook to a would-be seer who looked like an unmade bed.

When the rugby scrum of cooked chook fanciers finally had their tickets, and everybody had settled back in their chairs, Duffer resumed his speech, although he had rather lost the thread of it. "As I was saying, the way I look at it," he said, "the books of our lives have a number of chapters, and each one has something to tell us about ourselves if we stop and read their message. I know mine, Chapter 1, Parents and Growing Up; Chapter 2, Schools; Chapter 3, First Jobs; Chapter 4, Military Service; Chapter 5, Romantic Partners; Chapter 6, College and/or the University of Hard Knocks, with other chapters to be continued.

"Now, let me review these various influences and their lessons…."

Just as he said this, someone dropped their chook raffle tickets on the floor by mistake, and a beer was spilled on them by accident, and somebody's girlfriend got pushed, not entirely by accident, and then the man who pushed the girlfriend was pushed by her boyfriend, entirely on purpose, and then a wholesale brawl broke out by general agreement, and even Duffer had a go at it, because he thought it would be a shame to miss the fun.

The bouncer arrived soon with a few bartenders to assist. None of the security team was named Socrates, but they were philosophic about the trouble, because it was not an unknown event at a pub, and, besides, there's no peace for drinkers. Still, while nobody was hurt badly, the cause of human enlightenment was delayed a week, until Duffer came back another night to finish his speech.

And that is how his speaking career began in earnest, the story that was to play out over at least three continents. The beat went on, thump, thump, thump.

Chapter 5

Where Eagles Did Not Soar

"When you are a small kid, you seem to cast a small shadow, but when you grow older, you realize that your little shadow is that of a giant, and the huge shade of childhood covers everything you do ever after." Duffer's remarks to a kindergarten teachers' book club, Brisbane, 1973.

When Margaret called Sheila to tell her of Duffer's passing many years later, she made a claim that really irritated Margaret, although it went unchallenged at the time. Sheila claimed that she was the reason for Duffer's ultimate success, the very same thing Margaret thought about herself. In truth, both helped him to an extent, but his original motivation to take up his odd calling was very different. The child is father of the man, as the saying has it.

While Duffer never again mentioned the Six Steps to Wisdom and Understanding that he had teased the pub patrons with when he first started out, he never forgot the separate chapters of his life that shaped his thinking. "What you know is mostly from what you have lived," as he said to Wombat one day.

The first chapter in his getting of wisdom was, of course, what we all have, a childhood. It is our dream time or nightmare time, a time of laughter, excitement, tedium, confusion, tears, fears, doubts, insecurities, indignities, absurdities, notions, emotions, and adults telling us what to do. Duffer's was just a little more colorful than most.

He grew up in Eagle Junction, a northern suburb in the city of Brisbane, capital of the state of Queensland. There were no eagles to be seen in Eagle Junction. There was, however, a junction just past the Eagle Junction Railway Station, where the branch line to Eagle Farm, again, no eagles, diverted some trains from the main line north. The main line could be seen across the paddock from twenty-six Lewis Street, Duffer's childhood home. The trains came by every twenty minutes or so, chugging along in great billows of smoke and steam, this in the days before electrification.

Duffer's mum was never a lover of steam trains. The smoke got all her laundry dirty as it hung outside on the line. It was the same for everybody. Lewis Street was not on the wrong side of the tracks because the neighborhood was just as shabby and smoky on the other side of the tracks.

Only the Sunlander, Queensland's fabled passenger train on the Brisbane to Cairns route, pride of the Sunshine State, was hauled by a diesel locomotive. As much fun as it was for everybody except the likes of Duffer's mum to see the steam engines panting along like iron beasts, the passing of the Sunlander was always a special treat. The kids knew the train traveled for a couple of days before it finally reached its destination in the far north.

Some kid's father had told Duffer, and the tale was repeated with wonder up and down the street, that in the buffet car the service was so luxurious that people were served meat pies on a plate with a knife and fork. It wasn't like the tuck shop at the Eagle Junction State School, where at Big Lunch the meat pies sold there were eaten with grubby hands. Jeez, they probably served real peas on the train, not the mushy kind that the kids were used to glopping on their meat pies.

The Sunlander was a fleeting vision of the good life and in another world might have been an incentive for the kids to work hard, do well in school, grow up to make piles of money in business, then ride the Sunlander and look down on the less fortunate who couldn't keep their laundry soot-free. But Australian kids were born with a greater ambition. There wasn't one who didn't want to represent Australia in sport. It didn't matter what sport, any would do, even tiddlywinks would do, so long as it got you a green blazer embroidered in gold thread with the Australian coat of arms, with the kangaroo and emu. Duffer dreamed of one day wearing the coveted green and gold as a cricketer or Rugby League player.

His backup plan, if national selection proved not feasible, was to play for the state of Queensland, which got you a maroon outfit. Unfortunately, Duffer was hopeless at team sports, and his chances were slim of wearing any prestigious colors.

Life on Lewis Street was sort of a Garden of Eden, lush with subtropical plants. There were plenty of boys on the street and, as soon as school was over, they would all rush out of their houses barefoot and, depending on the season, play cricket or football until it was dark or their mothers called them for "tea," the universal word for the evening meal.

Brisbane today is a big city of skyscrapers and highways, but when Duffer was a child the city was in its civic adolescence. It was like a big country town and the tallest landmark was the City Hall clock tower soaring an incredible three hundred feet or so, which today seems more deserving of the adjective "paltry." Eagle Junction was not very far from the main business district and yet horses grazed in the paddock, which regularly flooded after the rains, and small marsupials such as bandicoots hopped about with a choir of songbirds providing background music. Together with a large area nearby called Kalinga Park, Eagle Junction had a country-in-the-city feel to it, despite the lack of eagles.

Once or twice after a cyclone, floodwaters came across the road from the paddock and filled the backyard of his parents' house. This was not a complete disaster, as it stood on stilts like most houses on the street, which was the Queensland way of allowing air to circulate underneath the house to cool it in the absence of air conditioning. Unfortunately, this clever architectural touch never seemed to work properly, it was always ninety degrees in the shade in summer and very humid, but it did lift the house above encroaching water.

His mum was never mollified. The house may have been dry on these occasions, but the water in the yard kept her from getting underneath the house to the boiler to wash the clothes or hang them out to dry in defiance of passing steam trains and their drivers, who Mum believed would maliciously let out greater belches of smoke whenever they saw washing flapping provocatively in the breeze. As she used to say, "Those bloody train drivers can't drive past sheets or underpants without making their statement!" In the annals of conspiracy theories, Duffer's mum, Shirley O'Grady, has a special place.

It was the time before cell phones, just a big black family phone, with its large receiver to listen and its formidable rotary dial for frantic fingers to call the fire brigade if the house happened to catch fire, and no malls, just the few corner stores up the road, and before TV or video games, just board games like Snakes and Ladders or Monopoly when the rain came in buckets.

Television eventually came, but it took its own sweet time in coming, and in the first few years it was black and white with limited service, although not so limited as to prevent the young Duffer falling in love with Annette Funicello of the Mouseketeers TV show.

Before all that, before all the modern amenities arrived to take out the tasty gravy from the stew of life, kids had to make their own fun, some of it in retrospect not so innocent.

That's the thing about Gardens of Eden: temptation comes by the apple-tree load, although on Lewis Street it took different forms. One temptation came in the form of a shuffling character known to all as Bullah. Why he was called Bullah, nobody knew. He appeared every few months from the direction of Kalinga Park, taking to two steps forward and one step back, as he ranted and shook his hands and turned every which way as he battled his demons, which seemed to be of the alcoholic variety. He looked like Charlie Chaplin's little tramp on methylated spirits. "Hey, Bullah," Duffer and his friends would call out at him, and then throw stones and duck behind a wall.

What spoiled the fun somewhat was the opinion of someone's dad that Bullah wasn't a drunk at all, that he had suffered shell shock in the war, and that made Duffer feel his first pangs of guilt. It was one thing to torment crazy people, quite another to make life more miserable for crazy heroic people. Of course, it was all wrong, but sometimes you have to do something wrong to discover what's really wrong about it. For a long time, Duffer didn't think he had the usual monsters that kids imagine hiding under his bed. He had Bullah.

But the greatest opportunity to make grown-ups swear oaths and use foul language came on Guy Fawkes Night, or Cracker Night, as it was more commonly known. In 1605, Guy Fawkes was what we would call today a terrorist who tried unsuccessfully to blow up the Houses of Parliament in London by placing a stash of gunpowder beneath the buildings, an act that led in the end to his torture and execution.

For centuries, kids in Britain had innocently celebrated his demise by burning him in effigy and setting off fireworks, and this was too much fun not to be exported to Australia. Everyone knew the rhyme: "Remember, remember the Fifth of November, gunpowder, treason and plot."

The aim of the Gunpowder Plot was to return a Catholic monarch to the British throne, a sectarian history that made the holiday unpopular with nuns but not with kids, who thought little about the past but just liked blowing things up in the present.

Unfortunately, November the fifth comes during summertime in Australia, so the fireworks always posed the danger of bushfires, to add to the maiming naturally occurring as a result of kids being allowed to roam free with explosives. Some years later, after Duffer grew up, Cracker Night was moved to a date less inflammable for the countryside. Unhinged from tradition, covered in the prudent blanket of safety, Cracker Night was snuffed out forever, and boredom descended on the land with not a single firecracker cracking.

But while it lasted, kids had more fun than anything they ever did before or since. Duffer himself later said that drinking and sex, the Big Two, were nothing compared to Cracker Night. Kids saved up their pocket money and bought rockets and bungers until they were armed like the Viet Cong of later notoriety. And the highlight every year was the ceremonial blowing up of Mr. Mitchell's letterbox.

Mr. Mitchell lived across the street. Nothing much was known about Mr. Mitchell's life, except that he had worked for Queensland Railways and was now retired. He was also known to be grouchy, but, to be fair, having your letterbox blown up every year might make a person grouchy. On Cracker Night, when it was fully dark and the coast seemed clear of grouchy old men, the kids would run over to the letterbox, stuff it with high explosives, as high as pocket money would allow, light the fuse, and run back behind the wall, the same wall used to hide from Bullah, until "Boom!" Mr. Mitchell came out in a flash, dressed in a suit of all things, and shouting, "You bastards, you bloody kids, I'll get you,", shocking language for the time, but he couldn't tell where the muffled laughter was coming from in the smoke and darkness.

Childhood doesn't get much better than this, and no guilt was attached, as Mr. Mitchell was a known grouch. The problem is that you grow up. The markers can't be ignored. One of them came in the fifth grade, when for the first time Duffer was allowed to ride his bike to school, a bike without gears, as bikes with gears were rumored to exist but thought to be in the realm of science fiction. It was a rickety old bike, and the pedals had a habit of falling off when he pressed down on them. Still, to have a bike and then be allowed to ride it to school up steep Park Avenue and past the train station was a matter of great kid prestige.

But this is where girls enter the story, hitherto a largely mysterious, unknown species, except for his sister, and she was mysterious enough.

On the first day that he rode to school, a trip of about a mile and a half, Duffer managed almost all the way without incident. He stood up on his pedals to climb the slope up Park Avenue without the pedals falling off, he flawlessly navigated the traffic near the railway station, and soon turned onto Roseby Avenue, up the slight slope to the entrance to the school.

Like most of the houses nearby, the Eagle Junction State School was also on stilts, not that it was in danger of floods on its little hill, but perhaps was simply holding the high ground against the general tide of community cluelessness.

At the breaks during the day, Little Lunch and Big Lunch, and before school, the kids sat on benches overlooking the street under the shade of the camphor laurel trees. This was the favorite roost of those mysterious beings, the girls in Duffer's class.

That morning, at the dawn of his independence, the girls made up the appreciative audience who saw him manfully stand up on his pedals to make the last of the slope to the school gates, feeling very important and good about himself, a young man come into his manhood. That was when one of his pedals decided to fall off, and he immediately crashed straight down onto the crossbar with his nuts leading the way. In this way, he learned that trying to impress girls had its perils.

Chapter 6

Old School Days

*"I have always wondered how come we are born into this world
without later feeling any sense of astonishment. We arrive into the
light from the dark, but we grow up accepting our situation with
a so-this-is-how-it-is attitude, as if it weren't extraordinary. Are
we not shocked because we knew consciousness in previous lives?"*
Duffer speaks to the Magic Puddling Club, Brisbane, 1973.

Although Duffer's dad was not very successful in any of his
professional ventures, he was one of those ambitious parents who
believed that his gifted children must be sent to a prestigious private
high school in order to succeed in life. And he had one in mind.

Situated atop a ridge above the city center, the Brisbane Boys
Academy had for a century trained droves of middle-class students for
university entry.

Duffer's older brother, George Jr., was the first to attend and he
thrived there, learning supposedly gentlemanly manners and making
the contacts that would propel him into future corporate leadership.
This did not surprise Duffer's dad at all. "That boy is going places in
life," he always said with sincere unoriginality. His daughter Margaret
was sent to a respected private girls' school, Saint Margaret's, where she

spent her time being asked whether she was the saint in the school's name.

Duffer was a different case altogether. In fact, George Sr. did not want Duffer, Robert, he insisted on calling him, to attend the Academy at all. "That boy is not going anywhere in this life, other than debtors' prison, and only there because he hasn't enough initiative to become a true criminal."

"They don't have any debtors' prisons anymore and it's a good thing they don't because your various ventures might land us in one," said Duffer's mother, Shirley. "You are being too hard on the boy. He seems a little distracted sometimes, but he's a good kid at heart and deserves the same chance as our other kids."

"Distracted? He is lazy. I reckon he's distracted by the thought of hard work, so he has made a union of himself and his Amalgamated Slacker Union is permanently on strike from his homework. Shirley, he should go to a state high school. He's never going to go to university. It will be wasted on him. And we can't afford to send another child to a private school."

But George Sr. knew that his wife was never going to tolerate sending George Jr. and Margaret to private schools to maximize their obvious potential and not sending Duffer too in the hope that he might surprise everyone by showing some potential in something. No way was that going to happen. Shirley would forgive train drivers for soiling her laundry on the clothesline before she would forgive a father for denying his youngest son an equal opportunity.

And so in due course Duffer, who didn't want to go to a fancy private school and would have preferred the local high school because that is where most of his mates from the Eagle Junction State School went, attended the Brisbane Boys Academy instead. By way of encouragement, his dad said, "Try and not get expelled."

It happened that the private school was not entirely wasted on young Duffer. He did not become a prefect or the top student in any class, he wasn't in the first XV rugby team or the first XI cricket side, he did not want to go on to university, his manners were not markedly changed, and he did not make many future contacts.

But in managing not to be expelled, which was actually more luck than good management, the school made an impression on him, which was to help him in its own way. The irony was that Duffer, not his siblings, was the one who was destined to go places in life and he became quite famous in those places, which they did not.

Duffer found the school very strange at first. For one thing, he wore George's old, hand-me-down school uniform for the entire four years he was there. George was big and strong enough to have played rugby for the first XV, and so Duffer never properly filled out his older brother's clothes, his father being too cheap to waste further expense on him. The boy who in theory had been sent to a private school to make a gentleman of him was always dressed like a clown.

In *The* Wizard of Oz, Dorothy knew she was not in Kansas anymore and now Duffer knew he wasn't in Eagle Junction anymore. The Academy, with its architecture, culture, and curriculum, was modeled after the British public schools, which are in fact private.

Most of the staff were good teachers and most, not all, were decent human beings but only a few were inspirational. Back then only men taught at this all-male school. They did the job the best they could, they were strict about the rules, and when the rules were broken, they sent offending boys to the assistant headmaster's office.

There lurked Mr. Eardley, known to all as Thunderguts, the head of the Lower School and a nasty exception to the prevailing decency. His office was the cave of the fire-breathing dragon. Duffer was sent there one day in his first year, and the memory of it lasted a lifetime.

Mr. Eardley was as dour a figure as ever despised the young men he was sent to oversee. He was never known to smile, though he must have taken some pleasure in his work only to disguise it with his permanent scowl.

Boys would line up outside his office and practice knocking on his door, only they would do it in the air before they dared to knock. As every kid knew, if you knocked too hard, you could be deemed guilty of the unusual crime of insolent knocking, if you knocked too softly, that was cowardly knocking. Either offense was an excuse for Thunderguts to get out his rattan cane. Corporal punishment was administered for all sorts of other rule infractions, not just for being flagrantly stupid, and Mr. Eardley was just the sadist for the job.

The headmaster at the Eagle Junction State School also had used the cane to enforce discipline, but he seemed to do it more sparingly and with a sad air of duty when he did. Of course, the girls never got caned, the one instance of gender inequality having some benefits.

Getting "the cuts" hurt like hell, but it was seen as a badge of honor among the Eagle Junction boys. Not so at the Academy, the hapless kids who got caned felt no honor because Thunderguts had them lean over his chair so he could hit them hard on the butt, a pose not conducive to thoughts of glory.

Duffer, being inconspicuous from an early age, did not receive any beatings at the Academy, but he came close once.

His French teacher was a young thin man who oozed conceit and was known by the boys as Bones. He taught with passion, but not a passion for the French language, which was as foreign to him as to his students. His passion consisted of irrational rages in defense of his own feeble hold on authority.

The day that Duffer was unfavorably noticed, Bones stood exasperated in his baking classroom surveying the rows of young oafs rendered brainless by the stifling heat of a Queensland summer with not one of them remembering any vocabulary. *Rien!* "What the hell is the matter with you?" Mr. Bones said to them. "You'd think that you were learning a foreign language!"

At this, Duffer exploded with laughter. The sheer lack of irony in this remark struck him as the funniest thing he had ever heard, at least since lunchtime. Several boys woke up from their half-stupor and wondered what the joke was. *"You'd think that you were learning a foreign language, and in a French class!"* Duffer repeated it to himself under his breath to savor the high comedy of it.

Duffer laughed some more and he only stopped laughing when Bones, predictably not amused, ordered him to walk over to Mr. Eardley's office and report his crime, of whatever variety of insolence it might be. Bones was now past mere rage and was in a paroxysm of anger that made his curling mouth appear a twitching, frothy maw. "We'll see how funny you think your wretched behavior is when Mr. Eardley is done with you."

It was a sobering thought. "Shit!" Duffer said as he marched to his doom. "Now I have done it."

He knocked on Thunderguts's door, without bothering to practice and trusting to beginner's luck, and was greeted with a fair impersonation of thunder. "Come in!" came the bellow from the lair of the beast. "What do you want? Explain yourself at once. I haven't got all day."

Fortunately, Bones in his fury did not tell Duffer the precise nature of the charge. He did not mention insolent laughing, subversive mirth, contemptuous disruption, all the things Duffer knew he was guilty of. Instead, Duffer had the luxury of reporting his indictment in slightly more favorable terms.

"Well?"

"I was sent here by Mr. Bones for laughing in class, sir."

Oh no, he thought. I used his nickname by mistake. Now I am really in trouble.

But Thunderguts did not react. He seemed not to notice, and Duffer wondered, *perhaps the teachers use the same nickname for the horrible bastard we do.*

"So you think French class is funny, do you?"

Thunderguts looked at his watch. It was almost time for the lunch bell to ring. He seemed to be weighing whether administering a good thrashing would stimulate or depress his appetite. Or perhaps he had the twinges of an early case of caner's elbow, close cousin of tennis elbow.

"What is your name, boy?"

"O'Grady, sir."

"Listen here, O'Grady. You will write me a seven hundred fifty-word essay on why laughing in class is rude and inappropriate and hand it to me first thing tomorrow morning."

"Yes, sir."

Duffer did write an essay, one that he later considered the best he ever wrote in high school, one that was cleverly satirical, vaguely subversive, and amusingly ironic. He figured that Thunderguts would never read it and, if he did, would not understand it. He never knew what part he had been right about because he never heard another thing about it.

This might have been the most lasting memory Duffer took away from the Academy if it were not for another teacher, Harry Armistead. He was everything that Bones was not.

He was a big, strong man who looked like a rugby prop forward and had a battered face of wrinkles and scars as proofs of past battles, only in those days, honorably at rest, he spoke only of the battles of brawn and brain chronicled in the books of history and English literature.

Mr. Armistead was a man's man and a boy's hero, especially a boy known as Duffer, who longed for the affection of his father.

There was not a boy who was not in awe of him. He tolerated no nonsense, and in this way, no serious nonsense came his way. He never sent a boy to the office because he never had to. By the sheer weight of his personality, he kept order in the classroom. Despite his booming voice and imposing figure, the fear the boys had of him was that they might not live up to his expectations.

Their respect for him was such that they paid him the ultimate compliment. He was never given a nickname. Every other teacher in the school had a nickname, they probably compared their nicknames in the masters' common room at lunchtime. There was Lurch, the headmaster, Thunderguts, assistant headmaster and head of the Lower School, Chrome Dome, also called Nude Nut on account of his bald, chrome dome, Bouncer, Buster, Dickey Bird, Hickey, Moose, named for his protruding jaw, and Pinky, to name but a few.

The other teachers may have asked Harry Armistead at some time what the boys called him behind his back. And he would have replied honestly, "Harry."

Duffer sat spellbound in Harry's classes for the two years he had this remarkable teacher for both English and history. No one person, with the exception of his mother, had such a positive influence on him.

Even little details of longer lessons made him think. Harry had one peculiar expression when it came to teaching history, which was modern European history mostly, as Australian history was a secondary concern, perhaps because Europe was thought to have a better class of battle. Harry would say something like, "I would argue that in a

Europe in 1848, the hold of the old order upon the populace was suddenly made uncertain."

Duffer was struck by that one phrase, "… in a Europe." Harry would say "in a Europe" in all sorts of different contexts, when he could just as well have said, "… in Europe" without the "a." It was just Harry's signature verbal tic, probably something he said unconsciously, but it prompted the young Duffer to ask himself, *How many Europes are there anyway? Is Europe some sort of metaphor for something bigger?*

In other words, he got to thinking, really for the first time in his life. All it takes sometimes is exposure to one great teacher, however quirky, to make a difference in a kid's life, a point exemplified by one such kid who was to grow up and impart wisdom by way of laughing and scratching.

Duffer graduated from the Academy with various notions forming, and all he required was a finishing school to set him on his way. The University of Hard Knocks was waiting.

Chapter 7

Taking It to the Bank

"School is where you go to begin the first part of your education. The rest of your life is where you go to complete all the other parts of your education." Duffer speaks to the Fitters and Turners Union, Brisbane, 1973.

In the nineteen sixty-seven Queensland Schools Senior Examination, Duffer received A's in both history and English, but he never sat for the mathematics exams because he was hopeless in anything to do with figures. He believed algebra and calculus had only been invented to humiliate people like himself. As plots go to foil the lives of ordinary people, it wasn't on a par with the steam engine drivers deliberately spoiling his mother's washing as it flapped on the Hills Hoist, but it showed promise.

So, after he had finished at the Brisbane Boys Academy, with his overall grades not being good enough for most university studies, as his father had predicted, he applied for and was accepted as a trainee bank teller, a career choice that was said to require some talent for counting, which, like all things mathematical, was not his strength.

Yet at the time, it seemed a good opportunity. In those days, a great emphasis was placed on personal references, and most of the boys asked

47

for one from the school headmaster when they left. To the surprise of himself and his family, Duffer received a fairly helpful one, not glowing exactly but faintly luminescent. The crux of it read:

"I am writing to recommend Robert O'Grady, who has completed four years of study at the Brisbane Boys Academy. He was a quiet but conscientious student who took part in inter-house debating and played rugby for the fourth XV and cricket for the fourth XI."

That would do. Clearly, the headmaster had no idea who Duffer was, as evidenced by the words "quiet but conscientious." He was not really quiet, only in the sense of flying under the official radar, the one incident with the French teacher long forgotten, and he was not particularly conscientious, certainly from a math teacher's point of view.

But armed with the reference, and with the urging and help of his dad, he joined the Moreton Bay Bank at its head office in Queen Street, Brisbane, soon after leaving school. Dad knew the MBB manager from golf and little was said about his son's lack of high achievement in mathematics. He had received passable math grades in the Junior Examination two years before and that was good enough.

How much calculus and algebra does a bank teller need anyway? Duffer and his dad figured it was the telling part of being a teller that was important. He could tell the older customers about cricket and football while they fussed around and tried to find their bank deposit books.

"Duffer, I hope you make a go of this. If you work hard, you could one day rise to be a bank manager and make Mum and me proud. True, you might have to learn golf and that does involve some counting of strokes, but apply yourself and you might not turn out to be a bludger after all."

Young Duffer was eager to please his mum and dad, knowing that his father would always be the harder one to impress. But one other person had an interest in his success at the bank, his First Girlfriend, as she was ever after known. Patricia Morris was short and thin with dark hair. Her eyes were hazel and her eyebrows were quite lush and could be impressively elevated when Duffer was being an embarrassment, which was often. In middle age, when she started to develop wrinkles, she put it all down to her First Boyfriend.

She was a student at the Brisbane Girls Academy, just across from the boys' school, but separated by a wide, deep, overgrown ditch, a poisonous snake habitat possibly seeded with landmines. Patricia, like Duffer, was from a relatively humble middle-class background and had parents who wanted their children's education to be the passport to upward mobility. They met at a birthday party in his senior year.

The Academy girls wore an old-fashioned uniform in the same shades of blue as the boys, but designed long ago by sadistic Victorian-era moralists to be a total, buttoned-down boy repellent. Unfortunately, the resulting creation with its dark blue skirt and stockings and virginal white blouse was strangely erotic in a penguins-in-heat sort of way.

Few boys looked over that ravine, the metaphoric castle moat protecting the maidens, without developing a severe case of the dreaded blue balls, although whether they were in the same school colors was a matter of opinion in the playground.

Duffer believed he had the most severe case. Patricia did not need a moat to save her virginity as she had the job well under control. He began calling her "No Petting Pat" to his mates, whom he believed were doing much better than he was in the back seats of cars at the drive-in.

For a year, Duffer dreamed longingly of her in school and when he started at the bank he dreamed of her during teller training. This did not endear him to his supervisors, who nevertheless were kind and friendly because they found him amusing, even if the tally of money at the end of the day didn't always conform to his counting of it.

Patricia heard these reports in between keeping Duffer at bay on Saturday nights and slowly began to think that the only way he was going to succeed in banking was if he robbed a bank.

But one day, Duffer, who was still living at home, got a letter from the federal government. He had been called up for National Service and needed to report for an army medical. Although Australia a few years before had taken the controversial step of drafting recruits to help out the United States in Vietnam, a young man's chances of actually being drafted into the army were relatively small.

But Duffer had won the lottery. What a lucky twenty-year-old he was. Here was a chance to escape a boring job he was not suited to perform. He was visibly relieved and Patricia was secretly relieved. His parents were not relieved but worried that he would never grow up to be a bank manager. But they could say nothing, because he was about to serve his country, perhaps in a war zone. The best his dad could come up with was this: "I suppose we should be proud that he will serve his country in whatever way born bludgers and wankers are likely to do."

"Don't worry about that," his mum said to his dad, "he's unlikely to become an officer."

Before long, Duffer reported for his medical examination where a doctor declared him fit for military service, Duffer's feet not being quite flat enough to be disqualifying, his slouching posture not at the level of causing parade ground laughter, his mediocre eyesight not bad enough to require the assistance of a camouflaged cane, and his intelligence not beyond learning how to assemble and disassemble an M-16 or an FN Self-Loading Rifle.

Before he put a tick mark on his clipboard at the part indicating Cannon Fodder, the doctor, a young civilian who seemed a bit guilty about doing this to someone not far removed from his generation, asked one last question: "Do you really want to go, mate?"

Duffer always thought that if he had answered "No," his feet would have grown flatter and his eyesight dimmer at a few strokes of the pen.

Instead, Duffer said: "Aw, I guess so!" This wasn't the equivalent of "I have but one life to lose for my country" but it was enough to put him in uniform for the next two years.

Soon enough, Duffer said goodbye to his mates at the main MBB office, slightly miscounting the money for old time's sake on his last day. Then they all went down to the hotel two doors down the street to lubricate the memories of their brief but happy acquaintance.

"Hey, Duffer," one said, "maybe you can get out of the infantry by joining the army pay office unit."

"The only problem," another observed, "is that even in the army you still have to be able to count." They all laughed heartily, there being nothing funnier than the truth.

The next week he reported for duty at an army barracks in the Brisbane suburbs. A good mate named Steve drove him there because Patricia, now out of high school but busy in teachers' college, had said her goodbyes the previous night, promising to be faithful while he was away. Duffer had no doubts she would save herself for marriage, as she had been very successful in that department for the past two years, but her chaste goodbye kiss gave no hint that he might one day be the one to marry her.

His mum couldn't come to see him off because she was too upset and that was fair enough. She gave him a big hug, and between sobs, reminded him to always change his underwear every day, as mothers traditionally do. His dad explained that he couldn't come because he had his weekly golf game. He did apologize for not driving him, and wished him well, and Duffer said he understood, and no worries, although of course he really didn't understand.

To be fair to his father, the old man had secretly felt a little bad about at least not taking Duffer to the recruitment depot and giving him a proper farewell. The first four holes of his golf game seemed a revenge of conscience designed to underline his shame. With his mind distracted, he played horribly and his golfing buddies took to calling him Captain Hook. "And you don't even have the captain's excuse of having to play one-handed," they said. At this cue, the kookaburras in the yonder trees all seemed to start laughing at him.

But on the fifth hole, a par-four tricky dogleg to the left, the Tinker Bell of golf apparently sprayed him with her magic stardust and he hit a wonderful straight drive off the tee, followed by a cracking five iron that landed three feet from the pin, from where Duffer Senior could make the birdie, and to his mind that birdie had to be a kookaburra confounded.

After the fifth hole, his dad never thought another thing about the manner of his son's departure for the army. For his part, Duffer never forgot it all his days.

Chapter 8

You're in the Army Now

"There's an old nursery rhyme song that goes: 'Oh, the grand old Duke of York, he had ten thousand men, he marched them up to the top of the hill, and he marched them down again.' This perfectly captures the experience of army life." Duffer speaks to the Young Labor Party of Queensland, 1973.

This was Duffer's introduction to the army on his very first morning in camp, the day after his induction. It was 0600 hours, and it had been explained to them already that 6 a.m. was not what you called it. Of course, it was still dark. Several loud, nasty little men were going through the huts and waking up the recruits. "Hands off cocks, put on socks," they yelled.

What the bloody hell?

"Hands off cocks, put on socks."

It was too early in the morning for bad poetry, but the din wouldn't stop. "Hands off cocks ...." The call echoed down the hall.

Once the sleeping men started to stir, the list of wardrobe requirements and instructions was helpfully expanded.

"Now get out of your farters and line up outside. Put on your boots and hat for the roll call parade."

Duffer realized that he had lived a secluded life after all. He had never heard anyone call a bed a farter. It did make sense, as much as anything did here. Blokes were known to fart in bed and probably some of their girlfriends back home could verify this. Yes, he got it, not bad comprehension for 0601 hours, or whatever they called it.

He clung for a moment to his one and only wool blanket before getting out of his farter. He put on all his new army-issue clothes, his khaki socks, his green underpants, his long green pants, his green singlet, his green shirt, his big black boots, his khaki sweater, his greenish, khaki-ish so-called Great Coat, his gray slouch hat, and his blanket, and still he was bloody cold.

It was even bloody colder outside in the dark, with the sun just now starting to glaze the tin roofs of the huts. He whispered to the bloke next to him, "No way I'd put my hand on my cock in that refrigerator of a hut. It would be like feeling an icicle." The fella laughed. "You're not wrong."

Just then, a large sergeant started the roll call ritual with the aid of a little flashlight. "When your name is called," he said in a growling tone, "you will answer, 'Present, Sergeant.'"

"Recruit Adams?" He looked at the frozen ranks for a response.

"Here, sir."

"That's 'Present, Sergeant,' Recruit Adams," said the sergeant. "Say it."

"Yes, sir, present, Sergeant."

It was going to be a long ten weeks.

And so it went on down the alphabet from there, soon to arrive at the Os.

"Recruit O'Grady?"

"Present, Sergeant, but a question, Sergeant."

"What, Recruit O'Grady?"

"Yes, Sergeant, precisely, recruit is the word I wonder about. We're not really recruits, are we, Sergeant? 'Recruit' suggests that we made a choice to join up. But we didn't, we were drafted, conscripted as it were. The government made us join."

The sergeant had listened amazed. There was a long, menacing pause while he appeared in the gloom to be considering all the possible foul and threatening words available to him as a speaker of sergeant-ese, the most colorful and biting tongue in any language.

The recruits stood at attention but shivered, not just because it was bloody cold but because they instinctively feared that this Mt. Vesuvius with stripes was primed to blast. They didn't know much about the army but they did know it was unwise to play silly buggers with sergeants.

"Recruit O'Grady," the sergeant said at last in a strangely calm voice. "Drop down and give me twenty push-ups, which will warm you up and teach you the first lesson of military service. Unless otherwise instructed, you are expected at all times to keep your mouth shut and your bowels open."

After which, Duffer and the whole of his platoon, 8 Platoon, B Company, 3rd Training Battalion, went on a run for a couple of miles. They were led by the corporals who harassed the stragglers with all manner of strange oaths perhaps learned from the sergeant, whose name was Sergeant Cleary.

Duffer's introduction to the army was much more different and baffling than he had imagined. The term culture shock didn't do it justice. A day ago he had been fancy free, and now he was neither free nor fancy, dressed as he was in a baggy green outfit that made him and everyone else look like bags of garbage, a fair clue to their new military status.

His fellow recruits seemed as disoriented as he was. The previous day several hundred of them had come to the mustering center in Brisbane and Duffer didn't recognize a single one of them, which surprised him a little. Surely he knew somebody. The thought dawned on him that most of his old high school mates had gone on to university, where they would no doubt stay for years until they were too old for military service, and he might be the only person from the Brisbane Boys Academy ever to be in this position. The bastards. Just because they knew calculus they got out of this.

That first day for the recruits was mostly spent in them being rounded up and transported by buses and planes to the recruit training camp in the south. They were like so many unshorn sheep plucked from the paddocks and put into the pens, with sheepdogs posing as corporals barking orders at them. Many of the recruits were still shaggy with civilian haircuts and facial hair, but that didn't last long. Once they arrived at their final destination, barbers with no talent for style beyond short back and sides descended on them all like so many crazed shearers.

Then they were marched off to the quartermaster's store to be given their uniforms. Off came their civilian clothes, on came their greens and boots and the rest of their kit, which included other uniforms for other occasions.

"OK, mate," a lance corporal would say, "you're a fatso, you take large. You like green?" And, not waiting for an answer, "Too bad. We only have green. Aw, don't look sad, we do have khaki, which is just green with bird shit mixed in. Here's your dress pants and shirt in a lovely shade of khaki. Next …."

"You like green, you like khaki? I can't tell if you're a large or a medium. Better give you a large in case you eat more cream buns."

They changed right there, no fitting rooms available. Later, Duffer would understand that the rank of private in the army was a little military joke, as privates enjoyed little or no privacy, and anyway they were recruits, lower than the lowly privates.

The buffoonish lance corporals handing out the uniforms showed little interest whether the uniforms fit the men at all. It was all quick guesses and somebody else's problem. Duffer ended up with greens that were too large and his more formal battledress and summer khakis uniform too short. The trousers on each didn't cover his socks and he was later forced to swap them back at the quartermaster store, not without some argument. Fortunately, he had been ordered to do so by Sergeant Cleary and his word carried weight. Those one-striped dictators were as afraid of him as everybody else was.

For the first few days, he was consoled in his new life dressed as a military clown by remembering what his mother would say when his clothes didn't fit. "Tell your shoes to throw a party and invite your pants on down."

Over the course of the first week, he had time enough in between marching about to scrutinize his fellow sufferers. In that era of Australian life, the recruits were mostly white, working-class kids who had in common their youth and general bewilderment. Although he came from a family with social pretensions, he fit right in, having himself no pretensions at all.

Most of them were individually defined by what they had run out of, good luck, educational exemptions, and medical excuses, but others had fully embraced the calls of adventure, glory, patriotism, or family tradition. Again, Duffer was all of the above to some degree.

Everyone there, the willing, the unwilling, the curious, and the indifferent, knew what it meant to become a Digger, an Australian soldier in the tradition of the immortal ones, the members of the

Australian and New Zealand Army Corps (ANZAC) who had stormed the beaches at Gallipoli in 1915. This was the way to receive enough social validation to last a lifetime, even in the time of an unpopular war like Vietnam.

But first you had to put up with a lot of personal abuse, presumably to make you strong in case the Viet Cong made cutting remarks. If a cartoonist were to draw a picture, the common thought bubble rising from the ranks of the new recruits would have said, "What the heck is this that we did not sign up for?"

Their new home was in New South Wales, outside the town of Singleton, north of Sydney in the wine country of the Hunter Valley, a region that today is the location of fancy restaurants and wine-tasting venues. There was nothing fancy at all about the base. Wine was not sipped but a hard-worked recruit could slurp a can of beer in the evening after a dinner meal slopped on a plate but still attractive enough to a hungry man to be eaten ravenously. Lights-out time was at 2200 hours. Rifles had to be cleaned and boots polished before the recruits climbed into their farters, the warmest place in a wooden hut that barely kept out the biting winter wind.

The contingent from sunny but now distant Queensland never stopped thinking they were in the vicinity of Antarctica. They routinely shivered on the parade ground and in the latrines, and they shivered waiting in line to use the one public telephone to call family and friends, including girlfriends.

They slipped into a routine. They ran after roll call at first light, then marched, learned to read maps and to clean and fire rifles, climbed ropes, in case, Duffer thought, the Viet Cong happened to be up trees, marched some more, and stood guard duty or did mess duty. All the while they learned to insert swear words into every sentence they uttered, excepting the most important of all as far as the army was concerned. Yes, sir, no sir, three bags full, sir.

Through this unnatural process, they got to know one another and they made friends, the barking corporals being the common enemy. Sergeant Cleary was not as bad as he first seemed and left the harassment to his peevish underlings, who always addressed Duffer as Not Recruit O'Grady as his penalty for being a smartarse at the first roll call. The joke wore a bit thin after ten weeks.

Chapter 9

Duffer Goes to War

"Common sense is not so common because apparently the obvious is not so obvious to some people." Duffer speaks to the Association of Retired Mail Carriers and Night Sorters, Brisbane, 1973.

When describing his two years of army service, Duffer, the once reluctant private schoolboy, was in the habit of quoting the seventeenth-century poet John Milton: "They also serve who only stand and wait." But he added his own twist that made more sense to his rough-and-ready mates who were clueless about poetry in general and seventeenth-century sonnets in particular. "They also serve who only sit down and type."

Duffer was to have the distinction of going to Vietnam, the war of his generation, as a typist in the Royal Australian Army Service Corps. The army had found out that he could type and it was a life changer. As Duffer also said, this time quoting Omar Khayyam, "The moving finger writes, and having writ, moves on. The moving fingers type, and having typed, they move to bloody Vietnam."

This posting was perfect in an absurd way, giving him a farcical part in the larger tragedy, making him more spectator than warrior with a desk-side view of the general folly, with some forays into fleshpots and countryside thrown in for entertainment or self-education.

Though he did not realize it at the time, familiarity with war is helpful to any would-be apprentice philosopher. Most everybody else in his platoon was sent to the infantry.

It seemed unlikely at first that he would be sent to Vietnam, as most army typists stayed safely in Australia. Something else had to happen before he was posted overseas.

For his specialized corps training, Duffer was sent to a base in Victoria colder even than Singleton but generally more relaxed. Instead of puffed-up corporals barking at incompetent recruits, the instructors were a little more civilized, as befitting those who were not required to turn their charges into men but clerk typists.

One of them was, in fact, a woman, a WRAAC, a member of the Women's Royal Australian Army Corps, who taught typing. Her name was Warrant Officer Beryl Ponsford and she was to have an influence on Duffer's life beyond that of making him a better typist. By odd chance, Duffer was a pretty fair typist to begin with. In his early teens, he took over a typewriter that his sister Margaret had used in her journalism classes at university and began picking out his thoughts about life. It was an odd hobby, but then Duffer was an odd boy.

Beryl Ponsford, who was unmarried and had grown middle-aged in the service, was nearing retirement by then, and in the next decade the WRAACs were integrated into the main army and served alongside men. Some men and women are rendered better-looking by putting on a uniform, but Beryl was not one of them. She was as plain as her name, Beryl, not Feral. Over the years, she had discreet little romances with several of those men and women who did look good in uniforms, but these never lasted, and every time she seemed to grow a little sadder and more defeated.

But she nevertheless took a shine to Duffer, whose uniform hung on him like a bag of wrinkles. This interest wasn't in any way romantic. She recognized him as a wayward duck who had flown in and settled on the wrong pond. Her maternal instinct had never before found its full expression, but now here she was wanting to mother him somehow. It did not hurt that he was her best student. All the other male privates in her class seemed to have pig's trotters for fingers and no enthusiasm to make them wiggle the keys.

What was the best thing she could do for Private Duffer, er, O'Grady? Her life was the army and so she naturally thought the best thing a man could do in the army at the present time was to go to Vietnam and prove himself. He could get a war service home loan when he got back to Australia and would be respected by all for his courage and endurance. She never thought that he might be killed or wounded, which was always a possibility, even for a clerk typist, because it was a war zone after all. Instead, she applied a brush of mental "whiteout" to any thoughts of him being harmed.

She asked his permission, of course, before bestowing this unlikely favor upon him. "Private Duffer, er, O'Grady, how would you like to go and serve in Vietnam? If you have to be a National Serviceman for two years, you might as well go to where the excitement is. It's much better over there than sitting around typing boring stuff back home. I can arrange it. One of my old friends is at Army Headquarters in Canberra and his job is to find replacements for various units. I could drop him a line. Would you like to go?"

To which Duffer replied, "Aw, I guess so!" These were the very same words he had said to the doctor who did his medical that got him into the army in the first place. Beryl beamed and surprised him and herself by giving him a hug. Duffer, who was not much for hugs, tried not to struggle too much.

And so it was made to happen, through the power of hug, hope, and hapless affection. On January 5, 1970, he arrived in Saigon on a chartered Qantas flight. His mother and father both came to the airport in Brisbane to see him off to Sydney, where he would get on the plane for South Vietnam. For once, his dad looked a bit sorry about his situation. His mother struggled to be brave. They weren't quite sure whether Vietnam was a safe place for clerk typists, and there was no Beryl Ponsford to point out the wonderful benefits.

Duffer was never fitter after all his training. He had done a three-week course for cooks and clerks and other inept but indispensable non-warriors at the army's Jungle Training Centre at Canungra, in the rain-forested mountains west of the Gold Coast and south of Brisbane. Here he learned all the skills he hoped he would never have to use, how to patrol, react in an ambush, search an enemy village, set off a Claymore mine.

But nothing prepared him for Saigon. He was met at Tan Son Nhat Airport by a lean corporal with a black mustache who was leaning against a green military vehicle, a VW Kombi van, the same vehicle favored by hippies in other parts of the world at that time.

At first glance, the corporal had a pissed-off, world-weary look about him, and that made some sense because it turned out that he had served a previous tour in the infantry before he fell into picking up clerk typists at the airport. Yet his was not a thousand-yard stare because he was not remote or withdrawn, instead he had the look of someone surveying the scene and calculating the odds of avoiding doing whatever he was doing, or else finding some fun in it.

The corporal had no description of the new recruit except this: "Look for a useless-looking bastard with the rank of private," the colonel had said. You might suppose that he recognized him immediately. But remember that Duffer had the talent for being inconspicuous.

Among the more than a hundred replacement soldiers coming off the Qantas 707 that had ferried them from Australia, and was already being readied for a quick turnaround to get the heck out of the war zone to keep insurance companies happy, a fair number of useless-looking privates were among the more soldierly-looking specimens. The others, however, had been told to get on a bus and he had been told that someone would pick him up.

What gave him away was that he was milling around looking completely lost. Of course, he did appear to be a useless-looking bastard, wilted now by the great heat and humidity of the tropical climate.

"Robert O'Grady?"

Duffer grunted in surprise and the soldier said, "Well, mate, welcome to Saigon."

"How did you know it was me, Corporal?"

"Just a stab in the dark there, mate. I'm Bill Berrigan, but some of my mates call me Wombat to be more formal. By the way, nobody in our unit calls me corporal except the colonel and you can call him sir."

"I'll make a note of that. My mates call me Duffer." They shook hands.

"Nice to meet you, Duffer," Corporal Wombat said.

Duffer paused to consider the trajectory of his military career. He had got from highly regimented basic training to the less regimented and more relaxed environment of training to be a combat typist, and now to a unit that seemed not very regimental at all, with the exception of the colonel. What was next? Was he going to be flashing peace signs at everybody?

They were soon driving through the chaotic and demented streets of Saigon, playing dodge-em cars with teeming cyclos, motorbikes, trucks, buses, cabs, even hand-held carts, and Wombat had just passed a woman taking a crap on a railway line beside the road and had said, "Ah, picturesque Vietnam welcomes you!"

"You mentioned 'our unit.' What unit would that be exactly?" He wasn't quite at the stage where he could call this fella Wombat.

He turned and looked at Duffer for a second in astonishment, a dangerous move in that traffic, and said, "They didn't tell you?"

A moment later he answered his own question. "Wait. Of course, they didn't tell you. This is the army."

"They told me that I'd be a clerk typist at Army Headquarters in Saigon."

"Yeah, they got that half right, but don't be thinking you'll be seeing any generals or typing up top-secret plans. Our unit is Army Public Relations. Last to the battle, first to the bar is our motto. We write press releases, take photos of the boys enjoying their carefree Vietnam holiday, write captions for the photos distributed to their hometown newspapers, make little films of the boys sending greetings to Mum and Dad or the girlfriend or wife at Christmas, generally promote the idea that everything is hunky dory despite what the protesters say back home."

Duffer was to realize later that this description of the unit did not give any credit to the courage needed to carry out these seemingly silly duties. The staff who were assigned to the Australian task force in Nui Dat accompanied troops on operations in the bush and shared their risks, often armed only with their cameras. They were not usually last to the battle but they were the first to the bar.

Oh, yes, whether based in Nui Dat or Saigon, they were first to the bar. Duffer was to find that out on his first night in-country.

Chapter 10

Good morning, Saigon

"'Old soldiers never die, they just fade away,' as General Douglas MacArthur said, but I would add not before telling their stories over and over to old mates." Duffer speaks to a reunion of his unit at the Criterion Hotel, Brisbane, 1973.

Because he arrived in the morning, Duffer was taken straight to the office of his new unit at the Free World Military Assistance Organization on the outskirts of Saigon. There he met Colonel Bingham, an amiable enough officer who did not seem very regimental, but he called him "sir" anyway to be on the safe side. Duffer learned that the colonel had been a newspaperman before joining the army as a PR officer, which explained his slightly crumpled and distracted look.

The colonel had one office, where the colonel did whatever it was the colonel did, mostly reading and waiting to be driven to lunch when he wasn't receiving his few visitors. The other ranks had the office outside, where the main work was done. A bulletin board was above the desk and the typewriter and folding chair that would be Duffer's. Mostly displayed were photos of various members of the unit at work and play and some cartoons clipped from newspapers. There was also a typed notice that was a parody of an advertisement. It read:

Is your country being overrun by communist insurgents? Do rude armed men in black pajamas spoil the fun of your tropical paradise? Does the Domino Theory threaten to drop heavy dominoes on your head? Affirmative? Then you need FWMAO! FWMAO, the Free World Military Assistance Organization, is the answer to your prayers. Trained experts dressed in green are waiting by the phones to come to your country and clean up your rebellion by applying a strong dose of funding and military hardware. Don't wait until you see the whites of your enemy's eyes or the red of his politics. Call FWMAO today!

Duffer took this note as a sign that creativity was not discouraged, that the members of his unit had extra time on their hands, and that the colonel did not inspect the bulletin board for signs of cheeky material that others might see as subversive. There was also a photo of a young, pretty, round-faced Vietnamese woman laughing and sitting on the unit couch at the far end of the office. The door opened and in walked the woman in the photo, dressed in an elegant *ao dai*, the traditional dress for Vietnamese women.

"Hey, Velvet," Wombat said, "meet the new guy."

"Very pleased to meet you," she said, in her high-pitched voice, extending a delicate hand to be shaken. "I am Miss Tran. I look forward to working with you to make the photographs." Velvet worked in the unit darkroom in a hut at the back of the base, where the photographers developed their reels of film.

"No, Velvet, this is Duffer O'Grady. He is the new clerk."

Miss Tran, aka Velvet, was expecting to meet the new sergeant photographer, Chris Fordham, who had recently been posted to the Australian Task Force base in Nui Dat but had not visited Saigon yet.

Velvet looked confused by this explanation. "He is a corporal, not sergeant?"

Duffer nodded now. "Well, welcome Crick," Velvet said happily, mispronouncing the name Chris, the person she mistakenly thought Duffer was, as Crick. This ridiculous confusion lasted for as long as Duffer remained in-country. From that moment on, he became Private Crick, not just to Velvet but to everybody in his unit, including the colonel, who didn't understand the joke but wanted to be in on it.

When the real Crick, Sergeant Chris Fordham, finally made his way to Saigon, Velvet called him Fordie, like everybody else did. Crick remained Duffer's *nom de guerre.*

Many years later, during a bout of late-night philosophizing over a few beers with his mates, Duffer suddenly had the inspired thought that this episode summed up the whole Vietnam experience for his generation: misunderstandings, confusion, things lost in translation, bad motives, good intentions, and wrong outcomes until at last everybody saw what it all added up to, disaster, by which time it was too late to change anything. Unfortunately, thanks to the beer, he couldn't remember this insight when he woke up the next morning amidst the wreckage of his brain cells, so his future fans were spared this particular wisdom.

Vietnam was not a disaster in the case of Private Crick, aka Duffer. All of it was grist for his philosophical mill, although he did not know it then. His lyceum was the Canberra Hotel on a busy street in Cholon, the old Chinese quarter of Saigon.

The Canberra Hotel was the Australian billet for all ranks from corporal down to private. It was a dilapidated building, five stories tall, with a ground-floor open space and a little restaurant staffed by Vietnamese women who cooked and served basic breakfasts and dinners that were not very successful attempts at Western food. The meals were not particularly healthy either, saveloy sausages being the special almost every night.

But the restaurant was tolerated because it served beer, Victoria Bitter, the Australian nectar of the gods, and Schlitz, an American beer that was said to have a following in America, presumably because its devoted drinkers had experienced amputation of their taste buds, or so it seemed to the Australians. Needless to say, residents of the Canberra drank Victoria Bitter until such time as the latest container ship was emptied of its precious cargo, and then they forced down Schlitz until a relief shipment arrived. Marijuana was not a big part of the Australian military culture at that time, but perhaps beer being 10 cents a can had something to do with that.

The Canberra was an oasis of beer consumption. But out at the Australian Task Force base at Nui Dat in Phuoc Tuy Province, the men who did the fighting had to stay fit and ready, and so their beer intake was limited. In other words, the soldiers who needed beer the most to relax got it the least and the non-combat pogos at the Canberra got it the most, another proof that life is indeed unfair.

Duffer was given a room immediately above the ground floor and facing the street. This was better for climbing stairs after a night at the bar but not for daytime sleeping.

Everyone at the Canberra had to do guard duty for a couple of hours at night once a week, plus another stint guarding the Free World Military Assistance Organization compound.

If yawn-o-meters existed, guard duty at the Canberra Hotel would set off the snoring alarm. Saigon was under military curfew that began at 2200 hours (10 p.m.), although it took a while for the vehicles and teeming crowds to go home. By 2300, the streets were deserted, except for the occasional Jeeps of military police patrols. A Digger roused from his bed in the early morning hours faced two hours sitting at his sentry post with an M-60 machine gun, looking out on the empty street, hoping that at least an obliging rat might appear to break the monotony.

Guard duty at the FWMAO headquarters offered more interest, but that required staying after work at the building and sleeping on cots on the top floor until it was time for a shift.

The guards also walked around the large compound in pairs, so you had someone to talk to, and everyone was aware that an actual enemy attack was more plausible. The compound was surrounded by a high barbed-wire fence that Viet Cong sappers could probably breach with ease. Moreover, the headquarters was on a road only in the front, with the back overlooking backyards and thickets of bamboo, so an enterprising enemy unit wouldn't have to walk down a lighted and deserted street to get there.

These concerns did not stop Duffer and whatever mate was with him from making a stop at the darkroom hut in the back of the compound, empty at this hour of night but conveniently equipped with a fridge full of beer and a tattered supply of porno magazines. After a short break, they would resume their rounds, refreshed in morale if not in alertness.

So both guard duties were tiring in their own way, one because of the walking, the other because of the idleness, so the rule was that on the mornings after guard duty, a soldier was allowed to sleep late in his own bed and go to work mid-morning. But Duffer, having a room one floor above ground level and right next to the traffic, found it hard to sleep any time after 0600 hours. The street always roared like an angry beast, and on Saturdays it was worse.

Every Saturday, a funeral procession went by, a very noisy and slow funeral procession with dozens of mourners, with gongs and drums, enough to wake the dead or prevent honest soldiers from sleeping after a hard night of being the watchdogs of freedom, notwithstanding the breaks taken to flip through porno magazines.

As Duffer wrote to his girlfriend, Patricia Morris, these processions seemed to include professional mourners dressed for whatever religious reason in flowing white robes and pointed caps like dunces used to wear, or for that matter like members of the Ku Klux Klan, who probably started out as dunce cap wearers in school.

For the first month, Duffer shared all his thoughts with his girlfriend, filling an aerogram a night in his scrawling hand with every conceivable detail. He even told her about Velvet....

Dear Pat,

I just got back from dinner where we had saveloy sausages at the Canberra bar. I washed them down with a few beers only because I think alcohol is the only antidote to the red dye they paint the sausages with. I certainly do not want to die of sausage poisoning. I want to come home to you, because I love you so much, and the only sausage I want to hear mentioned then is the game of hide the sausage, which I look forward to playing with you one day. (Duffer here decided that talk of playing hide the sausage was not appropriate, so he scribbled that out but not well enough that Pat couldn't read it.)

I have gotten into the swing of things here. I get up in the morning without an alarm clock because every jitney and cyclo in Saigon drives by my room to give me a wake-up call. We don't have much of a breakfast but there's toast and tea and that does me fine but you are supposed to bring your own Vegemite, which nobody told me. Apparently, it's not a big thing in Vietnam. Can you send me some in a care package?

After breakfast, we all jump on the trucks and go off to work at FWMAO. You can take a bus but it's nice to be outside in the open air, though everybody is coughing because of the diesel fumes. I like everybody in the unit. We have a Vietnamese girl working for us — she works in the darkroom helping the photographers. Her name is Miss Tran but everybody calls her Velvet. She returns the compliment by calling me Crick, like a pain you have in your neck.

She's a good-looking lass and I asked my mate Wombat whether any shenanigans go on, she working in the darkroom with the photographers who would root a boot given half the chance. But Wombat said that Velvet has a boyfriend in the Vietnamese army and gives every other man the stiff arm in order to save herself for marriage. She's just like you, but of course you don't do black market currency dealings like Velvet does.

Well, I'll say nighty night for now. The lizards are telling me to shut up anyway. We have these strange little lizards here that look like miniature crocodiles but climb up the walls and say fuck you, fuck you, fuck you at a great rate of knots. We call them fuck-you lizards. (Duffer also scribbled over any mention of fuck-you lizards and next to the scribble wrote instead: "These lizards swear at you.")

Love you more than meat pies,

Duffer xxxx

Two weeks later, Duffer received a Dear Duffer letter from Pat. She did not say she had met another man or had developed better taste in men while he was gone. She just said that she was very sorry but she didn't think their relationship was going to work and she could not write anymore.

Duffer, of course, was crushed. But, worse yet, he never got his Vegemite.

Chapter 11

Revelation in a Jitney

"Many things that happen in life are so absurd and unlikely that no writer could put them in a novel and expect to be believed."
Duffer's remarks to the Gold Coast Optimists Club, Burleigh Heads, 1973.

Duffer didn't savor any of the notorious Saigon fleshpots in his first three months in-country. He was not saving himself for marriage and would have gladly lost his virginity, had it been entirely up to him. But his new-found friendship with Wombat kept him mostly in the Canberra Hotel.

Wombat was a good influence because he was terrified of contracting a social disease, as it was quaintly called back then. He had a steady girlfriend back home and was a loyal soul by nature. Besides, explaining to the girlfriend that he had contracted the clap would be beyond awkward.

A stark reminder of the danger to health and morals was the presence of a green ammunition box kept at the front door of the Canberra. It was full of condoms, and soldiers departing into the night were urged to take some in case they met a lady of the night.

One morning, the residents of the Canberra came down for breakfast to find the ammo box turned over and emptied of condoms. But inside was a note, which read: *"I tried to place this box over my dick for protection but couldn't get the bloody thing on, so to heck with it."*

So, while tempted, Duffer stayed celibate in solidarity with his new mate, which was a wonder on a couple of levels. Duffer was 21 years old, which suddenly seemed to him very old to be in an unfortunate state of purity, so he naturally jumped to the conclusion that Patricia Morris, while she was still around, was his last best chance of ever having sex. He reckoned that if he got much older, he would be too feeble to climb into bed, his limbs grown gnarled with arthritis due to chronic frustration.

He, Wombat, and their mates did go out sometimes. They even went to bars and met the girls who said the notorious passwords to bliss: "You want to buy me Saigon tea?" But they never bought the girls a Saigon tea, which was really just a colored soft drink posing as a come-hither cocktail and, therefore, was expensive because even phony love does not come cheap. They also went to some good Chinese restaurants in the Chinese quarter of Saigon where they were billeted.

In the evenings, Duffer often went up to his room and wrote to his mum and dad because he had nobody else to write to after he got Pat's bucket-of-cold-water letter. He wasn't sure his dad read his letters, so he felt he was really just writing to his mum, as she was the one who always wrote back.

After three months of this, it happened that Wombat persuaded the colonel to send him to the Task Force at Nui Dat and try his hand at being a photographer, which he said he had experience doing. He didn't. His classification was army reporter, and his job was to write press releases and stories for the army newspaper. But at the time there was a need for someone to take photos on a temporary basis because Fordie, the sergeant photographer, was incapacitated due to his party trick of cracking beer glasses with his teeth, which led him, one inebriated night, to cutting his mouth badly. This came as a bit of a shock to him because previously the worst damage he had done while glass munching was making all his fillings fall out.

This was a big break for Wombat because temporary became permanent for the rest of his tour and gave him a new profession when he returned to civilian life, photographer/cinematographer.

At first Duffer kept up his old routine, he would climb on the truck in the morning for the trip to the headquarters building, marveling at the common sight of six or seven family members on a single motorcycle, then he would type letters and press releases all day, except for the time spent driving the colonel to and from lunch in the Brinks building in the center of Saigon, and then, after another day of not doing anything to win the war, came home to the Canberra Hotel.

At night, he would eat his greasy saveloys, drink Victoria Bitter, and often watch a movie. The movies were shown on an old-fashioned projector with reels the size of giant Mickey Mouse ears, and the screen was an old white sheet.

Good equipment wasn't needed to show the movies because they were the dregs of Hollywood, and possibly B movies only because no category of C movies existed. But they did feature a lot of scenes of pretty women without their clothes on, and these were very much appreciated by the residents of the Canberra and did a lot to encourage patronage of the green ammunition box.

And now Duffer no longer had his guardian angel with him when he went out in Saigon, and that inevitably led to trouble when he went out with other mates not so resistant to temptation. One of them was Mac Harris, a corporal reporter in his unit. Mac was a very talented writer when he was not goofing off, but the problem was that he was always goofing off. Duffer's horizons expanded, and not always in good ways, but he was collecting more stories.

His wild mate Mac featured in some of the stories, one of which he told years later, in February 2010, at the Pink Otter Cocktail Lounge in Monterey, California. The story, which he never forgot, though he was late in telling it, prompted Duffer to think about things he had never much considered before, chief among them, racial prejudice, fair play, fate, coincidence, shared thoughts beyond language barriers, and the possible existence of God, quite a load for one night on the town. After a preliminary recounting of what he was doing in Vietnam at the time, Duffer explained it to the audience like this:

"One night a mate named Mac and I went into Saigon and, when we had taken on a sufficient load of beer to satisfy an alcoholic camel after a long trek through the desert, we thought we better get back to the Canberra Hotel before curfew started and the MPs came out like mosquitoes after the rain.

"So, in the absence of any pedicabs or taxis just then, we piled into a Vietnamese jitney, a sort of little bus mounted on a motorbike that could take as many as 10 people in the tiny cabin at the back, all crowded in cheek by jowl, for a fare of only a few piasters each. Definitely a local mode of transportation. This was not the usual way we got around, and our unusual presence made all the other local passengers nervous. Well, Mac sat down and started to berate everybody just for something to do, and he soon focused on some poor little guy sitting directly opposite him. He and the rest had done nothing to deserve this abuse except being Vietnamese in their own country.

"So Mac was playing a game of bully-on-the-bus, and everybody else except me was looking at the floor of the jitney to avoid eye contact and hoping the drunk Aussie would soon get off and leave them all alone. This was especially true of the guy who Mac was personally berating. He was being called every racist name and swear word in the dictionary of prejudice, and the little guy was looking down at the floor as if his mother had written a personal message of encouragement down there for him to read.

"Well, I was no enlightened saint, but I reckoned I knew unfairness when I saw it, and I didn't like what I saw. So I said, in a perfectly nice voice, so as not to start a fight with my own mate, in a confined space no less, where it would be hard to punch each other anyway, 'Mac, don't be yelling at this nice Vietnamese gentleman over here. He is a very distinguished person. In fact, he attended Oxford University.'

"Now, if I had been living in the U.S. then, I would have said that the nice Vietnamese gentleman had gone to Harvard or Princeton or Stanford. I only said Oxford because it was just about the only prestigious overseas university I knew.

"No sooner had I said the magic word Oxford than he looked up at us, with his face lit with utter astonishment, and said in perfect English, 'How did you know?'

"It was the turn of Mac and me to be thunderstruck. What were the odds? I managed to say, 'Oh, I just made a stab in the dark there, mate.'

"Mac was too dumbfounded to say anything more to the guy, who got off at the next stop unmolested.

"Years later, I came across a quotation from Albert Einstein, who said, 'Coincidence is God's way of remaining anonymous.' Maybe that was why Mac couldn't think of anything to say, realizing that what had happened was so beyond the realm of probability that it was almost supernatural. Or maybe it just fused his alcoholic brain with one strange thought too many. At the time, I thought that was probably it. Now, I am not so sure."

Chapter 12

Goody Two Boots

"In Vietnam, I once went out on patrol in Centurion tanks. Each tank was like a traveling library, with books for the boys to read during down time. Most were of the Death in Black Panties genre, but I found a copy of The History of Western Philosophy by Bertrand Russell, a difficult book, but some occupations make you more philosophical than others." Duffer speaks to the Redcliffe branch of the Returned Servicemen's League, 1973.

Duffer was getting closer to the end of his tour. He only had one month more to go. His mates considered him a "short timer" and enviously treated him as such. So one night when he went out with his mates in Saigon for a few beers, the traditional term "a few beers" meaning many beers, his wild mate Mac asked him, "What was the most memorable thing that happened to you over here?"

Duffer had never thought about that, but now he fell silent and reviewed the long catalog of strange and ridiculous events over the last eleven months.

Mac decided to help him out, "Was it the time you stood up on a bar stool to toast one of the bar girls and almost got decapitated by the ceiling van?"

"No, not that one."

"How about the time the taxi driver chased you down the street for not paying enough for the fare?"

"No, I thought he had a gun, but I'd rather forget than remember."

"How about the occasion when you managed to drop a condom full of water on a passing Saigon policeman from the fifth floor of the Canberra Hotel?"

"I was aiming for one of those young, draft-dodging Vietnamese cowboys on their motorbikes down on the street, but the cop suddenly appeared out of nowhere. Not my fault. Besides, he didn't know what hit him."

"What about when you and Fordie were in the bush with the tank squadron and were sitting on the top of the turret in the middle of the night on guard duty and both realized that you didn't know how to operate either the radio or the .50 caliber machine gun and would have to run for help if the VC attacked?"

"Well, fortunately, they didn't attack, so it wasn't too memorable after all."

"So what then?"

"The day I went to the orphanage."

"What?"

"Yes, a trip to the orphanage. It was organized by Corporal Matthew Gooding. Do you remember him? Everybody called him Corporal Goody Two Boots, because he went about doing good works, to the irritation of all."

"Yes, I remember him. Perfect name for a moralist, I reckon. He did not swear, he did not drink, he did not buy Saigon teas for the late-night ladies of Saigon, and he didn't smile much as a result. He arranged Bible studies and community projects."

"Yes, and one of the community projects was a visit to a local orphanage to bring the kids toys and supplies."

"You went on that?"

"Yes, normally I would not have joined Goody Two Boots on one of his missions, but Wombat had gone bush and the colonel wanted someone to report on this event for the army newspaper and maybe write a press release, too.

"It was my first writing assignment. The colonel recruited me for the job on the theory that if I could type, I could probably write as well. Before I left on the assignment, I asked the colonel, 'Sir, is the angle that we kill people and then give their kids toys and lollipops afterwards?'"

"'Not exactly, Corporal,' he said. 'After you write it, show it to me first.'"

"'Yes, sir,' I said."

"So I went along with the group of do-gooders, and Fordie came, too, to take the photos. He was in Saigon at the time recuperating from his beer glass chomping. To my great surprise, the event turned out to be a revelation."

"Really?" Mac said.

"Yes. It was a Saturday morning on my day off, and I would rather have been in bed waiting for the 1100-hour funeral to go by outside. Instead, we all piled into the back of a truck loaded with the various toys and necessities for the kids and went off to the orphanage, which was in a part of Saigon I hadn't visited before.

"It turned out to be in an old French villa surrounded by a tall fence with feeble strands of barbed wire on the top, which I suppose were supposed to protect the nuns who lived there with the kids. The nuns were on the first floor and the kids were on the second floor.

"The mother superior, a tiny person in a white habit with a heavy crucifix around her waist that would sink her forever if she stepped into one of the drains in monsoon season, led us up the stairs where we were immediately met by the overwhelming smell of urine.

"Man, it was like walking into a bladder control experiment gone horribly wrong. I was amazed that the smell was so strong. I mean, the competition for smells around here, the drains, the traffic exhausts, and the boiling pho pots, is legendary.

"But this didn't stop me being astonished by what I saw. Every kid who could stand was standing up in his crib with little arms outreached, crying desperately to be lifted up and cuddled. You could see the primeval need for affection. I had no idea. I was the last kid of three in my family, and I haven't been around other small kids since I was in preschool. Sure, I sort of knew that kids need love, although my dad never seemed to get the message, I saw now that it was essential. A person can be starved of love as much as being starved of food.

"I don't fault the nuns for not picking the kids up more than they did, or even changing their soaked nappies more than occasionally. Each of them was outnumbered by about twenty kids to one. The poor nuns could spend all day walking around picking kids up and, by the time they got to the last one, the first one would need more attention again.

"It was incredibly sad. So, faced with this, I actually picked up a kid against my better judgment. I am not sure whether it was a boy or a girl, because I was more concerned about not dropping the kid or holding it too close and getting my uniform soaked, which I sort of did anyway. The kid seemed very happy for that brief moment, and was not even put off by me looking extremely uncomfortable. But before you think I'm some budding Mother Teresa, I did draw the line at changing the nappy of the kid I picked up.

"I suppose this makes me a bad person, but I did learn something that day about life, all you need is love, like those Beatle boys sang."

"A few hot dinners help too," Mac said.

"Yes," Duffer said, "but without love everything is screwed up."

He paused for a moment and went on, "I also realized something else that day, too. Corporal Goody Two Boots was a better man than I was, Gunga Din."

"That must have been very irritating," Mac said.

"Exactly," said Duffer.

Chapter 13

Love Is a Burning Thing

"Sigmund Freud posed the eternal question: 'What do women want?' Beats me. I think the answer is backrubs, but I could be wrong. This I know: Whatever women want is born of the special wisdom gained by feeling and seeing what dopey men do not." Duffer speaks to the Country Women's Association, Toowoomba, 1973.

Duffer came home from Vietnam a changed man in some respects, not traumatized by war but someone full of new thoughts and feelings and the desire to express them. He quickly decided that returning to the bank was not for him, because he didn't want to work on improving his counting to be a teller and he didn't want to take up golf to become a manager. So he went to Mulgabimbi to help Uncle Frank on his farm while he thought about what to do.

His speaking gigs began as a sort of hobby, a break from manual labor and something to do to entertain himself and others, which he did with some success. At one of his very earliest ones, he had charmed Sheila into accepting his hand in marriage, which incredibly she accepted. Not long after, while they were still engaged, Duffer gave another speech, which Sheila did not attend, and gave voice to an idea that became a key part of his thinking.

Coincidentally, or not, the theme was romantic love. Perhaps Duffer thought that being newly engaged made him an expert. Well, it was a new experience and Duffer believed that experience was the great teacher of life.

For once, he spoke not in the back of a pub but instead at a School of Arts, an institution long characteristic of Australian country towns. These were once thriving community centers dating from a time when a touch of refinement was felt necessary to offset rural isolation and the rough bush ways that knew nothing of art and literature.

There they still stand today, usually small, stone structures, yet sometimes quite impressive given the relatively small budgets that funded them. Having now been swamped by the tide of modern living, with its surge of apathy and commercialism, the high ideals that raised these stones sometimes live on in painting classes or basket-weaving demonstrations or little talks for retirees to mull mid-morning before lunch. That was where Duffer came in.

The crowd was small, maybe 10 older ladies and one man dragged along by his wife, but they had the advantage of being very sober and in some cases looked likely to have been sober for many years. Fistfights seemed unlikely and, if anyone was going to be knocked cold, it was going to be a nap that toppled them on the floor.

They also looked like the barely breathing antithesis of sex and romance, which mostly involves heavy breathing. The human mind, in all its inventiveness, could not imagine that anyone in this room, with the exception of the enthusiastic, smiling young woman who was to introduce the speaker, had ever been wrapped around the body of a lover and had felt the pangs of ecstasy.

Such are the ravages of time. If only old blankets and the back of vintage trucks, or once creaking sofas and beds, could be called to testify, then it would be clear that these old dears had learned more about love when they were young dears than Mr. Duffer O'Grady and his fiancé could ever learn in a month of Sundays, or, more to the point, a month of Saturday nights when the action is often said to occur. All Duffer's experience of romance amounted to his brief time with Sheila, then early in her sufferings, and his first girlfriend back in school.

Peggy Purvis, the young representative of the shire council that arranged this program for seniors, tried with her best perkiness to whip the crowd into, what?, a passing semblance of consciousness. "We are so pleased to have Mr. O'Grady come to speak to us today. He recently returned from serving in the army and being in Vietnam made him very thoughtful. He has started to share his interesting thoughts in some exciting speeches at the Mulgabimbi Post Hotel and now we have the pleasure to have him here to speak to us on the topic of 'Love Is a Burning Thing, and It Makes Divorce Lawyers Sing,' which is a song by Johnny Cash, if I am not mistaken. Ladies and gentlemen, please give a big round of applause to Mr. O'Grady."

A small round of applause followed. Duffer was not put off. "Thank you, Peggy, for the wonderful introduction and for all of you coming out here to hear me today."

"We come here every Thursday," said a lady in the front.

"Yes, but I bet you don't ever think about love and romance every time, and that's my topic today. You see, every life has its important milestones and none more so than our love affairs. I ask you all, were you ever in love? Do you remember how it felt?"

The lady in the front seemed baffled by the question. No previous speaker on a Thursday had ever asked. Others didn't know what to say either. Duffer paused for a moment before changing tack.

"So, where did you meet the first person you had a crush on?"

"He was hanging around the milk sheds," a lady with a hat said.

"Well, we met at the pub," said her sister.

"Bill and I were in the first grade together," said the lady who had brought Bill, the one man in the audience. "I never had a chance," Bill said, with little obvious joy.

Off to the side, young Peggy Purvis, who felt sadly stuck in the single state despite her nice figure, blond hair and cute upturned nose, listened with a perplexed look and wondered whether she should go to a farm and check out the milking sheds, as the pub had not worked for her.

Duffer's expression showed signs of relief. He was delighted with this sudden display of audience interest. It wasn't glaciers falling into the sea but it was a sign of the ice thawing just a little in that old, cold stone School of Arts.

"Interesting. For most people, I think, who we choose to love is foremost a matter of proximity. A bloke starts work on dad's farm. There's a kid at school. A lady goes to a pub with her girlfriend. Actually, that is how I met my soon-to-be wife, Sheila. We just got engaged a month ago and we met at the Post Hotel. Pure chance. We could easily have been somewhere else that night."

The lady at the front piped up again.

"So what? What does it matter if we find someone available nearby? That saves on the bus fare."

"Well," Duffer said, "I think it suggests that the one we love more than anyone in the whole universe might not be so unique after all. In different circumstances, but with the same old biological urge, we could have fallen in love with anyone suitable given the right circumstances. We might have dozens and dozens of suitable partners but we just didn't go to the right school, milking shed or pub. Think about it, even if you think your partner is one in a million, in a country of nearly 14 million people now, half of them will be the opposite sex, so there are at least half a dozen others walking around with eligibility. If you take one in a hundred as your yardstick, the number of potential partners becomes staggering." He wanted to let this idea sink in but the math was a little challenging, so he charged on.

"I know this idea is counter to the very notion of romance. I say this with sadness because I have lately become the most romantic person in the world, or at least in Mulgabimbi. I have bought Sheila so many flowers that she says to me, 'Duffer, stop making the florist rich. You are going to attract bees.'" Polite giggles were heard.

"One of the things that amazes me is how relatively little regard we human beings place on actual qualifications to be married," Duffer continued, in the absence of prolonged giggling. "Of course, many men and women consider the suitability of their potential partners, their place in society, if they can use a knife and fork, do they dress like dorks, do they hold similar beliefs, has their underwear fallen off too much on previous dates, how is their health, do they have a house and a job, especially a job, and sometimes sadly how rich are the respective parents. But in the battle between reason and rashness, between brain and biology, it's often the hormones that have the final word.

"If you were in the line for a job with potentially lifelong tenure, the person doing the hiring would do a long interview and go through your background with a fine-tooth comb. The hiring process for marriage usually consists of a few dates whereby the decision is mostly made on the basis of how frisky you were at the drive-in theater.

"In some ways, we are no better than the animals. We have our own mating displays and wait for the call of the wild. Oh, that reminds me, mating displays, just don't get me started. When I was a kid, everybody wanted to look like James Dean, well, the Aussie version anyway. We all put so much Brylcreem on our hair that it is a wonder flies didn't stick to us. Remember the jingle? 'A little dab'll do ya!' Yeah, it did me alright. Gave me a bad case of chastity that lasted for years.

"Just before I went into the army, bell-bottom jeans were all the rage. We all looked like long-haired sailors or maybe seasick clowns. I lived in vain for some girl to say, 'Hello, sailor,' in an actual fully fledged flirt. Didn't happen."

By now, the crowd had that look which signaled a cup of tea and a biscuit might be preferable to any more destruction of romantic myths, memories and the ways of courtship.

"But you know what?" asked Duffer. "Beyond all the biological urges we experience, something else has to be at work, something magical, and being magical, something romantic. We connect in ways that no one can understand, at least not yet. Do you know how you can stop at the red light in Mulgabimbi and the person with the car in the next lane is staring at you, you can feel it, and you look over and you are right? And it doesn't only happen when the town perv is in the next car, it happens with all sorts of folks.

"It happens when we meet the person we fall in love with. There's a connection made beyond words. Maybe it's what people call mental telepathy, but whatever you call it, it's our instincts speaking without us using words. I reckon this was our original language. Tens of thousands of years ago, long before there was actual speech, long before we had tongues enough to shape words, we had to communicate in order to survive."

The small crowd was somewhat confused by all this and probably communicated its only question via the lost art of mental telepathy, "What the heck?"

But being then blind to social cues, Duffer went on to speak for another 15 minutes before the tea and biscuits arrived. But it was this short sequence that established a theme which would recur in the future, how our minds navigate by feeling the invisible threads that connect all living things.

Chapter 14

Duffer Settles on a Career

"As everybody has a part of the human puzzle, even a seeming nobody is a somebody." Duffer's remarks to anybody who would listen, 1973.

Duffer's job on Uncle Frank's farm was always meant to be temporary, until something else came up. Besides, Duffer liked cows, but he didn't want to meet them first thing in the morning, and the cows probably felt the same way about Duffer.

As for his side gig as an apprentice popular philosopher and comedian, it did not pay well and it seemed likely it never would. But he was happy doing it, and at first he was in no rush to look for more sensible employment. Then he met Sheila and decided that he wanted to marry her, and only then did he seriously think about the future.

One evening, a few months before he married Sheila, Duffer and Uncle Frank took time out from doing nothing at that moment to discuss his employment prospects. Nephew and uncle settled back on wicker chairs on the veranda, with a bottle of beer in front of them and a couple of glasses retrieved from among the dirty dishes still stacked in the dishwasher. At Uncle Frank's place, the dishwasher rarely washed anything. It stored dirty glasses and dishes until the forgetful inhabitants of the house needed them in a hurry, at which point they washed them by hand. A wonderful invention was the dishwasher, but the thought of saving electricity was wonderful too.

Duffer once asked, "Uncle Frank, why do you have a dishwasher when you never turn it on?"

"It gives a veneer of civilization if anybody should come over," Frank said. Of course, Duffer was the only one who had ever come over, and yet he somehow missed the veneer of civilization.

The evening was hot, and somewhere far off thunder made low growls. As they looked out on the paddocks and bush, the birds were returning to their roosts and chirping their good nights, perhaps discussing the likelihood of rain in their trilling and chirping. It was contemplative o'clock, too early to make tea, too early to go to bed, but not too early for a cold beer and a good conversation.

"Ever given any thought to re-enlisting in the army?" Frank asked.

"No, Uncle Frank, I don't want to be away from Sheila. As it is, I had a pretty good time in the army, all things considered. I mean, I went to a bloody awful war and I had a good time, which makes me feel a bit guilty when I think of some of the poor bastards who did the fighting. But I was lucky, and in life it's all about the friends you make, I reckon, because they help you make the best of bad situations. I had good mates, and really the officers were not all that bad, considering that we all knew I wasn't a patch on a real soldier's pants. But I spent two years dreaming of the day I'd get out, so it would be a mockery of my feelings about the army if I were to turn around and re-enlist now. Heck, they would have to give me a new load of resentments as well as a new uniform."

Duffer poured himself another beer because he felt he had made a speech long enough to become parched.

"What was the best job you ever had?"

"Well, I've only had two real ones. The bank and the army. Wait. When I was in high school, I did work as a postman during the Christmas holidays. Did it for three years, starting when I was sixteen."

"How was that?"

"Best job I ever had!"

"There you go. I think you told me that at the time."

"Yeah, I never experienced such freedom. I would get a sack of mail in the morning and then ride a couple of miles on a bike from the Clayfield Post Office down to my delivery route, which was near the racetrack around Hendra and Doomben and the old woolsheds near the airport. Lots of big flies came with the job, of course, buzzing about for the horses and the greasy wool, so a passing postman was just a dessert for those bastards. I reckon some of the flies had tattoos, but they didn't bother me that much. I had a job to do and everyone was waiting for me when I did my rounds. I felt important for once, appreciated every time I blew my whistle to tell people their mail had arrived, and that made them happy. For a long time, I thought I should take a whistle to parties and blow it now and again to see if it worked the same charm."

"Did you whistle up any adventures as a boy postie?"

"Well, I always imagined that postmen made out like the proverbial milkmen with the bored housewives on the route. I dreamed that one day I would meet a comely lady in a diaphanous nightie who would come and meet me at the gate. I can't say I knew what diaphanous meant then, but it sounded pretty good-o. I was always on the lookout for the lady who would ask me in for a cold lemonade and ask me, 'Do you have a big package for me today?'"

"Did that ever happen?"

"No, of course not. There was no rooting on the route. I don't know whether that was just me or whether women are not much attracted to hot, sweaty young fellas covered in flies. Maybe it was a bit of both, and I suppose relief from boredom has its limits too. To tell you the truth, I am not sure the average milkman did any better delivering love as well as dairy products."

"Maybe you should become a postie again and re-live the dream?" Uncle Frank offered.

"Hmm," Duffer said, "I hadn't thought of that."

Frank said the postmaster down in Mulgabimbi was one of his mates and that he could find out how you applied and maybe put in a good word for Duffer. And so it was settled that night on the farm before the rain came. The job was perfect for Duffer. He would be outdoors meeting people and have job security and a regular paycheck. Better yet, a lack of arithmetic wouldn't burden him too much, as the only things he'd have to count were house numbers.

They drank a toast to Duffer's new career plan. They sat in silence for a moment and Duffer looked out on the scene and said, "What a grand sight!"

Uncle Frank said, "Duff, you can hardly see the paddocks in this light."

And Duffer said, "Oh, I don't mean the paddocks. I mean the big brown bottle of beer reflecting the sunset."

Before they retired for the night, Duffer said, "Hey, Uncle Frank, I have a question. Why do they call this place Mulgabimbi? As I understand it, mulga is a shrub found in Australia's semi-arid areas, yet this place has plenty of grassy paddocks and hills and a nice little creek. What it doesn't seem to have is any mulga."

"Good question, Duffer. I never thought about it before. Perhaps bimbi in the Aboriginal language meant that it was a place of no mulga. We will have to add it to the list of life's great mysteries."

With that, they got up out of the wicker chairs and put the glasses back in the dishwasher to be stored again until needed, probably quite soon, as contemplative o'clock came around pretty much every evening.

It all came to pass, although it took some time, because it involved a government department and the wheels of government tend to grind slowly, to the annoyance of everyone except the public servants. Duffer was sufficiently educated, better than most who applied, and his veteran status carried some weight. He got the job without being asked the meaning of diaphanous or the square root of nine.

He was told in advance that he would probably have to move, as Mulgabimbi already had its quota of postmen. But that would be no problem. Before he and Sheila were wed, a letter came in the mail saying that he had the job in Brisbane. This solved the problem of where the newly married couple would live. They could have stayed on the farm if it came to that, but Sheila, theoretically a country girl, was less enthusiastic about cows than Duffer was. As a nurse, she would have no problem in the city finding a job in one of the big hospitals, and Duffer would be glad to be closer to his family, which is to say mostly his mother.

When Duffer finally returned to Brisbane as a married man, he was delighted to discover that he would be working in his old territory out of the Clayfield Post Office, just as he had before when he was a teen helping out during the Christmas holidays. The only disappointment was that he would no longer be riding a bicycle on his rounds, because they were being phased out in favor of little motorcycles. That sounded cool, and was a bit, but riding a scooter did not make the same sexy impression as Marlon Brando did in "The Wild One." And without the pedal pushing to keep his figure slim, his beer gut saw its chance to expand.

Like Duffer's tummy, the sufferings of the Long-Suffering Sheila were not yet fully developed. The early days of their marriage were relatively happy, but they had their unfortunate moments.

Fresh from one of the most influential chapters of his life, army service, one that was going to inform his philosophy of life, he learned from experience not to discuss his time in military service in the presence of his wife. As far as Sheila was concerned, the army was as boring as a herd of cows.

One evening after they moved to Brisbane, Wombat, his old mate from Vietnam, came over for a beer and stayed for a bite to eat afterwards. Duffer cooked up some sausages on the backyard barbecue for an impromptu meal, scrounging up some leftover mashed potatoes to go with the sizzling snags, and they got to talking about their experiences. Sheila excused herself, "I am going to bed, boys, I'll leave you to it," and they went on talking and drinking and talking some more. It was Nui Dat this, and Vung Tau that, and do you remember that time in Saigon? Their voices became louder without them noticing, despite their many years of experience in drink-enhanced conversation.

After about two hours of this, Sheila suddenly burst out of the bedroom at the back like some opera singer appearing stage left to put the Valkyries to flight. Her hair was sleep-disheveled and she wore a flimsy nightie that barely covered her heaving chest. "Will you blokes shut up? If I hear the name Nui Dat one more time, I swear I'll take the broom to both of you." The more she bellowed, the more her breasts swayed with indignation.

It was an unforgettable sight. Wombat said, "Wow. If we'd had her in Vietnam, we might have won the war." Then he called a cab to take himself home, a swift retreat being the sensible option.

For his part, Duffer was speechless, but he thought, "She is magnificent. How I love that woman." And when he stumbled into bed, still aroused by the memory of her appearance, he gave her a hopeful caress, as clueless husbands are apt to do. And she said, "Will you stop tugging my nightie? It will fall off."

That seemed like a good plan to Duffer, but as her voice had the tone of a drill sergeant, he was wise enough not to press on. The better plan going forward was to keep his musings about the army to audiences that did not include Sheila.

His chance came up only three weeks later. The Benevolent Order of Pondering Possums invited him at short notice to speak in the same week as Australia's day of remembrance, Anzac Day, so a patriotic theme of honoring military veterans was needed. Their intended speaker, an army colonel, had developed laryngitis, and the club president had heard about Duffer and decided to take a chance.

Chapter 15

The Family Dinner

"I am not here to support any one religion, but there's one part of Christianity that's immensely human and touching. It's the Last Supper, where Jesus gathered his mates around him and had a good lamb dinner with bread and wine to say goodbye. Was Jesus the first Aussie? It's a question for the theologians." Duffer speaks to the Society of Retired Clergymen, Brisbane, 1973.

The first sign of trouble in the marriage of Duffer and Sheila, other than midnight complaints about wartime reminiscing, made itself known in the usual way. Sheila didn't get on very well with her new mother-in-law.

This was quite unexpected, as Duffer's mum, Shirley O'Grady, was otherwise loved by all. She was generally kind, cheerful, and helpful, and the affection she inspired wasn't just a matter of clearly being a better person than her husband, George, who was not loved by all, not even some of his golfing buddies. Nor did Shirley feel that a young woman was now replacing her in her son's affections. She and Duffer were very close, and she wasn't worried that anybody could change that.

In fact, she had felt relief that some young woman had taken on Duffer, given that he seemed happier delivering messages to drunks in pubs than to customers of the Postmaster-General's Department. Duffer seemed to her to be in need of a steadying female influence, and she was glad, in theory, that someone, anyone, had married him.

But in practice, cordiality was more of a challenge. On their very first meeting, before they were wed, Shirley asked Sheila what her parents, Trevor and Pam, did for a living. This question was not asked because Shirley cared about social standing, the bride's parents could have worked on a garbage truck for all she cared. She did it just to make conversation, as you do when you are struggling to make a connection.

"When she was younger, Mum was a typist, but stays home now and looks after the house," Sheila said. No surprise there. Shirley was a housewife just like Pam, as were so many others of her generation, their brains and ambition now locked in the laundry room.

Then Sheila said: "Dad is an engine driver for Queensland Railways."

Shirley processed this slowly, hoping somehow to soften the bad news. "You mean … on one of those new diesel engines?"

"No, the old steam engines, up in the cab with all the smoke and soot," Sheila replied, with a touch of pride in her voice.

"Does he ever drive the trains through Eagle Junction?"

"Of course. He does the northern routes all the time. Maybe you can wave to him next time he goes by."

And what Shirley, the good and amiable, the loved-by-all, wanted to say was this: "Maybe I can put a tree stump in front of his train. Maybe I can throw a piece of hot coal at his loathsome nut on behalf of all my soiled linens."

Instead, Shirley said: "Well, that's nice."

It didn't improve much after that. Now that Duffer and Sheila were married and living in Brisbane, the O'Gradys would regularly have their children over for tea on Sunday evening, as always, on the understanding that no actual tea would be served, just beer to wash down a full roast dinner, featuring a joint of lamb or other unfortunate animal that was cooked a long time, so as to avoid any outbreak of bleating. This was accompanied by similarly overcooked vegetables, and each dish was topped with a blanket of brown gravy that resembled the grimy residue that came out of Shirley's clothes-washing boiler after the train drivers had done their worst.

Shirley tried very hard to forgive Sheila's dad for the sins of emission in his job. When they would meet on social occasions, Trevor was inoffensive in his manner, and Shirley struggled to support her grievance. In her heart of hearts, and good-natured as she was, she knew better than to hold him responsible for anything other than trying to earn a living.

But when Shirley looked at Sheila, she couldn't help but think that some of her daughter-in-law's irritating ways could somehow be traced back to her father, the infuriatingly mild-mannered Trevor, Terror of the Tracks. Whenever a charitable thought came to Shirley about him, a nagging voice in her mind would say: "The apple does not fall far from the tree, and the coal does not fall far from the engine."

The most annoying thing about Sheila was her habit of being outspoken. She said exactly what she was thinking, which many people consider a good trait. But the problem with candor arises when the unfiltered one hasn't thought enough to extract any sense from the thinking process. That was Sheila. She often knew nothing, but still said everything.

As Duffer looked over those steaming Sunday dinner tables, with adoring eyes focused in his wife's direction, Sheila would come out with a series of silly statements that, by accident or design, skewered the personal pastimes and preferences of her new family. "Eating meat is a barbarous practice," she would sincerely declare, then ask Duffer to pass her the huge platter of dripping chops.

She told Duffer's older sister, Margaret, then single and living in a flat with girlfriends and trying to make her way at a public relations firm in the central business district, that she ought to get a real job instead of trying to make unpleasant companies look passably appealing.

Sheila often repeated the same offensive comments at consecutive dinners, just in case anybody had forgotten. She liked to tell George Jr., Duffer's brother and would-be coal baron, that the mining industry was raping the country, which George took with silent disdain, but his prim, delicate girlfriend, Judy, later to be his wife, looked like she had swallowed a pickled onion whole.

To her mother-in-law, Sheila once said that the crossword puzzles Shirley so much liked to do were wasting her talents, without ever specifying what those redeeming talents might be. When she said this, a cloud of doubt momentarily came over the love-struck face of Duffer, and he would venture a timid defense of his mum. "Now, now, Sheila, that's going a bit too far. Mum deserves to relax in her own way. She is a good person with not an enemy in the world." Just then, a train whistle sounded.

George Sr., Duffer's dad, was the one person Sheila did not offer hurtful advice to, and she was wise enough never to say one bad word about golf. The charitable view might be that she knew Duffer longed for the affection of his father, and she wasn't going to undermine his efforts. The baser conclusion was that she genuinely liked Duffer's dad, because he was as insensitive as she was.

If they were merely older man and younger woman, and not father-in-law and daughter-in-law, an outsider might conclude that they were flirting with each other, such were the exclamations of "Oh, George," and "Oh, Sheila!" that littered their overly affectionate banter.

If that were not gross enough, George Sr. invited Sheila to come to the golf course, meet his buddies, and play a round with him. But she said in reply, "Oh, George, I'm no good at sports, and if I could take a good swing with a club, I'd use it to hit your son." Duffer was impressed that she and his father got on so well, but felt a bit depressed that his father wasn't so warm in his company. "What does a man have to do to get a good word from him?" he asked his mate Wombat one day. "Grow breasts, I'd say," his ever helpful mate said.

Sheila's reference to taking a swing at Duffer with a golf club, perhaps the traditional nine iron that the locals used to clear Queensland backyards of pestilential cane toads on humid evenings, did not altogether seem like a joke at the time. She was hard on her new husband, more than she was on anybody else. Of course, she did not resort to violence, she was unfiltered, not unhinged, but her criticisms were unrelenting. In retrospect, their marriage seemed well on the way to death by a thousand cutting remarks.

But for the moment, they were a couple trying to make a go of it. Duffer enjoyed a regular sex life for the first time in his life, although whether Sheila enjoyed it was not so clear. She took to reading the Australian Women's Weekly while Duffer toiled gamely on.

Duffer didn't mind, in fact, he took it as further proof of how clever she was. "She certainly likes to read," he proudly told his mates, without telling them how he knew this. If ever it had occurred to him that reading the Women's Weekly might not be a common practice for a woman during love-making, he would probably have consoled himself by thinking that it was a very popular magazine.

One Sunday, after the men had devoured the ritual meat and potatoes and slithered off like pythons to digest their meal in another room, where a football game happened to be on the telly, Shirley decided to have a quiet word with her daughter-in-law.

"Well, here we are then, Sheila."

"Yes, here we are, Shirley." There was a pause as both waited for something else to be said.

Undeterred that her opening remark had not broken the ice, not so much as a crack in a glacier, Shirley pressed on, all hope and no expectation.

She had pondered what to say during the long, awkward moment. Maybe a simple "How's it going?", but everybody said that in Australia, and she might as well be at the front gate greeting a postman.

So she just asked the million dollar question: "Are you happy?"

"Happy?" Sheila said. She seemed surprised.

As she was waiting for a reply, Shirley was tempted to say, "Yes, happy, surely you have heard of it? It's a much sought-after emotional state."

Sheila finally said, "Yes, happy." Then she added: "Well, if you take ecstatic at one end of the scale, and a poke in the eye with a burnt stick at the other, I guess I am somewhere in the middle. Like most people. Why do you ask?"

"Well, I don't know, you sometimes say things that seem to be a bit harsh, hurtful, especially about Duffer, and I just wonder whether a happy person would say those things."

"What things?"

"Well, at dinner, you called Duffer the biggest slob who ever walked out of a rubbish tip."

"Well, yes, I admit that, but I was trying to straighten him out. But suppose I do say the first thing that enters my mind. I don't mean any harm by it. I am sorry if I ever offended you. By the way, I saw you wince the other day when I made a comment that quilters are all making up for their sexual frustration. I meant to apologize later, but then I said something else that probably wasn't very polite, and forgot about it."

That apology of sorts was enough to keep the fragile peace between the two most important women in Duffer's life for a little while longer. Sheila tried for a few weeks to keep her more obnoxious opinions to herself, but she eventually slipped back into her old ways. Shirley went back to her quilting, not because she was thinking about sex, but because she wasn't, she just wanted something to do.

Duffer went on being a slob, impervious to both kind treatment and harsh comments. But his wife's attempts to straighten him out made his mother realize that Sheila wasn't the whole problem. Shirley loved her son, but she had to admit he was exasperating, just like his father.

Chapter 16

An Old Teacher Receives His Mail

"Chance is everything. Sometimes you pick the winning number, sometimes you don't, although sometimes by chance the hand of fate appears to fiddle with the random numbers." Duffer's remarks to the Pigeon Fanciers of Queensland, 1973.

Duffer, the seeker-of-wisdom postman, was out on his rounds one summer day in his new career, riding his little Honda motor bike from letterbox to letterbox, when he saw a large, older man advancing toward him from down the street. It was a typically hot day in Brisbane, and even at a distance the man's body language indicated that he was hot under the collar, and not because of the weather.

"Crikey, what now?" Duffer thought to himself. The morning had passed routinely so far, and he hadn't seen many homeowners; they were either at work or had the good sense to stay indoors. His mail bag was full with Christmas cards, which were welcome, and the usual array of bills, which were as popular as dog turds.

The old bloke was waving his hand in the air with a fair display of indignation, and he held something in it. Duffer had figured he had confused the house numbers and delivered mail to the wrong person, as numbers were the familiar curse of his brief banking and mail delivery careers.

As the man came closer, something about him looked familiar to Duffer, despite his appearance now. He wore a big bush hat, a rough old undershirt, a pair of shorts too short for polite company, and on his feet a pair of battered flip-flops.

Only when he spoke, and Duffer looked closer at the angry face, did he make the connection. "See here," the man said, "What's the meaning of this?", and he waved the bundle of letters at Duffer, "I found these in the street."

"Mr. Armistead?" Duffer had delivered letters to a Mr. Armistead on this street before, but never imagined it was this Mr. Armistead, the one he knew when he was Duffer's history and English teacher back at the Brisbane Boys Academy.

The old man looked surprised, and curiosity took over from anger. He stared for a moment from under his big hat.

"O'Grady?"

"Yes, sir. Sorry, sir, I didn't recognize you without your suit. Are those your letters?"

"As a matter of fact, they are," said Mr. Armistead.

"I am honored to have delivered them to you, sir. I wouldn't want your Christmas cards to fall into the wrong hands."

"O'Grady, it is my understanding that most postmen put the letters in the letterbox, not plop them down in the middle of the street."

"Yes, sir, but I didn't deliberately plop them. I am still learning the postman trade, and I guess yours fell out of my bag inadvertently. I hope you consider this a special delivery of sorts."

Mr. Armistead looked on incredulously. Then he remembered the young Duffer and his legendary excuses, and he started to laugh, first as small chuckles, then growing ever louder into great guffaws and gales of mirth. Duffer fully expected the homeowners to start coming out to see what the joke was. He marveled that the neighborhood flies didn't leave the rubbish bins to see if a spilled lunch was being served with the joke.

And then Duffer remembered why he had liked Mr. Armistead so much back in high school. The man could be fierce and stern, but he had a sense of humor, he was fair, and he understood people, even young pimpled people just starting to understand life like Duffer. Mr. Armistead was a teacher, but he was something of a natural philosopher and, more than anyone else, he got Duffer thinking about the great riddles of life, such as, is our human existence a comedy or a tragedy, or a bit of both?

And here he was appearing unexpectedly in a flyblown Brisbane suburb, Old Harry, as no one called him to his face, sir in direct contact. His short shorts and grimy shirt with decrepit accessories were the traditional retirement uniform of old blokes.

This is who Duffer wanted to be when he grew up, minus perhaps the shorts, which were definitely an unflattering look. To Duffer, Old Harry was a god who came down from Mt. Olympus to fetch his mail.

They stood in the middle of the street, as occasional cars went by and talked. "Are you retired now, sir?" Duffer asked. It was a silly question because his retirement was obvious, but Mr. Armistead explained his situation patiently. The gist of it was that improving young minds had grown old over the years, along with Mr. Armistead, and now it was time for him to bother the fish with the help of a surf rod. "What are you doing, O'Grady, other than putting mail in the road?" Mr. Armistead said when he was done.

So Duffer told him about his banking career, such as it was, then his tour in Vietnam, typing press releases and trying not to be shot. Then, feeling rather self-conscious because it sounded stupid when spoken out loud, he told his former teacher about his odd hobby of making little talks in pubs, clubs and meeting halls, just trying to make people think and laugh with jokes and insights, the difficulty being that many people seemed to be unthinking and humorless.

Mr. Armistead listened with interest. "Why do you think you have insights that other people don't, O'Grady?"

"Well, sir, as you probably remember from school, I have always been the odd character out, the misfit, the onlooker, who sees it all because nobody is bothering to see him." So said the odd character who seemed even to fill his postal uniform differently from any other mail carrier. And he added: "Does this strike you as silly, sir?"

"Not at all, O'Grady," Mr. Armistead said. "That is a good answer. I don't know what you call yourself, but I reckon you *are* a philosopher, not the usual type I'd say, but I bet that in a Europe in the old days quite a few philosophies were hatched over a pint of bitter."

Duffer was elated. This seemed like the "A" that his old teacher had never given him in school. And for the first time, he was invited to think of himself as a philosopher. Up to that point, he didn't know what he was, maybe a comedian, entertainer, pundit, wanker, and now he was ... a philosopher? Whoa, that sounded pretty alright. Duffer wondered what the pay scale was.

"Where can I hear one of your secular sermons?" Mr. Armistead asked. Duffer told him that, in fact, he was scheduled to make a speech that very evening at a local meeting hall and the event was open to the public, but "I doubt you can catch it with this little notice."

"I'll be there," Mr. Armistead said.

Duffer was now beyond being flattered, but he was also suddenly a bit intimidated at the prospect of having his old teacher in the same room.

The meeting hall was not far from the Clayfield Post Office on Sandgate Road, where he had first worked part-time as a schoolboy during the Christmas holidays and now was back working there again as a grown-up of sorts. He had seen the hall from the outside many times, but all he knew about it was that it could be hired out by community groups.

Duffer was not initially successful in finding an obliging pub in Brisbane interested in hosting an apprentice philosopher, if that is what he now was. But community groups needed speakers to pass as entertainment when their official business was done.

So here he was on a Thursday night at the Northern Suburbs Football Supporters Hall, whoever the supporters were, speaking to a group of men, all men this time, for some reason, who belonged to the Benevolent Society of Pondering Possums, whoever they might be.

The hall itself was plain and unadorned; a small stage was in the back of the hall, suitable for amateur theatrical productions, and simple fold-up chairs for any audience that might be lured there by mistake or against their better judgment. The toilets were off to one side near a small kitchen, in case a wedding or retirement party might be held for unpretentious people who weren't expecting much in the way of décor.

How the Possums had found out about Duffer is not recorded, but they somehow knew he was a recent Vietnam veteran and that suited their particular purposes. When the president of the group, a little round man named Fred Roberts, contacted Duffer, he asked him if he could speak on the subject of courage. "I can speak on the subject of anything," Duffer said. "I don't mean to boast, as I am not sure it is a good thing, but my wife always says I can talk the leg off a piano at a moment's notice. She says the nicest things."

"Well, we don't have a piano in the hall," said Mr. "Call-Me-Fred" Roberts. "Our group likes to discuss issues, all sorts of issues, social issues, moral issues, things that come up in the newspaper, sometimes just people's traits, like courage. That's the pondering part of our name. And that's where you come in, having so bravely fought in Vietnam, and able to give us your battlefield insights. After you speak, we will discuss the topic ourselves and you can answer questions afterwards."

Duffer realized that Fred thought, as many well-meaning people do, that just being in the army and possibly being in harm's way made everyone who served equally a hero. Apparently, he did not realize that Duffer's official army job classification was clerk typist. He wondered to himself whether speaking to this group was an exercise in false pretenses, but he banished that thought: They needed a speaker and he needed to speak and he could talk the leg of a piano on any subject even in the absence of a piano.

"We start our meeting at 6:30 p.m. with our business part of the meeting," Fred went on. "When we Possums are not pondering, we are doing charitable work, that's why we are Possums, we are soft and cuddly and spend our evenings keeping busy and making a bit of a racket."

Duffer had duly turned up at the hall on time to find about 20 men, mostly middle-aged or older, milling about or already seated. The only one who fit the definition of cuddly was President Fred. He had evidently eaten quite a few meat pies and sandwiches in his life, and he wore braces to keep his pants up.

Apparently only one member of the public was not a Pondering Possum in the audience that night. That was Mr. Armistead. He was dressed more like he had when Duffer knew him as a schoolmaster, grey pants, white shirt and blue tie, black shoes, but no coat because of the lingering heat of the day. His short shorts might have helped, as air-conditioning was not common in those days, and a large fan would have been seen by the hall's owners as spoiling the guests.

Fred Roberts had spied Duffer as soon as he walked in, not too difficult because he was the only younger person in the hall. Soon everybody was urged to take their seats and, after several cries of "Shush, please," the business part of the meeting began. This went on for quite a while, and Duffer realized that the Possums were ponderous as well as pondering.

Finally, after a 45-minute discussion, they had talked to death the subject of how they might have a stall at a school fete to sizzle sausages to raise funds for their group and whether to have pork sausages or beef (it was finally decided to grill both), Fred called the Possums to order.

"As you know, the topic we agreed on last month for tonight's discussion is courage, and those of you who voted for promiscuity as a topic should not be frustrated as we'll get to that in May. As it happens, we have a gentleman ideally suited to talking about courage as he has recently served with our Diggers in Vietnam …"

At this point, a voice from the back said loudly: "Maybe he can talk about promiscuity as well because those bar girls in Saigon are said to be really something." The Possums all laughed and, as advertised, made a bit of a racket.

After a slight pause, President Fred pressed on: "So, it is our great pleasure to have as tonight's speaker Robert O'Grady, although I think everybody calls him Duffer, so I reckon we should too. Possums, put your paws together for our speaker who will tell us about courage. What is it and is it something we need to be afraid of?"

A polite round of subdued applause followed. At the back, Mr. Armistead looked on with an inscrutable expression that challenged Duffer's confidence as he went up to the podium.

Chapter 17

Duffer Speaks to the Possums

"According to Bertrand Russell, René Descartes, often called the Father of Modern Philosophy, was caught in a cold spell in Bavaria around 1619 and got into a stove and stayed there until he had finished half his philosophy. As Russell wrote, 'Descartes's mind only worked when he was warm.' So I reckon it's a wonder that Brisbane hasn't produced more philosophers." Duffer at the Friends of Kalinga Park, 1973.

Duffer went to the Benevolent Order of Pondering Possums in two minds about what to say. He had been invited to speak as a Vietnam veteran on the subject of courage, when he had never fired a shot in anger. His speech was in the same week as Anzac Day, one of the country's most sacred holidays, a day of remembrance honoring the heroes, living and dead. Duffer's challenge was to tell the Possums a story that would make them think, and perhaps laugh, as a prelude to an occasion that was supposed to be about solemnity, and not comedy.

His initial thought was to tell one of his stories about the few times he had left his Saigon duties and gone on patrols in the jungle, because tales of typing press releases and visiting orphanages might not invoke the Anzac spirit.

But the one story he had that was exciting about a rare patrol he was on with the infantry did not end in a gripping firefight. Alone on sentry duty in the middle of a very dark night, atop a sand dune, with a platoon section fast asleep around him, he saw and heard an AK-47 round fired straight upwards about 50 yards to his front, perhaps an accidental shot fired by a Viet Cong as inept as he was in the business of soldiering.

Duffer was terrified; he had been thinking about his old girlfriend at the time, and was suddenly brought back to reality. He was puzzled, as well as scared. He realized that this random shot, a tracer round that he had seen shooting into the sky, didn't quite fit the definition of a contact with the enemy. While he probably should have opened up with the M-60 machine gun immediately, he couldn't see any target in the pitch dark. So instead, he decided to wait and see what happened next. Nothing happened. Asked later by his mates why he didn't shoot, he said: "I didn't want to wake up everybody in the section. They all seemed very tired."

This also didn't seem sufficiently gung-ho for an Anzac Day story, although it was touchingly thoughtful concerning his sleepy companions. The story he did tell, he called "The Bravest Man I Met in Vietnam."

This was a very odd story too. It was a war story without the usual trappings of war. The hero of the tale, the Bravest Man of the title, was none other than Corporal Matthew Goody Two Boots, as previously mentioned, the benefactor of orphanages. His field of battle was a meeting in the Canberra Hotel.

Duffer explained all about the Canberra Hotel in his speech, who lived there and what happened there (which is to say, copious consumption of saveloy sausages and beer).

To the surprise of the residents, it turned out that every beer drunk and paid for at the Canberra went to a welfare fund for the benefit of the men. The bank account had grown to thousands of dollars, and a meeting was called to decide how to spend it. The commanding officer, a kindly, gray-haired major going through the motions before his imminent retirement, presided over the meeting, all the while wishing he were somewhere else, and hoping to speed up the proceedings.

The major asked for suggestions, and the men had a few. One of them was to construct a swimming pool on the roof of the hotel. But that plan was not feasible, and would probably cost more money than was in the fund.

This is how Duffer explained the rest of the story:

"Then a corporal in the Catering Corps came up with a brilliant idea. 'Christmas is only six weeks away, sir,' he said. 'Why couldn't we use the money to put on the biggest prawn feed ever seen as our holiday treat? We could also have lashings of roast beef and plum pudding later.'

"A cry of delirious joy went up seemingly from every throat. A prawn night! Washed down with beer! Beer and prawns, the culinary match made in heaven! It was a suggestion that embraced the most cherished memories of every Australian soldier overseas … prawns, beers, meat pies, sausage rolls, pasties, Chicko rolls, cream tarts, Vegemite, and various sweets and lollies of nostalgic dreams. Maybe there would be enough funding for those, too.

"If the Canberra had actual rafters, the cry would have gone up to them. As it was, the enthusiastic cries echoed through the old building. 'Prawn night! Prawn night!' the crowd chanted.

"Clearly, there was a winner. All the prawn night needed to become a reality was the formality of a vote. The major was just about to call for a motion when another corporal rose to his feet and said, 'Excuse me, sir, but I have another suggestion.'

"It was Corporal Gooding, a well-known do-gooder, up to his old tricks. The major looked up, surprised and a little saddened, because now he wouldn't be leaving in a minute or two. Protocol had to be followed.

"'Yes, Corporal, what is your suggestion?'

"'Sir, together with some other Diggers, I have helped deliver toys and necessities to an orphanage in Saigon run by an order of nuns. They do not have much money, and the need they serve is great. I propose that we give our beer money to them to dispose of as they best see fit. While we believe our cause is just, war nevertheless brings suffering and pain, and we, as transients, can make a real difference long after we are gone by helping these poor kids who are victims through no fault of their own.'

"A troubled silence fell over the assembly, troubled because everyone knew these were righteous words, the words of God transmitted through some annoying do-gooder bastard with two stripes, as even the atheists in the crowd were inclined to believe. Someone murmured: 'He never drank a beer to support the fund himself,' but that could not hide the great moral weight that had suddenly been put upon all of them.

"'Thank you, Corporal, for your compassionate suggestion. Is there any discussion? Does anyone have anything to say about that?'

"There was not a peep. They looked at their boots instead. Not a man in the house, as much as he liked a prawn night, was going to be the one to speak out against orphans, something that the Almighty might hold against a person on Judgment Day, or at least something that would probably incur the wrath of a girlfriend or wife who eventually heard the story, setting off the marital trumpets for

Relationship Judgment Day, which is always around the corner and often arrives when least expected.

"So the vote was taken by a show of hands, the hands operating while the heads were still bowed in shame and boot inspection. With two suggestions still in play, the major took them in order.

"'Who is in favor of the prawn night?' he asked. Hands were counted. Then, 'Who is in favor of the donation to the orphanage?'

"'The motion in favor of a prawn night was 114. The orphanage got five votes. There were some abstentions. I am not saying how I voted.'"

Duffer paused a few seconds for dramatic effect, then he went on to finish the story.

"Corporal Gooding was the bravest man I ever met in Vietnam. Daniel in the lions' den had it easy compared to that irritatingly good corporal. Those lions were pussycats compared with the crowd he faced at the Canberra. So maybe you should ponder this when you start pondering: Courage comes in different varieties, and the strongest might be moral courage. Thank you for inviting me tonight."

The Possums were dumbfounded. They had expected a John Wayne-type story, and instead they had got this … a puzzling story, shattering every expectation, somehow outrageous, yet morally uplifting, bad and good, challenging, and worse yet, funny in an absurd sort of way, although not to be admitted. They muttered to themselves, "What the heck was that?" Their eyes were as round and wide as their namesake marsupials. They clapped a little, only out of habit.

Only one man timidly put up his arm to ask a question. "Can you tell us now about those bar girls in Saigon?" he said.

When the meeting was done, Fred Roberts, the President Possum, presented Duffer with a fountain pen embossed with the image of a ring-tailed possum looking down from a tree with a quizzical expression, as well it might in that company.

Several of the Possums then gathered around Duffer to thank him for his talk, which some said was "interesting," the only good thing they could think of. Finally, the last of them dispersed until only two people remained, Mr. Roberts, who was jangling the keys to the hall in what was his cartoonish attempt at a subtle hint, and Mr. Armistead, standing near the front door with his arms folded in an attitude of impatient patience. Duffer said goodnight, and he and his old teacher walked out together into the humid night full of stars and dark flying shapes, birds or bats, off to their own rendezvous.

"Where did you park?" Mr. Armistead asked. Duffer waved his right hand vaguely in the direction of the shops a few hundred yards away in Clayfield's commercial strip. "Good, we can walk together." They walked on in silence. He must be collecting his thoughts, Duffer thought to himself. … He's taking his time. … How many thoughts can he possibly have? … Maybe he doesn't want to hurt my feelings. … But that didn't seem to stop him when I was in high school.

"Well, O'Grady," Mr. Armistead said at last, "I thought you did very well. I am glad I came. You have a natural gift for public speaking, which came as a surprise to me, because I never saw any evidence of that back in school, except when you were delivering the lamest excuses ever heard in Christendom. I found your remarks very daring and thoughtful.

"I don't know what you are going to do with this previously unremarked ability of yours," Mr. Armistead went on. "You could go into politics, I suppose, but first you'd have to get elected." The old teacher gave a sideways glance to Duffer, indicating that this seemed doubtful.

"You could become a teacher, if you studied part-time for a degree, but I got the sense at the Academy that you didn't really like schools all that much. Perhaps, as they had you writing stories in the Army, you could go into journalism, because someone who delivers a fluent speech probably can write facts coherently. But I don't know where speaking to drinkers in pubs or groups of Possums in halls will get you."

Duffer was generally elated, and was not put off by Mr. Armistead's pessimistic view of his career prospects, as he shared them himself. Then Mr. Armistead said: "Now for some constructive criticism ..." Duffer was instantly less elated, knowing from experience that constructive criticism usually had a destructive-to-morale aspect to it.

"Your story about the vote for the prawn night was in the worst possible taste, for arguably putting our Diggers in a bad light so close to Anzac Day. On the other hand, it was disturbingly funny, although I felt bad about laughing.

"Overall, while your story gave listeners a strong sense of being there, it was a bit of a one-point wonder. You should concentrate on stories that have more than one point. Sharing insights about life is your strength, and you may have the makings of being a populist philosopher, although I can't think of anyone you can model yourself after."

He stopped next to an old Hillman sedan parked on the street. "Here I am," he said. "Good luck to you, O'Grady. You have surprised me once. I think your life's trajectory will surprise me again." And he shook his hand firmly, and was off.

Duffer thought about what his old teacher had said all the way home. Being still excited by the effort of making a speech, Duffer stayed up and waited for Sheila to come home from her shift at the hospital. When she finally did wander in just past midnight, he got her a glass of milk and an Arnott's biscuit, and they sat together at the kitchen table. Outside in the yard, the fruit bats were feasting in the mango tree, and were making a heck of a racket. "Bloody flying foxes," Sheila said, "they sound like a bunch of married couples."

"So how was your night?" Duffer said. "Routine," said Sheila. "How was your speech to the bandicoots?"

"Possums," he answered. "The Benevolent Order of Pondering Possums. I think it went well, it's hard to tell. One odd thing, though. This morning on my delivery round, I ran into Harry Armistead, my old history teacher from school. He was one of the few teachers I really liked and admired, although he thought I was a dickhead then.

"He told me he's retired, and we got to talking about things, what I had been doing and so forth. He could see I was a postie now, but I told him how I was making public addresses from time to time to different groups, one that evening to the Possums, and he said, 'I'll come along.' And he did. I was amazed."

"Jeez, Duffer," said Sheila. "Not content to talk to a group of bizarre people posing as furry animals, you have to drag some old teacher of yours out of retirement to bore him to further distraction. How did that go, anyway? Did he confirm that you are still a dickhead?"

"Well, no," he said, "Mr. Armistead said I had talents he hadn't seen when I was in school. He was impressed, and said my talk was thoughtful."

"Thoughtful? Oh, high praise indeed! Let's immediately get you a talent agent and sign you up for your own TV show, so we can go live on the Gold Coast and eat sherbet and wait for other postmen to deliver you royalty checks."

"Actually, he said that he didn't know where all this public speaking was leading me."

"OK, well, his judgment is still sound after all. That's exactly what I've been saying." She sighed theatrically. "I am tired. I am going to bed." Outside, a possum, a real one, not the pondering variety, made scratching noises as it made its way onto the roof.

Chapter 18

Ship of Fools

"The ocean is the biggest metaphor in the world." Duffer
speaking to members of the Surf Life Saving Association
(Queensland Branch), Noosa, 1973.

Duffer's mate Wombat, making idle conversation in a New Farm
pub on a hot Brisbane afternoon, had early on suggested the idea
of going overseas to London for a working holiday. They both liked
their jobs, but they felt restless, the adjustment to civilian life being
a special challenge for many veterans. Wombat's suggestion fell like a
seed in ready soil, growing slowly at first, but inexorably. It took hold
of both of them and Sheila, too.

Two years later, Duffer was standing on the deck of the Chandris
liner RHMS Patris, with Sheila and both sets of their parents, who had
made an unaccustomed trip out of their usual range to say goodbye. The
call for friends and family to go ashore had been made, and awkward
goodbyes were now being said. Wombat was below decks trying to
find an open bar. He had said his goodbye to his mum and dad back in
Brisbane with less theatrics than now on display.

The men were pretending to be stoic, making jokes, being
optimistic, while the women, who their whole lives had lived closer to

their feelings, tried to put on a brave face, hiding their tears or smiling bravely through them, as best as they could manage.

The uncertainty surrounding the future added to the pathos of the ship's leaving. As it was, the departure of a passenger ship in those days often had a built-in capacity for pulling the heartstrings. This was no casual cruise; the passengers were going to another country on the other side of the world to live for a long time, perhaps forever. Their baggage was more than their clothes; they carried their memories and dreams.

The Patris was a Greek ship, the RHMS stood for Royal Hellenic Mail Ship, and she had taken many migrants to Australia and Australians to England many times since the late 1950s. She was a pretty ship, with a white hull and single blue funnel with a sideways white cross on it, but she was not a many-tiered wedding cake at sea, a fanciful floating palace of water slides and late-night banquets for the benefit of sea-going tourists on short cruises. She was more a no-frills, floating home to long-distance travelers who wanted to travel the old-fashioned way.

Even then, the age of the long, sedate sea passage was coming to a close, with more and more people flying instead. The Chandris line offered the best of both worlds; the Patris would take you on a two-week voyage from Sydney to Singapore and then put you on a charter flight on British Caledonian Airlines to Gatwick Airport in London. The combination of ship and plane, charm and convenience, appealed to Duffer and Sheila as the best way to go.

When their loved ones had at last all gone ashore, almost all the 1,000 or so passengers on the Patris hugged the rails and threw paper streamers to those waving from the dock, and, as the ship eased from its moorings when the ropes were cleared, the streamers parted, one by one, until at last only one remained, and when it broke the last tie to home seemed to be broken for everyone. Passengers boarding planes out at Mascot that evening were missing all this fun and the benefit of a good cry, too.

Sheila and Duffer stayed on deck for a while as the ship began to steam up the great harbor. "Do you think we are doing the right thing?" Duffer asked.

"I dunno," Sheila said. "I am excited, though. And we are doing what thousands of Aussies have done over the years. The Great Australian Overseas Working Holiday. I am worried about you resigning your job as a postman after only three and a half years. Nursing is my career; I can do that anywhere, but that was your career, and now you don't have one."

"I reckon I can go back. I was a good postie and only left a few bundles of mail in the street by mistake, and they were all found by understanding people. I turned up, did the job, didn't complain, and they liked me. I got a nice reference from the postmaster, so I think I'll be OK."

The ship cleared Pimlico, where she had berthed, past Darling Harbor, and soon enough was under the Sydney Harbour Bridge, with Luna Park and Taronga Park Zoo on the port side, and the naval docks and Rushcutters Bay on the starboard side. Just then the public address system crackled into life, calling all passengers to their lifeboat stations for the mandatory lifeboat drill. Assembled with their life jackets on, they had a parting glimpse of Double Bay and Rose Bay on the starboard side before they were dismissed.

They guessed now why the lifeboat drill was called early before the first sitting for dinner. In the fading light of the evening, the Patris hit the big swells as she left the protection of the harbor and headed for the heads and the open ocean. The wind was gusting, and the sea was growing rougher. A few hundred yards ahead of them, they saw the South Steyne, the famous old Manly Ferry, taking the full blast of the sea, dipping and rolling with the spray of the whitecaps above her two funnels. They decided that this would be a good time to go inside, as the ship could withstand the elements, but Sheila's hairdo might not. Besides, they had to go and find Wombat. He had long ago lost the girlfriend he had in the army and now was unattached, or at least he was two or three hours ago.

They found him at a bar in the main lounge and saw that he had found a new friend. Her name was Denise, and she said her hellos while tightly clutching a green-colored cocktail glass in case the little umbrella floating in her drink acted like a sail every time the ship pitched.

Denise was a short, pretty blonde. She said she was from Newcastle, where she had worked for an insurance company, and was traveling by herself and sharing a cabin with another single girl whom she hadn't yet met. As she gave the abbreviated version of her life story, she smiled wanly every time the ship heaved, and they wondered whether her complexion would soon match the color of her drink.

By contrast, Wombat looked the picture of health, which was a bit annoying for the rest of them. After downing a few too many beers, he was full of friendliness and mirth and showed no signs of queasiness. He reckoned nothing was going to deter him, not even an angry ocean, in pursuing his full flirt with Denise. She, by contrast, was looking more and more pained as she felt her stomach turning into a personal bilge.

She lasted until the second sitting for dinner was called. "I think I will excuse myself now," she said; "I 'd better go to my cabin and meet my bunkmate. Nice to meet you, William," she said, using Wombat's real first name, the one his mates had largely forgotten.

"You aren't hungry?" Wombat asked.

"Ah, no," she said. "See you again soon." She walked off unsteadily on her little feet, grabbing passing furniture for support, as the floor went this way and that until she reached a ladies' room.

She did not reappear on deck for three days.

So the others went to the second sitting of dinner, which turned out to be sparsely attended, as Denise was not the only one to confound the immediate chances of shipboard romance.

Duffer and Wombat ate and drank heartily. Sheila picked at her food, consoling herself with the thought that those with cast-iron stomachs would be the first to sink to the bottom of the sea if the ship sank in the storm.

"William, is it?" said Duffer, with exaggerated, taking-the-piss sarcasm.

"Well," said Wombat, "a bloke's got to impress. He can't give the first impression that he's a hairy creature who likes to root about."

"But that's true on all counts, isn't it?"

"Right you are, Duffer. But if I have to be called William to add a touch of class, so be it. I admit that it hasn't got me very far. Tonight was a terrible waste of a bloody good flirt."

With dinner over, Sheila made her excuses and left to go down to their cabin four decks below in the bowels of the ship, where the economy class passengers had to share loos and could only dream of portholes. Duffer was not tempted to follow her, reckoning that she was unlikely to want to read the Women's Weekly in her bunk with the ship bouncing about.

"Want to walk outside on the main deck to clear our heads?"

"Good idea," Wombat said.

It was, as usual with these two, a bad idea. As soon as they opened the heavy door to the deck, they were almost blown inside again. The wind was howling, and walking was nearly impossible, with the wind strong enough to blow dogs off their chains and the deck going up and down and sideways.

Yet Wombat started walking toward the bow. Duffer would remember this walk for years to come. What was remarkable was that Wombat, inebriated as he was, walked dead straight, his body perfectly synchronized to the motion of the heaving deck. The deck leaned sharply to starboard; Wombat drunkenly lurched to port. The deck leaned to port; Wombat staggered to starboard, giving the appearance of a man striding along in a flat park. Only a drunk could have done it.

"That was amazing," Duffer said to Wombat when he came back to the hatchway.

"What was amazing?" he replied. "Did Denise come back?" No such luck.

The next morning, Duffer and Wombat came down to breakfast. They were among only a few passengers not nauseated by the prospect of fried eggs. Sheila did not make it. Duffer had left her softly moaning in the bottom bunk with a sheet over her head. Wombat's roommate, who he had yet to meet, was likewise incapacitated, but thankfully kept his moans to the minimum.

Ocean liners today have stabilizers, but seasickness remedies were the only thing to stabilize passengers on the Patris, at least until they grew their sea legs. Those who didn't immediately grow them got some respite when the ship docked in the port of Melbourne, 628 nautical miles south of Sydney, to embark more passengers and let the current ones have a new but brief appreciation for the stability of the land.

When they sailed again, the ocean was waiting for them in all its bad temper. Its rowdy helpers, the Bass Strait and the Great Australian Bight, did their tumultuous best to keep most passengers infirm, but slowly the rolling came to seem like normal.

When the ship stopped briefly in Adelaide to take on a few more passengers, a local bike gang was waiting on the dock to see two of their own off. Their names were Rabbit and Buster, both in their twenties, long-haired, heavily tattooed, and suitably scruffy. The rest of the passengers figured that they weren't going to England for the culture.

Buster was a big bloke and looked menacing, but he turned out to be good-natured and quiet. Rabbit was small and talkative, but he too was amiable, which for him was a better choice than fighting everyone in the bar as a bantamweight.

Fremantle was the last port of call in Australia, but very few people got on. The routine of shipboard life became settled. Even the sickest of people now ventured out of their cabins, even Denise, albeit cautiously and not for long.

During the day, people played Scrabble and Monopoly in the salons, strolled the decks and saw the sea, smoked like chimneys, played un-athletic deck games such as shuffleboard, swam in a small metal swimming pool that sloshed in any sort of sea, and drank beer or mixed drinks until the lunch or dinner gongs sounded.

The entertainment at night was a small band with a female vocalist of uncertain age who wore a sequined dress left over from the fifties. She struggled bravely to be heard over the crowd of drinkers and sometimes succeeded.

After the ship entered the Indian Ocean for the longest part of the voyage out of sight of land, the passengers were invited to the Captain's Dinner. As the captain would look very distinguished in his braided uniform, it was suggested that the passengers should take a stab at formality too, coats and ties for the gentlemen, nice dresses for the ladies.

Duffer and Wombat duly scrounged up respectable outfits from the bottom of their bags, and Sheila put on a colorful party dress.

Most of the passengers did something similar, although the meaning of formal was stretched pretty thin among those in the lower cabins. It was enough for the party organizers that a guest had obviously tried.

The ones who tried the most, and in a creative way, turned out to be Buster and Rabbit. Buster wore his motorcycle jacket, black jeans, white shirt, and what looked like an old school tie. Rabbit looked like Mandrake the Magician from the comic books. He had gotten from somewhere a long black coat with tails, which he wore with a silk shirt, a bow tie, and his black leather motorcycle pants.

Denise, dressed conventionally in a pretty frock and now fully recovered, took one look at Rabbit and was smitten. The feeling was obviously mutual. The two of them danced together all night, kissing and hugging in between numbers. Denise, the sickly and cautious one who was seldom seen, became the healthy, conspicuous huntress seen everywhere, until she and Rabbit left at the end of the evening to rendezvous behind the lifeboats in the traditional manner.

Wombat witnessed this sudden romance and was amazed. "Crikey," he said, "I told her my name was William in order to look classy, when all I needed was axle grease behind my ears."

However, Wombat's evening was not a total disaster. He made friends with the singer in the band, her name was Doris, and they became constant companions until finally parting after the ship arrived in Singapore a week later. As she was not on duty, Doris came ashore with him in Singapore for their brief day there, and he bought her a new dress.

Duffer had stopped in Singapore on the way to Vietnam, but had seen only the airport. Now, he, Sheila, Wombat, and Doris toured the Tiger Balm Gardens, and Duffer asked whether Tiger Balm was an ointment put on tigers to cure their ailments, but Wombat said, no, it was made out of tigers.

Then they walked around the old quarter near the Singapore River, before going to lunch at a Chinese restaurant, where Duffer and Wombat ordered Singapore noodles to see if they were as good as the ones served at the Fat Dumpling All-You-Can Eat Chinese Buffet in Fortitude Valley.

Finally, it was time to fly. Buses waited to take them to the airport. And Duffer marveled at how Singapore was again his unlikely last jumping off spot for another great adventure with an uncertain outcome. Wombat said goodbye to Doris, with more fervor than he had mustered for his own mum and dad, promising her ever-lasting love, guaranteeing they would be together just as soon as it could be arranged. They never heard from each other again, although Doris did keep the dress Wombat bought for her.

Chapter 19

The Mother Country

"You never really realize you have an accent until you go somewhere else where people have a different accent." Duffer speaks at the Dying Swan pub, Richmond, London, 1974.

The British Caledonian charter plane left Singapore late at night and arrived early the next morning at Gatwick. Its contingent of passengers from the ship, tired and grumpy from the cramped and noisy flight, were met in the time-honored way by British immigration officers who had little excuse to be grumpy, but were anyway.

Having been taught to believe that Britain was the Mother Country, Sheila and Duffer soon got the impression that mother was in one of her moods. Sullen was the word to describe everything and everyone they saw. The sky was overcast and threatened rain, a threat that soon became reality, and the ordinary English people looked depressed. They were supposed to be chirpy, like in the English sitcoms, but the simplest pleasantries were unpleasant.

It was a time of civic malaise, a pervasive damp rot of morale and motivation. Countries, like people, have their moods; in Britain, the euphoria of winning the war had given way to the dull, belt-tightening '50s, then to the fun-while-it-lasted Swinging Sixties, then to the who-knew-what-the-heck early seventies. Then the coal miners went on strike, which led to a three-day week imposed by the government to conserve energy, not that the people showed much sign of energy themselves.

Sheila and Duffer's first priority was to find a cheap place to stay and then look for jobs, or could the job seeking be left to later? A fateful decision had to be made, and Wombat needed to be consulted. But he had not been on their plane. Because one flight could not carry all the ship's passengers bound for London, flights left on a staggered schedule, and Wombat was on one of the later ones.

They anticipated this. To stay in touch in the time before mobile phones, they had arranged to meet him a few days after arrival at Australia House, a stately building in the Strand that was home to the Australian High Commission.

Wombat was planning to stay with an old mate who was renting a flat in Lambeth in South London. Sheila and Duffer planned to find a bed and breakfast in Camden Town in northwest London, which a mate of theirs had recommended as being clean and reasonable. It was centrally located to other parts of London, and the area sounded interesting, with a market and a canal and the requisite number of pubs and shops.

Their first real glimpse of London, up close and impersonal, this being standoffish England, was when the train from Gatwick arrived at Victoria Station, which was teeming with people trying to avoid close contact with other people. The scene was strangely foreign and bewildering, but they found one of the iconic red English phone booths. The familiar charm of the red phone booth, featured in every tourist brochure they had seen, was spoiled by the fact that in reality it had the smell and feel of a small stall for a large camel.

After putting much of their change into the coin box and tediously dialing the number of the rotary apparatus, and having to do it again when the call did not go through because of an extra digit, Sheila called the recommended lodging to inquire whether a room was available. One was … "on the top floor, last one available, dear."

So they hailed a London cab, another stereotype of the London experience, and found a Cockney driver wearing a flat cap, of course, as central casting would have it no other way. "Goin' to Earl's Court, guv?" he said, before Duffer even had time to fracture a vowel or two in authentic Australian.

Earl's Court was the one place they had vowed not to live. It was known as the notorious haunt where all expatriate Aussies supposedly ended up. It was a living cliché with pubs, and had been satirized to death by the great Australian comedian Barry Humphreys.

"Promise me that we won't live in Earl's Court," Sheila asked Duffer when they first started planning their trip. "No worries, darling, we can do better than doing what every other Aussie arriving in London does."

So the ground-breaking, independent-thinking couple who had left Australia by ship, which up to that time almost all Aussies did, and who were planning to buy a van and drive around Europe, as every Aussie and his mum did, said they weren't going to live in Earl's Court because it was too predictable.

"No," Sheila quickly replied to the cabbie with pride, "we are going to Camden Town." Whatever the cabbie replied was unintelligible, but had the tone of being unimpressed.

Camden Town was a good location for new arrivals, but the words clean and reasonable, which their mate had mentioned, were clearly matters of interpretation. When they arrived at their hotel, they handed over a fistful of pound notes, which still had the novelty of seeming like Monopoly play money, but were not. So much for reasonable.

Duffer suppressed the thought that a hotel in Earl's Court might have been cheaper, perhaps just half a fistful of pound notes. They did not own credit cards, they were not yet universal, and clearly the next stop on their tour itinerary would be a trip to a bank to exchange their travelers' checks for more cash. The cab ride took a while and also cost a fistful of their funds. The queen smiled at them from the banknotes, but they were not amused.

The bed and breakfast was a dilapidated, narrow, tall building sandwiched between other crusty buildings of similar vintage. They soon discovered that all bed and breakfasts in London, if not England, were apparently built before lifts were invented. They were at least five stories tall, meaning the hopeful visitor usually had to climb the narrow staircase with his luggage, because the vacant room was always the one on the top floor.

A porter was supposed to be on duty, but he was nowhere to be found, conveniently for him and only him. Duffer had to carry the bags, making several trips, and wondering all the while if Britain's National Health Service covered the cost of hernias for visitors.

Sheila encouraged him with helpful exhortations: "Jeez, Duffer, hurry it up, will ya? Our clothes will be out of fashion by the time you get our bags up here."

"Don't worry, Darls," Duffer said cheerfully between gasps of air, "my clothes were never in fashion." She didn't reply, but realized that never a truer word was said.

Their bed and breakfast in Camden Town followed the general pattern of such hotels in other ways. It was an old Victorian building heated by ancient gas radiators that did more gurgling than heating. The brochures said the beds were comfy, but they only came in two varieties, neither of them comfy: the mattress was a sinkhole for sheets, or else it was a trampoline masquerading as a bed.

Duffer and Sheila had the second type. After lying down for a quick nap, Duffer theorized that these beds were built as a type of stationary contraceptive device by prudish Victorian engineers who knew that lovers might bounce up during the act, colliding with the ceiling and hitting the dim and dusty light fixture, which would quickly put an end to all thoughts of romance. As for the alleged cleanliness, the carpet was there to refute that hope. It may have been red when tread by visitors to the coronation of Queen Elizabeth II some 20 years before, but it was a very dark and morbid shade of black and brown now.

To add to the shabby appearance, the air was heavy with residual smoke, because, as you know, the words "No Smoking" were unknown to that generation. To be fair, though, no bed bugs were encountered, perhaps because their little lungs could not process the fumes.

The bathroom and toilet were in a room down the hall to be shared by the two or three other guests on the same floor. On the first night, Duffer decided to take a bath, literally a bath, because no shower was provided. He took off his clothes, ran the bath, and settled in, but the water was a bit chilly. He turned on the hot tap, but there was no hot water. Apparently, he had filled the tub with the last of the hot water from the previous occupant.

Then he saw the sign and the little meter: "For hot water, please insert 20 pence." Being naked and his wallet back in their room, Duffer had to bellow down the hall to Sheila to come running with a bag of 20 pence. Of course, he had to get up out of the tub, dripping and cold, to let her in, and she didn't have many coins, only enough for one bath.

He had a very quick bath that night, and Sheila followed him for the second sitting to use the second-hand water while it was still warm. She was not pleased once again, and clearly there would be no bouncing tonight beyond that provided by the mattress.

Over the next couple of days, they toured the sights. The British Museum, Hampstead Heath, Greenwich, Covent Garden, the pubs, Soho, Hyde Park, Hampton Court, the pubs, London Zoo in Regents Park, the pubs, and the Changing of the Guard at Buckingham Palace, where Duffer felt obliged to say, "Christopher Robin went down with Alice," and Sheila said, "I know she did , Duffer, I read Winnie the Pooh, too," and Duffer added as a retort, "A soldier's life is terrible hard, says Alice," because he agreed with Alice, who in the poem was marrying one of the guard. After all, he had some experience of army life himself.

They only stayed a couple of nights in Camden Town, because the bed and breakfast was more expensive than they anticipated, and the canal made Duffer nervous, or so he said. "If I fall into the water with all my collected 20 pence pieces for the bath, I'll go straight to the bottom and you'll never see me again."

They moved into a small flat in Kilburn, where you could turn on the tap for hot water. Miracle of London miracles, the new digs didn't require naked bathers to search their pockets for coins in order to wash up. The flat was rented by none other than the daughter of Sheila's Aunt Dottie. The daughter, who had the same name as her mother, but was simply called Dot, was in her early 30s and had been living and working in London for five years. She had a little room she wanted to sublet to someone she knew, and the fact that Sheila was her cousin was perfect. The rent was only a quarter of a fistful of pound notes per week.

So when, as previously arranged, they met up with Wombat again at Australia House, they felt well placed to make decisions about what to do next. The plan always was to buy a van and tour Europe, but should they get a job first, or should they go immediately?

It was lunchtime when they met, so they walked over to The Wellington, a convivial pub a short walk away, where they could grab a drink and a bite and plan their European campaign. As always, Wombat was in an upbeat mood, despite his disappointments in love. They swapped stories over pints, and the common chord was that they were spending more money than they thought they would. "I say we make a run for it while we still have the money," Wombat said. "England is not going anywhere. We can tour around here later."

"Where will we go?" Sheila said.

"Where do you want to go?" Duffer asked.

"I want to see France, Spain, maybe Switzerland, Germany, Austria, then down through Yugoslavia to Greece. I want to do the Greek island thing."

"The Grand Tour is certainly going to be grand," Wombat said. "We better leave tomorrow."

"Not tomorrow, we need to buy a van first," Duffer said, striking a rare note of practicality.

"I know just the place," Wombat said.

Chapter 20

Duffer, Sheila, and the Fried-Out Kombi

"We prize individuality as a species. Everybody wants to be different. But most of us are remarkably like each other, and no ridiculous haircuts or silly clothing can change that. Our strength lies in being a community of individuals, each a link in a chain." Duffer speaks at the Mermaid and Merkin pub, Oxford, 1974.

In the folktales of the '60s and '70s, the VW Kombi van rides a golden highway through a fine mist of memories. Under-powered, affordable, strangely attractive for a rolling metal box with just enough room to sleep several dreamers, this was the era's iconic chariot of surfers, hippies, and sundry other adventurers, especially Australians making their traditional European tour.

Duffer and Sheila bought their Kombi at least eight years before the band "Men at Work" immortalized the vehicle in a song about a man from a land Down Under "traveling in a fried-out Kombi." They did not know they were buying a piece of a cultural legend. All they knew was the price of 300 pounds seemed about right, a nice round sum they could afford because Wombat was going to be riding with them and would pay 100 pounds for his share.

They should have known better. Little Nellie and her dog would have known better. Their Kombi looked old and was old, even then, and the hippies and other kindred wayfarers who were the previous owners were obviously not much for car maintenance. Their Kombi, like the one in the song, was fried-out.

The ones they went to see were all fried-out in varying degrees. They were parked all around the side streets of Australia House, a short walk from The Wellington. Wombat led them there after their pub lunch. "Look at this," he said, waving his hand at the fleet of fried-out vehicles. "Look at the variety."

And he was right. On sale were the completely fried-out, moderately fried-out, and a few just partially fried out. Every vehicle had been around Europe multiple times in the frying process, and most stayed in Britain for the winter to be sleeted and snowed on, to add the finishing touches of rust and ruin.

Every so often, the parking meter attendants came around, and the vans were coaxed into life, and everybody drove around the block and parked in a spot near where they were before.

Not all of the vehicles were Kombis; some were Bedford vans or similar vehicles suitable for camping and touring adventures, such as breaking down in foreign locales.

The buyers were all Australian. They came to Australia House to attend to whatever official business they had, and then they went outside and found an array of vehicles suitable for making the big European tour. What better place to buy a car than from fellow countrymen who knew the ropes and could give advice on what type of vehicle was needed? Aussies felt better about dealing with other Aussies, because they were still suspicious of English people.

This happy theory forgot that Australia has had its share of suspicious people ever since it was founded as a convict settlement. Most of the van owners could not afford virtue, as they had paid excessive prices for fried-out vehicles, and had to recoup their savings from their initial swindling by repeating the procedure with others.

It took a day or two for Sheila and Duffer to make their choice, and it came down to which owner was the friendliest, which is to say, the biggest amateur con man. "How are the brakes? Oh, they are excellent. Had them fixed just last year." … "How is the engine? She purrs like a kitten. Had it tuned two months ago when the brakes were done." … "What's that? Did I say last year for the brakes? No, three months ago. This country warps your sense of time."

All this was delivered with a grin worthy of the Cheshire Cat, and, like that cat, soon the ex-owner disappeared into the ether, only with the 300 pounds in his pocket to make up for his own folly the previous year.

Once they bought the van, Duffer and Sheila stayed two more weeks at Dot's Kilburn flat to organize themselves, and, as it was still April, wait for the weather to become a little warmer. In the meantime, Dot decided to throw a little party to introduce them to some of her English friends.

Duffer was interested to see if English people at a party would behave like people at home. Would the men be gathered around the keg at the back, tenderly monitoring its flow and talking about sports, while the women would keep to the living room, talking about what bores the men were?

Sadly for the drinkers, there was no keg, although plenty of suspiciously dark, un-lager-like beer was carried in, along with a few bottles of cheap cider of such low alcohol content that they couldn't inebriate a squirrel enough to fall out of a tree. There was also a bottle or two of sweet wine, and a cheap whiskey, and a cheese ball, and some stale crackers.

The guests were dressed in what might be called disco casual style. Duffer fell into conversation with a long-haired, very English bloke named Nigel, who wore a black turtleneck, bell-bottomed jeans, and desert boots, a sort of uniform in the early '70s. With some variations, other men in the group had on shirts of some ersatz material, overly large ties loosened at the neck for festive effect, regular work pants, and the traditional gawky Englishman look of open-toed sandals with socks.

When Duffer first saw the guests, he said to Wombat, who had taken the tube from Kensington to come to the party, "I think this is the first time in my life I've attended a casual social event without shorts on."

"Spoken like a true Queenslander," Wombat said. "But it's just as well. You don't have the legs for shorts, mate. We were just afraid to tell you."

Nigel introduced himself about this time, and Wombat wandered off to get himself a beer. Nigel, who, as it turned out, worked with Dot in the same office, asked him how he liked England. "I saw snow the other day when we took a drive into the countryside," he said, with all the excitement of an archaeologist finding a new trove of Dead Sea Scrolls.

But this didn't seem to impress Nigel all that much, so they went on to other topics. Nigel had attended Oxford University, and Duffer was tempted to ask him if he had ever met a Vietnamese fella there that he had met once in Cholon, a well-spoken, mild-mannered little bloke who liked public transport. But he thought better of it. So they kept talking about other things, including how Duffer liked to visit pubs, especially ones which had back rooms where people might make entertaining speeches.

Nigel's usual face of polite reserve suddenly became animated. "My favorite local in Oxford regularly holds meetings like that in the back bar, a sort of Speaker's Corner with ale, where various odd characters get up on a Saturday night and take their turn as the crowd good-humoredly heckles them with smart-arse comments."

"Jeez," Duffer said, "it sounds like Mulgabimbi with ancient spires."

"Well," said Nigel, "I don't know anything about Mulga, what? Mulga-bimbo, but I'm going back to Oxford to see some old pals on Saturday, and we were going to drop by for some laughs. Any chance you'd like to come?"

This was Nigel's way of asking if Duffer had a car and could give him a lift to Oxford. Clever bastards, these English people. Of course, not only did Duffer have a car, he had a Kombi wagon, the mythical vehicle, the chariot of the age, so arrangements were made, subject to the approval of Sheila.

When Duffer asked her later, she was full of enthusiasm for a road trip to Oxford. "That's a great idea," she beamed. "It's supposed to be very picturesque." Then Duffer told her about the pub with the meeting hall in the back where people made speeches.

"No thanks," she said, her nose suddenly scrunched up in disdain. "I'll stop here with Dot." All the ivy-covered old buildings in the world wouldn't move Sheila to watch gasbags led by Duffer making fools of themselves. She thought she had left all that behind her. Why couldn't she have a husband with conventional hobbies?

Chapter 21

Duffer Makes His Debut

*"Whoever created the world, and my mum said it was God, and
I can't say she was wrong, made humans in many colors and
varieties, so we wouldn't all die of boredom. So if you don't like
the color scheme of your fellow humans, you mock the hand of
God, which Mum said is never a good idea.",* Duffer speaks at
the Mermaid and Merkin, Oxford, 1974.

The following Saturday, Duffer drove the Kombi over to pick up
Wombat, who didn't have any other prospects for entertainment
that weekend, and together they picked up Nigel and his previously
unannounced girlfriend, Fiona, a very thin, short-haired blonde trying
to look like the model Twiggy. She did not say much but was perhaps
thinking of a way to politely ask for a sandwich.

The Kombi was not the fastest vehicle on the road; it chugged
along in suitably laidback fashion for laidback travelers, and the journey
took about an hour and a half or so. Nigel and Fiona were dropped off
at their friend's house, and Duffer and Wombat went off to explore the
famous town.

They spent the whole afternoon wandering about, stopping only
for a sandwich that Fiona could only dream of, and a pint of bitter to

wash it down. Then they took the Kombi wagon to scout out where to park for the night, and headed for the Mermaid and Merkin, the pub where they would meet Nigel and his mates that evening.

The pub was not of the old quaint sort, but rather dilapidated and grimy, a dank place where charm had gone to die. They staked out a table and got some beers placed on coasters to save it. At the bar, he made immediate friends with members of a college rugby team. Duffer had played a bit of rugby, badly, because he was neither fast nor big, but he liked the game and the camaraderie that it encouraged after the happy violence was done.

The crowd started coming in a great variety, as if Noah's ark had become a franchise and was now taking odd human creatures aboard two by two.

The organizer appeared, a large man with a big black beard, and he started a sign-up sheet, because in the land of queues, naturally, you had to queue up to speak. Each speaker was to be allowed five minutes maximum, but the presiding beard was allowed to stretch the definition of maximum. While religion was allowed to be discussed in a general way, sectarian appeals for a particular religion were discouraged by the man with the beard, who, come to think of it, looked like an Old Testament prophet. The last thing he needed was a pub full of Jehovah's Witnesses handing out pamphlets.

As early as they had arrived, Duffer found that he was number nine in line to speak. With gaps between speakers to allow the audience to go back to the bar, it took about an hour before he was called up.

In the meantime, he listened to short speeches in favor of vegetarianism, the lasting advantages of British imperialism, the benefits of eating meat, denunciations of colonialism, anti-war messages, in particular concerning the Vietnam War, chastity as a satisfying way of life, the need for Britain to have strong military forces, and the importance of having lots of sex. As these were random speeches not delivered in subject order, you had to listen intently to remember that one was contradicting another that you heard 10 minutes or so before.

It was just Duffer's luck to appear after the discussion of the benefits of sex, which the crowd obviously loved. What made it all the better was that the speaker was a young man with round spectacles, a bad case of acne, and long pants cinched somewhere up near his armpits. In short, the champion of unfettered sex looked like he had never actually had any, and his presentation seemed like a pathetic invitation for someone to take pity on him and do something about this. He was not rushed by inquiries after he finished.

Duffer's speech started badly. The crowd had filled out, and lots of people were either seated or milling about now, and among them were two leather-clad fellas who had faces only a mother could love, shaven scalps, bad tattoos, visibly bad attitudes, scars, studded rings, the whole punch-me-if-you-dare thing. They were not there to make witty interjections, but to throttle any joke or attempt at reasoned conversation.

They had commandeered two chairs that kind and gentle people had previously occupied, but had left vacant to visit the loo. They were bloody hooligans, louts, bodgies, in the old Australian way of saying. Duffer had hardly said "Good evening" when the uglier of the two uglies yelled "Ya mean 'Good f…ing riddance,' you Jewish prat."

Duffer, for all his experience at handling hecklers, was taken a bit aback. Usually, hecklers allowed you to say more than "good evening" before heaping their abuse at what you said. And "Jewish prat?" He had been called many things before, but never Jewish.

The crowd was shocked too, and waited for what Duffer would say, that is, if he did not run terrified into the night, like a reasonable person might do.

But Duffer remained very calm. He left the microphone, to the surprise of all, and marched right over to the two on the chairs, and put his arms on his hips as if he were the intimidator, all 5 feet 8 inches of him.

And he said in a firm and unafraid voice, first softly, then louder and louder: "Yes, mate, I have to come clean. I am Jewish. As you don't seem to like Jewish people, I must also admit to being some other things you probably don't like. I am black. I am Chinese. I am also homosexual. I am a woman, too. I am a Tory or a Labor supporter, not sure which, just the party you don't like. I also support your footy team's arch rival. Let me spell it out for you dumb-arse fellas, I am happily anything you don't want me to be."

The crowd erupted in cheers. They had never seen anything like it, and neither had the two skinheads, who looked around them, not quite knowing what to do. They were up to fighting a bar full of poets and pansies, but the rugby team looked likely to come to Duffer's aid, with a bit of kicking in the rucks to be expected. And coming closer was the Big Beard, and he was pounding the palm of his hand with a big heavy stick.

"Ah, fuck the lot of you," said the uglier of the two, and they both got up and left amid a chorus of hoots and hollers.

"Thank you, gentlemen," said Duffer, "I think that's the same advice our last speaker was giving us."

The really ugly guy pulled a hood over his head as he left, either to cover his shame, or to take his last, best shot at looking menacing. Then they were gone into the night, and good riddance.

After the tumult had subsided, Duffer spoke for his allotted five minutes, but nobody later remembered a thing he said, other than it was generally pleasing and funny.

At the end of the night, the beard, his name was Walter, came and congratulated him, and invited him to return. "I'll be gone for two months or so touring Europe, but I'll certainly take you up on that," Duffer said. And he added: "Do you know a pub in London that also does this sort of thing?"

"I certainly do," said Walter, "my brother is the publican there, and I'll introduce you when you get back."

So, for Duffer, the worst beginning of a speech turned out to have the best ending. As he and Wombat were walking out, the little man who endorsed sex stopped him to say: "Hello, my name is Teddy Cowslip, and I just want to say that you were wonderful." Teddy looked like he had found love at last, which made Duffer a little nervous.

"Thanks, mate," he cautiously replied.

Suddenly, Nigel and Fiona were there. "Terribly sorry we are late. Can you pick us up at 9 in the morning? And, oh, how did it go?"

"A night to remember," said Wombat, before Duffer had the chance to reply.

Chapter 22

An Odyssey to Greece

"Travel, they say, broadens your mind, but if you travel like a tourist and never meet real people, all it does is broaden your stomach while slimming your wallet." Duffer speaking at the Mermaid and Merkin, Oxford, 1974.

Off they went at last, headed for the continent, the Lord willing and the Kombi's well-worn internal mechanisms allowing. That May morning was not the typical one of English springtime lore. True, it had warmed up a bit, but it wasn't all daffodils and robin redbreasts. It was overcast and drizzling, once again causing the visitors to wonder how the rain-averse game of cricket was ever invented in this land of leaking clouds.

Even though it was early on a Saturday morning, Dot, Sheila's cousin and now their landlord, came out of the flat to say goodbye. She stood on the pavement holding an umbrella and was genuinely sorry to see them go. It helped that they had given her 50 quid to keep their room until they returned in July or August, but she had liked having them as company and looked forward to their return.

Sheila insisted on driving. The traffic was light and they got down to Dover without incident and took their place in the queue for the ferry. The clouds cleared up a bit as they sailed across to Calais, the weather gracefully accepting it was not in England anymore. Soon enough they were on the road to Paris, marvelling at the strangeness of driving on the right-hand side of the road.

They stayed four days in Paris speaking the bad French they learned in school, and they kept the Kombi parked on a side street, as if it were Australia House back in London, moving around from time to time in case they ran afoul of the no-parking rules. They walked or took the Metro to the familiar sights and they went to cafes and wondered how they might order a croissant without resorting to mime.

From Paris, they drove south down to Biarritz, which has a beach with a respectable surf, and to their astonishment it reminded Wombat and Duffer of Manly in Sydney without the Norfolk pines. They even managed to hire some old wooden surfboards and, as it was early in the season, they had the waves pretty much to themselves.

At night they parked the van in cul-de-sacs and again the gendarmes did not bother them. They had croissants for breakfast and pomme frites for lunch and they cooked pasta on their primus stove at night, which they supplemented with sardines out of a can. Sheila felt sympathy for the sardines as they reminded her of their sleeping arrangements, all packed in the Kombi van with Wombat.

In fact, the forced coziness of the situation led them to stay only two days in Biarritz and then go back on the road to seek a campground where Wombat could curl up on the ground outside. Another incentive to leave, no greater one for surfers, was that the waves went flat.

Next stop was Spain. They crossed the nearby border and headed for Madrid across the Pyrenees, the rocky barrier separating Spain from the rest of Europe. If ever the Kombi was going to fail them, this was likely to be the place, but it wheezed over the mountains at a sedate and chugging pace, every mile anxious but every mile passed.

They liked Madrid. They stayed a couple of nights in a campground on the outskirts, with Wombat in a sleeping bag outside. They used the campground as their base and at night drank sangria and beer, which made for a novel change.

The campground was full of Kombi vans and various foreigners like themselves, Australians, Brits, Americans, French, Germans, Italians, Spanish, and Scandinavians, all a bit unwashed and unkempt. "Crikey," said Duffer. "The youth of the Western world is on the move this year."

"Yeah," said Sheila, "I'm glad we are not like them."

But their favorite city was Barcelona, with its beachfront, flower markets, and Antoni Gaudi's eccentric basilica called La Sagrada Família, which by then had been under construction for nearly a century.

When Wombat saw the endearingly strange structure still in its forever scaffolding, he said, "It must be a government job." When told that, in fact, it was privately funded, he said, "OK, it must be a union job then."

But all roads lead to Rome, and it was in Italy where the Kombi started to seriously misbehave. At that stage the van was running unevenly, but at least it was running, so they stopped to see the sights in Rome with mechanical anxiety a gathering dark cloud. Sheila was disappointed that they missed seeing the pope. "Maybe if we got blessed, it might extend to our vehicle."

No such luck. They decided to keep going, but as soon as they got on the open road the Kombi chugged slower and slower, with the engine making louder noises in complaint. They drove the next few hundred miles heading south at a pace not much more than putt-putting along. Sheila didn't take this well, and so they stopped in a couple of towns along the way to seek help, not so much in the hope of a mechanical miracle but simply to appease her.

These attempts seemed to follow a familiar script. They would arrive at a garage, a swarm of mechanics who did not speak English would come out to inspect the engine, and the Italian-deficient Duffer and Wombat would explain the problem with gestures and theatrical noises, and the Italians would make all sorts of gestures that the engine had to be replaced and this would require lots of lira, and when it was finally conveyed that the travelers had only a little lira, the mechanics would all rush off and leave them standing there alone, except for Sheila, who was leaning against the van doing a fair impression of Mount Vesuvius, smoldering and likely to erupt.

So they puttered on and, finally, just outside Brindisi, they stopped at a last-hope garage before they abandoned ship and looked for a bus timetable.

A mechanic came out from the inauspicious-looking premises, no swarm of mechanics this time, just one guy in greasy overalls, and he looked in the engine, paused, scratched his head, and then disappeared into the back of his shop. Two minutes later, he returned holding a cable, then proceeded to take a cable out of the engine and replace it with the new cable.

He now gestured for Duffer to turn on the ignition, and the engine burst into life like it was new from the factory. The motor purred, and that noble mechanic, apparently the Patron Saint of Kombi Wagons, smiled modestly while the band of Aussie wayfarers beamed, even more so when the mechanic indicated that the price was just the cost of the new cable, a trivial amount. It did seem like a miracle. Maybe the pope had left a blessing in St. Peter's Square from a previous appearance and they had somehow soaked it up.

When they took the ferry to Greece from Brindisi, they were still smiling, even Sheila. Once on the mainland, they drove to Athens without any problem. But they didn't stay long there. It may seem strange that an apprentice philosopher didn't want to spend more time in the ancient cradle of Western thought, but Duffer knew he wasn't any Socrates or Plato; they didn't work the pub and club circuit.

Duffer was just a tourist walking around the Parthenon in the relaxed and unsupervised manner you could back then. Indeed, having just been up to the great edifice on the hill, Duffer and company went down to the Plaka that evening to eat lamb on a skewer and to discuss where they might go next. "I thought we all agreed we'd go to the Greek islands," Sheila said.

"Yeah," said Wombat, in between contorting his face after a glass of retsina, the Greek wine famed for tasting like turpentine. "The thing is, a lot of these islands are small. We don't want to spend our money taking the van on a ferry to places where it won't be needed. And Athens doesn't seem like a place where we can easily park a vehicle and forget about it for two months."

"Agreed," said Duffer, and he pondered the situation a bit. All around them the Plaka was raucous with crowds milling about, Greeks and foreigners, some of whom may have been at the Madrid campground. An onlooker might have assumed that Duffer was distracted by the colorful party scene. But presently he said, "Crete."

"What's that, Duffer?" said Sheila, straining to hear what he said over the hubbub in the outdoor taverna. "Are you too much on the Greek version of turps to say anything but one incomprehensible word when a helpful sentence might do?"

"Crete," Duffer said again, only louder.

They seemed not to understand. "It's where the minotaur lived," Duffer added.

"Oh. What's a minotaur?" Sheila asked.

"A half bull, half man, a beast who lived in a labyrinth, which is a big maze underground, with lots of different pathways and dead ends. It required human sacrifices."

"Sounds like the motor vehicles department when you get your driving licence," Sheila said. "Are you blokes minotaurs? Half bull, half man and heading for a dead end?"

With no better suggestion, it was settled, they would go to Crete. The next day they motored down to Piraeus, the port of Athens, and put the Kombi on a big ferry. This was the second Greek ship they had been on in three months, but the ferry was no Patris. This vessel was so bare bones it made the old Patris seem like a luxury liner.

They did not have a cabin. Once they parked their van down below on the vehicle deck, they came up to a large public stateroom, where they put down their backpacks on a table and chairs to stake out a little space where they might sleep later. The obligatory snack shop and bar was at the end of the room toward the stern.

Throughout the afternoon, the stateroom was packed with another army of young travelers in jeans and T-shirts. All afternoon they smoked, drank beer, danced to the popular songs of the era, and ate sandwiches and pistachio nuts from little cones.

By 10 p.m., the bar had emptied and those who had splurged a few extra drachmas went off to their cabins. The music stopped playing and the lights dimmed as the sounds of Crosby, Stills and Nash faded.

Wombat appeared with a small, brown-haired girl who looked to be in her early 20s. "I am Malena," she said, giving a little wave. "I am from Sweden." She smiled wanly.

"We are going to sleep out on the deck. Malena wants to come with us when we get to Crete."

"Oh," said Sheila, wondering how they would all fit in the van at night.

"It is OK," Malena said, sensing that Wombat's friends might be worried about adding another body, even her small body, to cramped quarters. "We like to sleep outside."

"No worries," said Duffer. So with the introduction made, Wombat and Malena picked up their sleeping bags, opened the heavy hatchway to the windy deck, and went out to find a place to snuggle and sleep, the snuggling perhaps not helpful to the sleeping.

Twenty minutes later, a gust of strong wind filled the stateroom and Wombat and Malena stumbled inside, wet and wind-blown. "We like to sleep inside now," Malena announced.

When dawn broke, the sea was still rough, but the rising sun gloriously illuminated Crete over the bow, and in another half hour the roofs of Heraklion could be distinctly seen.

They had slept fitfully on the hard floor with the boat pitching, but now they were awake and excited. They grabbed some coffee and pastries in the snack bar and soon enough drivers were called down to the car deck as the ferry was about to dock. With Malena in the back with Wombat, Sheila sat in the front with Duffer, whose turn it was to drive. As they waited to clear the boat ramp and enter the city, Duffer asked the obvious question nobody had thought to ask, "So where do we go now?"

At first glance, Heraklion did not seem a good choice to stop and explore, as they could only see the area around the port, which was unappealing.

Malena had said little up to now and had mostly spent her time holding on to Wombat as if he might lose interest and wander off. Now she said, "A man said there is a place on the coast with a cave and beach."

"I reckon there's many caves and beaches on Crete," Sheila said. "Did the man say where this beach was?"

"To the east," she said. "Past the town of Chania, far as road goes."

"Well," Sheila said. "If a man said it, what choice do we have? Men know everything. Just ask them and they will tell you."

But sarcasm alone could not scuttle Malena's suggestion because again they had no other plan to consider. They saw a road sign for Chania and they took it.

Crete is mountainous and the road to Chania along the coast was not so good then, so the going was slow, but they were in no hurry and clearly Crete was beautiful and something to savor.

Three hours later, they found themselves in Chania. The town looked a bit run down, but they decided to explore on foot, and maybe find a bank and a post office. After parking the van, they didn't go far before finding themselves in a charming little harbor, ringed by ancient houses atop open-air tavernas that were serving lunch.

They found a table in the first taverna they came to and took in the fine view, with fishing boats bobbing at their moorings and splendid old residences bearing the weight of history. Indeed, as they later discovered from a tourist pamphlet, Chania was a melting pot of cultural influences, including the Venetians, who had left their own graceful mark centuries ago.

When lunch was done, Wombat got out a battered map and unfurled it, not an easy task with Malena still clinging to him possessively. "Hey, Mal," Wombat said, shortening her name in the usual way of Aussies, because he figured Malena was a name way too long for social purposes, "Did the man say what the place he liked was called?"

"I don't … remember exact." These were the first words she had spoken all lunch. "I think it begins with F." She made F sounds. "F… f… f… f … Falopia? Fallopian?"

"Could it be Falasarna?"

"Maybe, yes, I think maybe."

"Where did you come up with that name from what she said?" Duffer asked.

"It's the only name on the map at the end of that road."

"OK, Falasarna, here we come then."

They hadn't driven long out of town before they realized that this was the fabled road less traveled, more winding, more mountainous, and not so wide. They passed through little villages with women dressed in black, Greek Orthodox priests with big beards and flowing black robes, farmers sitting on donkeys or drinking coffee in chairs while working their worry beads, but mostly big mountains staring down at the sea.

Finally, after about 20 miles of bends, they came over a grade and there before them was a wonderful vista spread out below, the road going down a long hill to the coast, the land spreading out with hundreds of olive trees, and in the distance a golden beach and some sort of low building.

"Crikey," said Duffer. "That man may have known what he was talking about."

"Not so much," Malena said. "He was a horrible man. He was my boyfriend last summer. He went there and I was supposed to go back with him, but I did not like to do that. Womb Bat is a better man."

Before long, they were all calling Wombat "Womb Bat," pronouncing it like the place babies come from.

Chapter 23

Anna's Taverna

"Ancient Athens had a slave economy, allowing an idle class of people to discuss philosophy at their leisure. One day all our daily tasks will be done by slaves of our own invention, robots. Will we gather in forums to discuss universal truths when the robots do the work? Or will we just discuss sports? Yes, I suppose it will be sports." Duffer speaking at the Eternal Optimists Club, London, 1975.

The low building they had seen from the top of the hill turned out to be a taverna. No visible sign was at the front door, but they discovered the proprietor's name was Anna, so for the foreign visitors it became by default Anna's taverna. It was perched on the top of a small rocky outcrop overlooking the beach. Just below the steps leading up to the taverna was a well, where a donkey was drinking from the trough when they first arrived.

Anna was a small, thickset, talkative woman with a high-pitched voice of command that was respected by donkeys and men. She had several small children to whom she assigned various domestic tasks in the kitchen or dining area. She had a husband, Andreas, who tended the vines and olive trees planted around the building but was otherwise a study in immobility. His main job was to be a man-in-waiting, and what he was waiting for was instructions from Anna. In a sense, many husbands are men-in-waiting, but Andreas took his vocation to a new level of tedium.

If guests wanted milk in their coffee, which the locals seemed to regard as an abominable habit of outlanders ignorant of the local custom of drinking strong black coffee, Andreas was summoned by Anna in an explosion of imperative Greek phrases that meant he should now milk the goat, which was kept out back with the donkey.

Andreas always had a resigned look, but his world-weary way somehow intensified when sent on an errand. He would slowly pick up his pail and plod out to the yard like Sisyphus eternally rolling the boulder up the hill. Unlike the ancient king, he was not doomed to fail in his appointed task, but it always took forever.

So impressively did Andreas assume the role of aggrieved and put-upon husband that visitors who did not even want milk in their coffee took to ordering it to witness the pathetic spectacle. Male friends would chide the person for adding to the poor man's misery, but the women would say, "Never mind the poor man! What about the poor goat?"

Down from the taverna, past the donkey trough, the track sloped down to the beach. About 100 yards further up the beach was a roomy cave, which bore the signs of previous habitation in the form of graffiti and soot stains from beach fires. Being early in the season, the cave had not yet been claimed, so Duffer and Sheila and Womb Bat and Mal occupied it.

Or rather, they plopped down their sleeping bags outside the cave, which inside was rather smelly and claustrophobic and, besides, Sheila feared that it might be home to bats, and it was enough that she had to sleep with a husband who was batshit crazy.

"This looks all right," Duffer said, as if confirming her opinion. "We have a nice view of the beach. The taverna is just up the hill. We got a cave to put our backpacks in and retreat into if it rains. What else could the human heart desire?"

"Toilets," said Sheila. "I don't see any of those."

"There are probably some up in the taverna if human needs are the same in Greece as they are elsewhere."

"Showers," Sheila said. "I don't see any of those either."

"Well, there's a nice spring-fed trough up the way that the donkeys seem to like."

Not being a donkey, Sheila was impressed by none of this. She had hoped to land in a place more resembling the song Joni Mitchell had written a year or two before, on the other end of the island in Matala. Her song "Carey" made Crete's caves seem very romantic, not like this at all, although in fairness her lyrics had mentioned beach tar. Falasarna had that too in grimy abundance, as they were soon to discover.

Sheila wondered whether Joni's Mermaid Café had a donkey trough where you could take off your clothes and rub the beach tar off your skin. That became the daily ritual below Anna's taverna, as long as Andreas and the donkey were not in attendance.

On that first day, the four of them were the only travelers camped on the beach, but in the next few days others arrived. A Dutch couple, Marie and Jan, came, then a Canadian woman and her French husband, Liz and Philippe. They met while having dinner at Anna's taverna, but later they all went down to the beach where they made a fire in front of the cave, and Womb Bat, formerly known as Wombat, played his guitar. He wasn't very good, but he played "Chantilly Lace" with great enthusiasm, and everybody joined in the chorus and were charmed.

Thus encouraged, particularly by Malena, who got so close to him he could hardly strum, he played some more tunes, not so well but with the same wildness, and before the end of the evening the newcomers decided that this part of the beach, outside the cave, was more fun than where they were. So they moved their sleeping bags and took up residence there too in what became a sort of spontaneous United Nations of wayfarers.

Fortunately for the foreign language-challenged Aussies, everybody spoke English, except the Frenchman Philippe, but his partner Liz translated when she could for him and left the rest to context. He seemed to enjoy life better when he couldn't understand. He was a large bear of a man and his loud "Chantilly Lace" chorus echoed down the beach, and it did not matter that Chantilly was the only part of his lyrics understandable to all.

A sort of routine set in, sort of because routines are usually made up of a series of tasks and the cave dwellers didn't have any set task or agenda beyond getting up and moving about, and that none too strenuously.

After a raucous evening of singing "Chantilly Lace" over and over, and drinking Fix beers purchased at the taverna, they usually woke up early. The sun came up bright in the morning, having the blue and cloudless sky all to itself, and they had no shade outside the cave, but it was not the rays that woke them.

Their wake-up call was the sound of gentle bells on the beach. A lone goatherd would lead his flock along the beach every morning. Where he came from, nobody could figure out. Where he went, nobody knew, and nobody understood either why he never came back by the same route in the evening.

The goatherd was a man of mystery. If he saw the cave people, he would call out *"kalimera,"* good morning, but he was evidently not curious about the strange folks living on the beach. He restricted any further remarks to the goats, who moved slowly along, the bells on a few necks providing their marching music, rhythmically pooping on the beach as they went. It was very picturesque, except arguably the pooping.

After this parade, the early risers might retreat into the sand dunes because nature calls whether porcelain is present or not, and a leisurely bit later they would go up to the taverna for breakfast. They always ordered the same breakfast to save their drachmas, *psomi marmeláda*, bread and marmalade, and plain Greek coffee, or Greek coffee rudely adulterated with milk to the greater sorrow of Andreas and perhaps the distress of the goat.

The breakfasters often stayed in their wicker chairs for a couple of hours after their Spartan meal was over, reading books and chatting before they went off somewhere else to do more of nothing.

One morning, having just seen the goats troop past, Jan shared a thought that compounded the mystery. "I wonder if Andreas keeps more than one goat," he said. "Maybe there's a small herd back there where he goes to get the milk. Maybe his goat is one of those that go by in the morning. Maybe the goatherd is his brother. None of us ever goes back there. Maybe we do not have to worry about exploiting one goat."

Jan's idea was something to consider. He was very tall and studious-looking and perhaps he had a towering intellect too. He was taller even than the Frenchman Philippe, but the Dutchman was thin, whereas Philippe looked like he might formerly have played in the scrum for the French rugby team.

After a long pause, Jan said, "Do you know that the ancient Greeks believed in *panes,* who were nature spirits that had some of the features of goats and people?"

"I know," said Duffer, shocking everybody. "They also had the god Pan, who had a goat head and a human body. They were virility beings, so they were often depicted with a big erect penis, like satyrs."

At the mention of the word penis, Philippe, who had been happily uncomprehending the conversation, suddenly took an interest and asked Liz to translate. When she was done, he smiled.

Typical French bloke, Duffer thought. And then he pondered whether penis is one of those universal words, understood in every culture, like beer or bastard.

After breakfast and ideas were digested, they would go off and have a swim. For variety, they would sometimes leave the beach and walk along a track through a field of olive trees and down to a rocky cove. Inside the cove lay a World War II landing craft, wrecked and three-quarters submerged, which made a great place for snorkelers to explore.

They would come back to the taverna about 1 p.m. to have a cheap Greek salad, always a Greek salad, and perhaps a bottle of Fix beer or two. In the late afternoon, they usually had another swim after the day-trippers had gone home. During the week, there weren't too many of these casual visitors, but on weekends quite a crowd of Greek families would arrive and take over the beach with beach balls and blankets.

When the cave dwellers weren't discussing goats and/or the virile powers of Greek gods, some of them played chess, and Womb Bat was one, as unlikely a chess player as could be found. This was usually in the afternoons.

Womb Bat had never played chess in his life but had always wanted to because he thought, against all odds, that it might add an air of intellectuality to his unvarnished manner. In his earlier years, he had tried smoking a pipe to impress the girls, but he never could keep it lit, so chess seemed to promise better results.

He had brought a little wooden chess set from home and now he reveled in playing with his new European friends. They didn't revel in playing him much because Womb Bat was naturally terrible at chess. He played the game like he played the guitar, quickly, with wild exuberance and no real understanding of how to do it. Worse yet, he knew no series of impressive moves that could be his "Chantilly Lace" of marvelous opening gambits.

The problem was that the Europeans were good at chess and they were totally bewildered by his opening moves. They had not been trained to counter such nonsensical play. They realized soon enough that Wombat was not an idiot savant of chess, he was just an idiot. They quickly adjusted and soon won their games, and while there is no honor in beating idiots, they kept playing him every morning because they thought he was a nice guy and wanted to humor him.

And he was humored. When they took half a dozen moves to defeat him, he took this as a great victory, proof that he was getting better. "That's better than yesterday. Jan beat me in four moves yesterday," he would say to Malena. "You are not bad man, Womb Bat," she would say. "You are very smart and good-looking." Perhaps, he thought, chess had helped smooth his rough edges.

At least once a week, Duffer, Sheila, Womb Bat, and Malena would pile into the Kombi van and drive back to Chania to check for mail hopefully sent by their friends and relations care of the Poste Restante and drop off any letters they wrote between *psomi marmeláda* and Greek salads at the taverna. They would then go to the bank to cash travelers' checks and use some of the proceeds to have lunch in the restaurant they first found beside the harbor.

The idyll lasted about seven weeks. The other couples went back to their own lives at different stages. Jan and Marie left first after about two weeks to go back to Holland. Liz and Philippe left for Paris a week later. Other couples came and joined the cave dwellers too. Two Americans and two Germans stayed for a while, plus one or two single travelers, and they were mostly nice, but the bond was never quite the same as the original group.

There was one visitor who was not nice, and he came early on while the original group was still there. His name was Gunther and he was very large, blond, and truculent. Unfortunately, he was Malena's old boyfriend.

He had made inquiries at the taverna and strode down to the cave and found Womb Bat and Malena sitting outside on the sand, holding hands and looking dreamily at each other. He started shouting at both of them, first Womb Bat and then Malena. Womb Bat was puzzled for a moment as his brain tried to puzzle out how he had offended this very large man. He wasn't unaccustomed to offending people, but usually there was an obvious reason and generally he tried to offend people who were smaller.

Ah, there was an obvious reason. Context explained it all. Womb Bat suddenly understood every word the guy was saying in Swedish, even though his Swedish studies had only recently begun and were limited to certain body parts. The gist of it was that Womb Bat should bugger off before the giant killed him and Malena should go with Gunther the Gargantuan.

Womb Bat stood up to his full height of 5 feet 10 inches just as Malena was explaining that Womb Bat here was a good man and he, Gunther, was a very bad man.

"Yeah, she's right, you bastard, you shut your cake hole!" Womb Bat said, looking up at the twisted snarling face of the 6-foot-6-inch Norseman. This remark made Gunther even angrier, and Womb Bat, as he prepared to enter unconsciousness for the sake of his girlfriend's honor, briefly wondered whether cake hole was a special insult in Sweden.

Just before he expected to go down fighting, or at least making a show of it, the cavalry arrived just like in the old movies at the Odeon cinema in Brisbane. They came in the beach-tar-splattered form of Jan and Philippe, both large men, and Duffer, who was not particularly big but was good at appearing tougher than he was, like a frilly lizard back home when cornered. They had heard the commotion and galloped in their flip-flops to the rescue.

Gunther saw he was outnumbered. As big as he was, he couldn't fight everybody, and now some other women were running up to join the group. He realized his old girlfriend was not going to go with him and was therefore not worth his further humiliation, which he attempted to cover up with a torrent of Nordic oaths as he retreated.

Looking back years later, Duffer saw this as the moment when his mate's holiday romance became something much bigger. Without hesitation, Womb Bat had jumped up to be the pawn sacrificed for the greater victory, and now it was checkmate, old boyfriend. Malena could not forget it.

That night around the fire, as Womb Bat played "Chantilly Lace" for the umpteenth time, he realized that Malena had a new wiggle in her walk and a giggle in her talk, and that was what he liked, just as the lyrics said.

The summer continued without further incident and the cave dwellers followed their usual routine of eating, drinking, singing, talking, swimming, reading and playing chess, and nobody paid any attention to Duffer, who, as always, was making notes in an old exercise book.

Eventually, in early August, it came time to leave Falasarna and drive back to London.

Chapter 24

Back to Britain

"I am not much for conspiracy theories. It seems to me that conspiracies require two things to work, people with high IQs and the ability to keep a secret. Yet these are the two qualities most missing in life. Ours is a world populated by mostly stupid people who can't keep their mouths shut." Duffer speaks at the Dying Swan pub in Richmond, 1975.

"So how was it?" Dot asked back at the flat in Kilburn. "Really good," said Duffer, "but it had its ups and downs."

"So what were the ups?"

"Crete was amazing. We sat around the beach all day and at night sang songs and drank beer outside our cave while Wombat played his guitar, well, one song really."

"You had a cave?"

"Yes, we went prehistoric for two months."

"And the downs?"

"The Kombi misbehaved through most of Europe. We finally got the engine problem fixed, but on the way back here the brakes decided to pack it in. We rolled down the Alps all the way to the English Channel."

"It was terrifying," Sheila interrupted.

"Oh, it was all right, darling," Duffer said, "we made it here. I admit that I did lose a bit of shoe leather pressing the brake pedal down hard on the road."

"You are joking," Dot said.

"Not much," Sheila told her cousin.

"Well, glad to have you back. Not much going on here in Kilburn. What happened to Wombat?"

"We dropped him off at the tube station with his girlfriend."

"He picked up a real girlfriend, one that will hang around?"

"Yes," said Sheila, "amazing, eh? The age of miracles is not yet dead. She's Swedish."

"Swedish, you say? There must be a national hot water bottle crisis in Sweden if one of them wants to share a bed with Wombat."

"She calls him Womb Bat. When we were in Crete, we all called him that, but the joke has become a bit stale, so he's Wombat again, at least to us."

"Womb Bat. Is that some kinky thing?" Before Sheila could reply, Dot added, "Oh, Duffer, before I forget, a letter came for you." She got up and retrieved it from the kitchen table.

"Is it from Mum?" Duffer asked hopefully.

"No, it has an English stamp."

Inside was a hand-written note scrawled on notepaper. It turned out to be from the pub owner in Oxford.

Dear Mr. Duffer,

Hello. Walter here, from the Mermaid and Merkin, the pub in Oxford where you spoke. I hope you are back and in fine fettle. I had a word with you after your great little speech after our philosophy and pints event back in April. I said at the time you should come back here or else go to my brother's place in Richmond, the Dying Swan. I told Fred about it and he said to invite you personally as he has started doing the same sort of thing on Monday nights. Give him a tingle when you come back. Here is his number ...

It was signed.

Walter Boggs

P.S. After you have seen Fred come back here.

That same night Duffer did call Fred and said that he'd be delighted to come to his pub the following Monday.

Several days later, Duffer took the Northern Line tube train to Richmond and walked from the station to the Dying Swan. He was by himself as Sheila wasn't interested, she and Dot were going out to the local Indian place for a curry, and Wombat was at his place with Malena, where things were hot enough without curry.

It was the same arrangement as in Oxford, except that Fred, who turned out to be a thinner version of his large brother but just as hairy, saw to it that the allegedly random list for speakers gave Duffer one of the best spots in the line-up, not too early for a fair-sized audience and not too late for the crowd to be largely inebriated. He also was promised that he could go on a bit longer than the other speakers because Fred was the one who rang the bell to stop.

Duffer had thought about his speech but he had nothing written down. He decided to speak more or less spontaneously about his summer in Crete, guided only by the memory of the notes he made in his exercise book at Anna's taverna while Andreas milked the goat.

It was the adult version of essays he had to read to the class back at the Eagle Junction State School: What I Did During My Summer Holidays.

This time he had more material to work with. He had seen naked women frolicking in the surf and taking baths in a donkey trough and if that didn't wake up the drinkers, nothing would.

"Good evening, everybody. My name is Duffer O'Grady. I am from Australia."

A chorus of boos greeted these remarks.

"Hang on. Fair go. It is not my fault we play cricket better than the people who invented it."

More boos.

"Anyway, I am just back from Greece and I thought it might cheer you up tonight to hear what a wonderful time I had there while you were walking in the rain to your dull jobs in London."

Yet more boos. As always, Duffer thought to himself: *This seems to be going well.*

Ignoring the groans and insults, Duffer happily went on.

"I was in Crete, at a little place, just one little cafe really on a beautiful sandy beach. It was called Falasarna, a rustic, unspoiled place where anyone can go sleep in a cave for free. If you order a cafe au lait, it comes with goat's milk. It is called café au bleat."

Groans.

"You should go there right now. What? You can't go there now? Then forget about it. If you wait until next year, someone is sure to tell you that you should have been here last year. This is apparently a law of nature. Everywhere I have been in the world someone has told me that.

"We went to another place famous for its caves in Greece, Matala it's called, and Joni Mitchell sang a song about it. Yeah, you guessed it, a fella told me that I should have been there when Joni was there. 'When was that?' I asked: 'Oh, I dunno. I think it was last year.'

"Well, I reckon it was two or three years before that, but he was a bit of a hippie guy, and they are not famous for keeping time straight.

He did get the principle correct, however, wherever you are at, it was always better before you got there according to somebody else.

"I took a holiday in Vietnam a few years back, all expenses paid courtesy of the Australian government. It turned out to be a strange sort of resort, all the guests had to wear green or camouflaged shirts or pants. It was hot as buggery and the amenities weren't all that great either. To top it off, the locals had a disturbing habit of firing guns and setting off bombs, which is not much fun if you are having a quiet beer or a nap. I said to one of the other guys dressed in green, 'This place is no bloody good at all.'

"And he said, well you know what he said. (Duffer paused here and gestured to the audience to say it along with him, which they all did, in one loud, combined voice): 'YOU SHOULD HAVE BEEN HERE LAST YEAR!'

"Now I am thinking that maybe, just maybe, that the place you are at, the place that is not as good as last year, could have been exactly the same last year, or different in no appreciable way. What I am saying is that the people who are such an authority on how things were last year are maybe gilding the old lily a bit. I reckon two things are at work. It's either that their lives are so pathetic that they have to claim some advantage over you, or else time has played tricks on them, as in the expression 'distance lends enchantment.'

"Unfortunately for both my theories, there is a third theory which must be admitted into evidence: It is possible that you really should have been at the place last year. That is because all across the world there is a creep going on. Some will call it the march of progress. I call it the creep of ruin. Our economic system demands it. This is the way of things. The process is inexorable.

"Imagine a blue sea and a beautiful beach on a wide bay, with mountains as a backdrop and olive groves on the sloping hills. There is one little café. Some enterprising person says, what we need here is a little hotel and some good toilets. No more bathing in the donkey trough. It is a reasonable thought, as we should not make life harder for donkeys than it is.

"People are attracted to the new facilities, but they want to buy souvenirs and they want to have fancier meals than were previously available. So other people come and provide these services, and before long holiday homes appear and more hotels, shops and restaurants and movie theaters go up and the big ball of alleged progress gathers speed. People have jobs now and they can get their children's teeth fixed and it's all good except it isn't. As Joni Mitchell sang in another song, 'They paved paradise and put up a parking lot.'

"So one day, an old local bloke will be sitting in the pub in this new little city and he will say to a mate, 'What is it that attracted all these people to this place?' And his mate will say, 'The charm and natural beauty, of course.' And then they will both look out into the street where throngs of tourists, dressed in ridiculous clothing and eating ice cream cones, are strolling past the trinket shops.

"And they will both say at once, 'Yeah, but you had to be here last year to see the charm.' Of course, as they are old in my little story, four decades would seem like last year to them.

"I have seen this unfolding where I live in Australia. I have seen the charm of the Gold Coast south of Brisbane fade into the shadows of high rises. I have seen the Sunshine Coast to the north covered with 'for sale' signs in the bush land.

"This is going on all around the world. It is not going on solely because of greed, although there's surely a bit of that. It is going on because we, the prime beings on the Earth, want it to go on. We want jobs. We want good plumbing. We want our children to have good teeth. It is natural to want these things, the blessings of prosperity. Heck, I want those things and I don't even have any children.

"And as this process is inevitable, we can't just hold up a sign saying 'Stop whatever it is you are improving!' We have to manage change, balancing what we are getting against what we are likely to lose, saving the pristine places if we can. I know that some people in our rebellious era would meet unbridled capitalism with extreme opposition. I get that and I hope that I am not too immoderately moderate for you.

"But if old Aristotle were still around, I reckon he'd agree with me; he counted moderation as a virtue.

"I do not know if the creep of so-called improvement will ever happen to Falasarna, but I reckon it is a prime spot for someone to come along and make it a place you should have visited last year. I do know that when I lay awake at night in front of the cave where we lived, I thought I heard the creep advancing. Of course, it's possible it was just the goats farting, but it made me think.

"The problem is that we never visit a place for the first time last year. We always visit it in the present that first time. This year will be someone else's last year and wisdom must come now if it's to do anyone any good in the future. I think the first thing we have to recognize is that all progress isn't progress.

"Thank you for your attention. Beer is available at the bar to alleviate your suffering. And if you didn't like my comments, remember, come on now say it with me, 'YOU SHOULD HAVE BEEN HERE LAST MONDAY.'"

The crowd roared and whether it was approval or disgust didn't matter. They were engaged and, having paid nothing except the cost of their drinks, they had clearly got their money's worth.

Chapter 25

Margaret Comes to London

"An old saying insists that the road to hell is paved with good intentions. Yes, sometimes. But I think that bad intentions always pave a road to hell. And if good intentions didn't exist, the whole world would be hell." Duffer speaking at the Mermaid and Merkin, Oxford, 1977.

Much to Duffer's surprise, Margaret arrived in London. It was four years later and here she was, appearing without fanfare.

Dot was the one to open the door and there was Duffer's sister standing in the rain with two old suitcases at her feet. "Well, blow me down, it's Margaret. What are you doing here?"

"Hi, Dot, I thought it was time for a change in scenery, so I decided to come to England and see what my brother was up to."

"Duffer is out at the moment, but this is a welcome surprise. I'll put the kettle on and make us a cup of tea. Do you need a place to stay?"

"That would be great. Have you got room for me for a night or two?"

"Sure. It's a bit crowded here with Duffer and Sheila parked in the spare bedroom. But there are two single beds in there and you can sleep next to Sheila. Duffer can sleep on the couch. He won't mind."

He did mind, of course, when he came back tired that evening from his day job. In the years since he had left Australia, Duffer had reinvented himself. The former bank clerk (unqualified), soldier (conscripted), and postman (inefficient) had become, since his arrival in England, a bartender and now a feature writer for a weekly newspaper. That was his day job.

His night job was still entertainer, comedian, philosopher, although it was intermittent and did not always pay. Sometimes he was slipped a few quid by a publican or else a hat was passed around the crowd to support the unorthodox struggling artist. It was the biggest hat he could find this side of a sombrero and its largeness was supposed to encourage donations. Instead, it only made the few paltry pounds received seem smaller lying in the depths of the hat.

In lieu of pay, Fred Boggs, proprietor of the Dying Swan pub, had hired Duffer to serve the bar, but you were not supposed to drink much on the job and Duffer wasn't very good at that. It seemed a waste of a good pub to him if you weren't drinking with everyone else.

That job only lasted six months, but he did make a contact that led to his latest occupation. The publisher of a weekly newspaper in London, Harold Beamish, happened to be a regular at the pub and he and Duffer became friends of a sort. Duffer told him interesting stories about Vietnam and his reporting stints in the army there, although he left out the part that he was a clerk typist just filling in.

The Crouch End Crusader wasn't The Times of London. Mr. Beamish was happy to have someone who told a good story and as a bonus he had some experience, although stories he had written about soldiers wouldn't be the same as writing about church fetes. He could type too and might even be able to spell. Best of all, whatever small wage he paid Duffer, it would seem like a raise for him.

Duffer thrived in both his day and night jobs. He hadn't ever intended to stay away from Australia so long, but Sheila was doing well nursing at the Royal National Throat, Nose and Ear Hospital and had made lots of her own friends. It amused Duffer that she worked in a hospital named for particular body parts, royal ones at that, and often teased her about this. "This is what you get when a country has a royal family with big noses and ears and a long neck in the case of the Duke of Edinburgh," he said, to which Sheila always replied, "Humpf!"

To cheer her up, Duffer said, "Well, at least you are not a nurse at the Royal National Penis, Testicles and Vagina Hospital." This warranted another "humpf."

Duffer's jokes were clearly wearing thin on Sheila. Sadly for him at least, they had begun to live separate lives. They slept in separate beds, and as Sheila couldn't find a replacement for the Australian Women's Weekly for her reading pleasure, their sex life suffered, although just maybe there was a bigger problem.

The day that Margaret arrived unexpectedly from Australia had been a good one for Duffer. He interviewed a local man who had worked full-time as a clown, but had to quit that line of work because everything about life now seemed sad to him. "I can't even fall over my giant shoes without crying. And when I get hit by a cream pie, my tears mix up with the meringue and make a terrible mess that makes the kids cry. I keep thinking, is life a comedy or a tragedy?" It was, of course, the very question Duffer had asked himself many times.

"I don't know, mate," Duffer said, giving the ex-clown a handkerchief to wipe his face. "It is one of life's great mysteries. Let me know if you find out." And as if a cream pie had suddenly hit Duffer in his own face, here was Margaret suddenly in their small flat. "Hello, Duffer," she said. "How's it going?"

"What...? How...? Why...?" he stammered.

"Well, nice to see you too. I thought I'd take a working holiday overseas, like every other Aussie in the world. I'll be spending the next couple of days here until I can get my own place."

"Hi, Margaret, it's just a bit of a surprise, that's all. How's Mum?"

"Mum and Dad are great. And your brother sends his regards. They were expecting that you would have come back to visit them before now."

"I was expecting that too. And I meant to. But I just got settled into a job earlier this year and there's the little matter of the plane fare, which we need to save up for."

"OK, well here I am. What's your new job?"

"I am working for a small weekly newspaper. I write features on eccentric characters, and thankfully England has no shortage of them. In fact, I think that there's a law that every second person over here has to be an oddball."

"Well, you aren't going to run afoul of that law, are you? I reckon the eccentrics accept you as one of their own and immediately tell you their goofy stories."

"Personally, I'd say it's just my natural charm at work."

"So are you still making idiotic little speeches to drunks in bars?"

"Certainly, and sometimes I get paid for it."

"A fool and his money are soon parted, as they say, but apparently fools lose their brains too as part of that process."

Margaret didn't stay long at Dot's. She had girlfriends from back home who had come on working holidays to England and several days later she moved to leafy and wealthy Hampstead, where her pals had a flat with a view of the heath, not the Sainsbury's supermarket up Dot's street. One of the factors, unknown to everybody else, was that Sheila and Margaret didn't really like each other. Long ago, just after Duffer and Sheila were married, Margaret had occasion to express her dismay about Sheila's scornful treatment of her brother, justified though it might be.

As much as Margaret thought Duffer was a goof who was wasting his life, she liked him and felt sorry for him and felt the need to stick up for him. Sheila had taken this rebuke surprisingly well at the time, but an uneasy peace existed between them.

After she left and Duffer got his bed back, Margaret became belatedly curious. She had never seen her brother perform, if that is what it was, in public. So when they next met, Dot having invited Margaret back for dinner at the Kilburn flat, they had a conversation that was destined to be more important than most.

It started out with Duffer asking Margaret about her new job. Always one to land on her feet and make a favorable impression, Margaret had already secured a position with one of the better public relations firms in London.

"It's going great," she said. "They are more formal than back home. I have to pay attention to dressing smartly all the time and I can't say bloody hell when I spill the tea."

"Bloody hell," said Duffer, "but congratulations anyway."

"Duffer, talking about jobs, I read some of the articles that you wrote for The Crouch End Crusader. You seem to have found your talent at last. The one about the clown who cried his way into unemployment, well, I didn't know whether to laugh or cry. It was great. And the one about the woman who painted rainbows on condoms, hopefully not used ones, to decorate her flat, that was fairly hilarious, in a guilt-inducing sort of way. Obviously, the lady is nuts but you humanized her just enough so as not to make fun of the mentally ill, maybe not completely, but I couldn't quite be sure because I was giggling so much."

"Yeah," Duffer said, "but just because people have strange hobbies and beliefs doesn't mean they are actually mad. It may mean they are just fulfilling the human need to stand out, draw attention to themselves, because they can't think of a so-called normal way to do it. They want to belong in a strange sort of way, by seeming not to belong. If you are the outsider in the group, you are still in the orbit of the group. I know a bloke who craves attention so much he gets up in pubs and tries to make people laugh and think between hoisting beers."

This was Margaret's opening, as she was wondering how to bring up the subject, which to her way of thinking was as strange as painting rainbows on condoms. "Funny you should mention that. I know that bloke too. I just don't know what to think of that."

"Why don't you come along and see for yourself? I don't think that you have ever been to one of that bloke's lectures."

"Lectures, you say? That's what you call them now?"

"I am not sure what to call them. Mindless rants, incoherent rambles, talks, discussions, verbal wanks, mouth spasms, symposiums, enlightenments, narratives, stories… many descriptions are available but you can see why I might want to settle for lectures."

"Where can I hear one?"

"Can you come to the Dying Swan in Richmond next Thursday night at 7:30 p.m.?"

"Will Sheila be coming too?"

"Not bloody likely. She says she suffers enough hearing me talk at home."

"Do you mind if I bring one of my girlfriends?"

"Why not?"

Margaret could think of several sane reasons why not, chief among them the perils of bringing one of her friends into a den of drunken wankers, but the arrangements were duly made. She and her friend Paula took the tube to Richmond, had dinner at a little bistro, and then walked over to the Dying Swan.

The pub was more crowded than they expected for a Thursday night, but more surprises awaited them.

Chapter 26

Duffer Assists the Police

"The eternal struggle between good and evil reminds me of the old matinee movies I saw as a kid: the goodies always won in the end and the baddies always lost. But unlike the movies, when good would triumph in less than two hours, evil in real life is agonizingly slow to lose, perhaps because the triumph of good is heaven's work and therefore a government job." Duffer speaking at the Dying Swan, Richmond, 1978.

The event room at the back of the pub was quite large and, even though they had come a little early, it was already half full when Margaret arrived with her friend Paula. The two women bought themselves glasses of wine from the bar and found chairs in the middle of the auditorium.

People streamed in steadily, mostly men but a fair number of women. They didn't seem to Margaret to be the usual pub crowd, a little better dressed perhaps and more of a variety of characters, but she hadn't been in England long enough to judge properly. Through the open door, recorded music could be heard playing faintly somewhere else on the premises, but mostly the noise was a dozen conversations.

Then there was a commotion at the door. People jumped out of their seats to greet someone and a few of them were shouting with enthusiasm or alarm, it wasn't clear which. The crowd was milling around and it was hard to see what was going on. Maybe it was some celebrity who had wandered in by mistake.

Then a dishevelled man came into sight, his nose bloodied, his shirt hanging out, his pants creased, his long hair obviously a stranger to a comb. Paula thought now that he had to be a vagrant, but vagrants weren't usually so important to people. Everyone seemed to be wanting to shake this bloke's hand or console him.

"Good lord!" said Margaret with a look of horror and surprise. "It's Duffer!"

"That's Duffer," said Paula, who had never met him. "Why does he look like that?" she asked, pointing in his direction.

"He didn't last week," said Margaret. "He's no fashion plate but now he looks like he fell out of the back of a dump truck. And why is everyone making so much fuss about him?"

They caught Duffer's eye and he came over in a minute or two when he had shed the last of his admirers, if that is what they were.

"Love a duck, Duffer," said Margaret, "what happened to you? Looks like you were in a fight."

"I was. In the back alley."

"What? Don't tell me it involved the police."

"It did. But not in the way you think."

"Not in the way I think? I think that the police will be after you."

Just then a policeman came through the door. He was looking a bit beaten up too and when he spied Duffer he pushed his way through the crowd.

"Sorry to interrupt, Mr. O'Grady. But I will need a statement before you leave tonight. What did you say you'd be finished, 9 o'clock? I'll stop by again then and drive you to the station. It won't take long.

Good luck tonight and again, thanks for all you did tonight. I really appreciate it."

"Thank you, Constable," Duffer said. "I'll be here."

Margaret and Paula were now completely dumbfounded. Margaret tried to stammer something but in her confusion the words wouldn't form properly.

"I'll explain," Duffer said.

Then he saw Paula.

"Oh hello, I'm Duffer, Margaret's brother."

"Nice to meet you," Paula said. "I'm your sister's baffled friend. Can I get you some ice for your face? Here, take my handkerchief, you are bleeding just a bit."

"Thanks, I am really OK. It was sort of fun really, except for being thoroughly pummelled, of course."

"Well?" Margaret said.

"Well, what?"

"Why didn't that constable take you away on the spot?"

"Constable Jones? I was on his side in the fight."

"You were on the side of the police?"

"Let me explain. I was in the back alley …"

"What were you doing in the back alley?"

"If you must know, I was taking the opportunity to shake hands with the unemployed."

She looked sideways at Paula. "That means he was taking a leak."

"Anyway, as I was about to relieve myself, I heard punches and shouts, so I zipped up and zipped around the corner where I found three nasty-looking youths getting stuck into Constable Jones."

"Did you know Constable Jones before?"

"Sort of. He always gave me the evil eye when I saw him on his rounds. Looked like an officious little bastard trying to think of ways to cop me. Anyway, as he had not actually done anything in the past, I decided to help him out."

"Whatever did you do that for? It seems you didn't even like the man."

"I didn't like the odds. Three against one. It didn't seem fair and the constable looked like he needed some urgent help. So I started swinging."

"After that pub fight you had in Mulgabimbi, you promised Mum you would give up fighting as you always lose."

"I know, but Mum wasn't around to ask her permission. But Mum's right, I always lose."

"You lost?"

"Well, yeah, my bit of the fighting, but we ended up winning. It was a lose-the-battle, win-the-war sort of thing. Two of the youths were so affronted by me coming to the aid of a policeman that they left the constable alone and concentrated on giving me a beating. This left Constable Jones with just one to fight and he managed to get the better of that clown. So it was now two on two, although I wasn't too effective, lying down on the ground getting kicked as I was.

"But just then, a bunch of other coppers arrived. I guess the constable had managed to call for support or else some neighbour had made a call. They got two of them and the third will probably be found running as fast as he can out of town. He was a nasty-looking character, although it was hard to see his face because he was wearing a hoodie."

"All's well that ends well?" Paula asked.

"Not exactly, as I looked suspicious, the other cops jumped on me and put me in handcuffs, before Constable Jones had a chance to set them straight. I must say they were very apologetic later."

"Tell me, Duffer," Paula asked, "if you had come around the corner, and three cops were beating one youth, would you have joined the youth's side against the police?"

"Probably, Paula. But I don't want to give you the wrong impression. I don't go looking for fights, which is good because I am not very good at fighting as Mum has told the world. And if someone insulted me, I'd just laugh it off most likely. But when others are involved, I'll be on the side of fair play."

"It seems Australians have a very strange sense of honor," she said, and she went back to the bar.

"Strange and personally useless," Margaret added. "Tell us, Duffer, what did you get for your trouble other than cuts and bruises?"

"Well, a constable is my new best friend against the odds. And I might translate that into a gig at the Policeman's Ball, being as they must be starved for entertainment. But you are right, Margaret. Now I have a big PR problem."

"What PR problem?" said Margaret, the PR expert.

"Well, I reckon the people who like what I do see me as a sort of a rebel, the Wild Colonial Boy of pub philosophers. Now that I saved a copper from a beating at the hands of louts, it would be a bit like Jack Duggan in the Wild Colonial Boy song having a beer with troopers Kelly, Davis and Fitzroy. My reputation is no doubt in shreds."

Paula reappeared with a pint of beer for him. "Here, drink this. It will revive you."

"I don't usually have a drink before I speak, but I'll make an exception just this once."

And it did revive him. All it took was one beer, a comb through his hair, a shirt tucked in and a few running repairs to abrasions and he was fit to play on.

Very soon he was up in the front of the crowd, apologizing to everybody for the delay and thanking his well-wishers, of which there seemed to be many, much to Margaret's amazement. And there wasn't any PR problem. All was forgiven for his taking the side of the police in a fight, at least as long as he didn't make a habit of it.

Duffer's talk that night was naturally inspired by the recent events:

"Talk about rude interruptions. As you may know, I was just in the back alley, siphoning the python so that I wouldn't have to step down later from the podium to read the latest graffiti in the men's toilet, when I heard a ruckus going on. So I think to myself, how impolite to have a ruckus without inviting me. So I went around the corner and saw a constable and three ruffians who were helping the police with their inquiries, or probably would as soon as they stopped beating up the policeman. Now, I have to confess, I have never thought of the police before as sympathetic characters, they are not usually all warm and cuddly and have an annoying habit of telling people to stop doing what they are doing, but I suddenly thought that these young bastards might just as easily have turned on me if I were in a dark alley trying to undo my pants.

"Now, of course, I think violence is no way to settle disputes, whether in a back alley with a few bozos or on the international stage where the bozos wear better suits. I certainly agree we should avoid violence if at all possible. I am a pacifist at heart but my nose does not necessarily agree if it is the one being punched. Then it will call on my fists to get involved.

"So there I am in the alley in a bit of a moral dilemma. In the interests of peace, I am inclined to give the youths a piece of my mind in order to forestall violence but suspect that might not work. Suddenly I recall a helpful quotation that fits the circumstances, 'A foolish consistency is the hobgoblin of little minds, adored by little statesmen and philosophers and divines.'

"Who said that? I think to myself. I reckon it was Roy Emerson, no, he's the Australian tennis star. It was the other Emerson, Ralph Emerson, no, Ralph Waldo Emerson.

"I look up and see the hobgoblins are winning the fight. I realize then if I have one other thought, they are going to beat up on me when they are done, because that is what hobgoblins do. Besides, nobody is going to call me a little philosopher because of my consistency.

"To heck with consistency. Once more unto the breach, I say, and I am immediately clobbered and fall down. Two of the bastards then start kicking me and I yell, 'Wait a second, I've fallen down, how about a bit of fairness?'

"Then the cavalry arrived in the form of more policemen. Now I expect that the hobgoblins are really helping the police with their inquiries.

"What can we learn from this adventure? No matter how bored you are with the graffiti in the toilet, you might be better off coming up with your own rather than take your chances in the alley. Also, give peace a chance, as John Lennon has instructed, and if that should fail, consider other remedies."

Duffer went off on another tangent after this and the crowd stayed with him for a full hour. They laughed and shouted out periodically and clapped enthusiastically at the end. Margaret had been told that Duffer was just one of many speakers who took their turn but apparently he was beyond that now. He was the sole attraction.

She and Paula were both impressed and surprised. Not only did Duffer hold the crowd in the palm of his hand but he also had a core group that clearly loved him. He left as he entered, mobbed and slapped on the back, and the women trailed behind him. The germ of an idea formed in Margaret's head. "Duffer," she said, "I think I can help you."

Chapter 27

Duffer's Fans

"No matter how odd you seem to others, never forget that you are contributing to the pool of human wisdom, as carried like a torch from one generation unto the next. 'What have I ever done, Duff?' said a man at the back, adding, 'I can't think of anything I've done for humanity.' 'Nor can I,' Duffer replied, 'but you were smart enough to come here tonight, so I reckon you have potential.'" Duffer speaking at the Mermaid and Merkin, Oxford, 1979.

Duffer's speaking engagements steadily attracted fans, which the self-deprecating people's philosopher took as proof that there really is no accounting for taste. They were never a huge group, but they were loyal and enthusiastic and made him feel like he was doing something worthwhile, which was not the prevailing view among members of his own family. Some of his fans graduated to being his friends.

The excitement that they brought to his gigs had impressed Margaret when she first encountered them at the Dying Swan. Deep down, she still shared their father's feeling that instilling wisdom into laughing drunks was a fool's errand and Duffer would be better off with a more conventional profession.

True, Duffer's job as a writer on a small weekly newspaper was conventional, the trouble being that it was both conventional and poorly paid. She took Duffer on as a project not because she thought he was the prophet of a new age of wisdom but because he might have commercial potential. Against all odds, it seemed that he had a knack for popularity and that, she thought, could be monetized.

Unusual people are apt to attract unusual people, or so one would conclude from the roll call of his new admirers. When he went to Oxford, which he did once a month or so, his fans were often associated with the various university colleges. They were either students or former students, or would-be students in their wildest dreams, and they were mostly men. For women, a night out to see an uncouth gent in a pub making ironic remarks was not generally their idea of an ideal date. Women can be funny that way.

Not too many professors were in the crowd either; they apparently had their academic standards and these did not allow for folk philosophers in pubs. Quite early on, some in the crowd took to wearing artificial beer bellies in solidarity with their now well-rounded idol. That look was so uncool that, of course, it eventually became cool. But that didn't happen for years.

Teddy Cowslip, the first admirer he ever made in England, remained a big fan. He was the strange little man who had spoken on the benefits of sex, without giving any hint he ever had any, at the Mermaid and Merkin in Oxford before the Kombi tour of Europe.

Teddy gave Duffer the creeps a bit, but he never had the heart to tell him to go away. A fan was a fan, and Duffer thought he didn't have so many fans that he could discourage any of them.

One of the friends he made in Oxford was to become very influential later on in Duffer's life. His name was John Foley, which suggested Irish heritage but not as much as his face and fair complexion did.

As it turned out, Foley was actually an American from Iowa. He was married to an Englishwoman at the time, but what he did for a paying job in England was never clear. He was simply called Foley, not John, by nearly everyone, except, of course, the quirky-minded Duffer, who called him Cowboy.

Foley asked Duffer why he alone called him Cowboy. "You are a laconic type of bloke and have this easy way of walking and talking. And you are my idea of an American."

"Not all Americans are cowboys," Foley said.

"You'd never know from your foreign policy or your lax gun laws."

"You got me there. But most cowboys aren't vegetarians." Duffer at that time didn't know that Foley liked a good salad more than most people.

"Well, I reckon you are one of them cowboys who rides the range singing 'Get along little soybeans, get along.'"

"I did work in a rodeo."

"See? The name Cowboy fits."

"I was a rodeo clown."

"Is that an actual profession?"

"Of course, it is. I went to rodeo clown school."

"If you are a politician, can you avoid going to rodeo clown school?"

"Probably not, but I went to rodeo clown school to get the only qualification that fitted me for the job. I was one of the guys distracting bucking bulls after the rider had been thrown, so that they wouldn't gore the guy."

"Why did they want to do that?"

"The bulls blamed the cowboy for the flank strap near their testicles, among other things."

"I might be infuriated too if I were a bucking bull with endangered testicles."

"That is why I became sympathetic to the bulls and became a vegetarian. I gave up my clown job and became a humane officer with the SPCA."

"How did the cowboys react to that?"

"They thought I was just a different sort of clown." And after a longish pause he added, "Being a humane officer clown was more dangerous than being a rodeo clown."

"How so?"

"Cowboys who have their livelihood challenged… heck, a rope around their testicles wouldn't make them any madder."

"You know, Cowboy, I think I'm a rodeo clown myself. I try to make people laugh as I state the obvious about life, I enter an arena, I hear hoots and hollers, I wear strange clothing, or so says my wife Sheila, and I am the sworn enemy of bullshit that afflicts harm."

"Maybe you are."

Cowboy was never one to put on a false beer belly as some of Duffer's fans began to do. He was too lean and handsome to spoil his popularity with the cowgirls. Besides, he didn't like beer, he liked chardonnay.

Ernie Burley, a fan Duffer had in London, never wore a false beer belly either. He didn't have to because he had grown a most impressive one on his own, thanks to the English dietary staple called the chip butty, French fries lathered with tomato sauce between two slices of white bread, washed down with copious pints of bitter beer. If he went on a picnic with his mum, he would have lard sandwiches as a treat with a thermos of tea.

"You shouldn't eat those, dear," his mum would say.

"Dad used to eat them all the time, Mum."

"Yes, Ernie, but he died at age 43 and you're in your forties now too."

"He was in a motor accident with a bus, Mum."

"Yes, dear, but he was unpacking his lard sandwiches on his lap when the bus hit him."

Ernie had a job with British Rail, which was more than was known about Cowboy's employment, but it was still not clear what duty Ernie performed. Presumably, his job did not involve communicating with the public as he had a Cockney accent and he mumbled. Duffer never really understood a word he said, other than "pint of bitter, guv'nor," and "cor blimey, eh?" Duffer just smiled and that was enough for Ernie to be his pal.

Gladys, an ardent female fan in London, had a beer belly, but whether it was real or not no man knew. She may have had a false bosom as well, because both her belly and bust stood out prominently on her otherwise thin frame. Some of her male friends wondered whether she might be pregnant. Gladys, who had a peroxided hairdo piled high and enough makeup for a kabuki theatre character, appeared to be at least in her fifties so pregnancy seemed unlikely, but none of the men dared to ask, although Ernie may have asked and not been understood.

Gladys gave Duffer a lot of affection, which he craved. Somehow, she seemed like his mum back in Eagle Junction, although she looked nothing like her. "Oh Duffer, you were great tonight," she would say, her long eyelashes flapping in appreciation. "But then you are always wonderful. My boy! Come and give me a kiss!"

Duffer was not one for polite kissing. As he once said to Wombat, "I don't mind a good kiss if it is a prelude to a bit of serious slap and tickle, you know, a real knife-and-fork job you can get stuck into, but not if it's just like another excuse for a casual handshake. Besides, you can easily catch a cold from too much kissing, especially if it leads you to taking your clothes off later in the evening."

There was no chance of that with Gladys. While Duffer's relationship with Gladys remained platonic, unwanted kissing aside, it was fortunate that Sheila never met Gladys. Although his wife did not kiss him much, she would have become territorial if confronted by a female admirer, no matter how bizarrely dressed and adorned with thick makeup apparently applied with a paint roller.

Fred and Walter Boggs, the two brothers who separately owned pubs in London and Oxford, also were his friends, but they were something more valuable, they were patrons. They knew lots of people, drinking people to be sure, thus not always reliable, but they helped plant the seeds of his modest fame. Fred and Walter, as much as they liked Duffer, were not such good friends that they paid him properly for this entertainment, but Duffer was happy to speak for not much more than a kind word. This made them all happy.

But his greatest fans and friends were Wombat and Malena, who against all the odds were still together. Malena had gone back to Sweden briefly to explain to her parents that she had a plan to waste her life on a man named for a furry marsupial, and they now were sharing a flat together in North London. She was working as an au pair and he had a job as a photographer.

That Wombat would be a loyal mate was no surprise, that is the job description of a good mate, but Malena's interest was baffling. She didn't understand Duffer's humor and didn't think much of his insights as best as she understood them. But love is blind, and sometimes crazy, so she was always with Wombat when Duffer made his speeches, and her Swedish accent began to take on a North London tone.

They came to every public event Duffer spoke at, whether in London or in Oxford. Wombat started taking photos and eventually he acquired a video camera. Much of what we know about Duffer is owed to his recollections or the tapes he recorded. He was to Duffer what James Boswell was to Dr. Johnson, the biographer.

The only problem was that Wombat had a habit of focusing his camera more on Malena than on Duffer, but that made a certain sense as she was better looking than Duffer. She did not look bored; her pose was Scandinavian serious, an air of enigmatic beauty, cigarette in one hand, a glass of beer in the other, her attention focused but strangely distant, thinking of other things perhaps, maybe the things she loved, fjords, herrings? At the Mermaid and Merkin in Oxford, Teddy could be seen silently worshipping her, his tongue not actually hanging out, just seeming to do so.

Margaret was rarely there; she was back at her flat planning how to make Duffer's fans more numerous and ardent. Like the lady in the garden with the wheelbarrow, she had the job in front of her.

Chapter 28

Misery Does Not Like Company

"So do we live after death? Speaking as someone not yet dead, I reckon it's not what we think. I believe everybody shares in the collective wisdom, and also the folly. Our immortality lies in our genes and our thoughts. Every generation passes on knowledge to the next. If we do have souls, they are recycled and only the good in us survives in an evolution of the spirit." Duffer speaking at the Mermaid and Merkin, Oxford, 1983.

Margaret's promotional work for Duffer was always conducted after her day job at the public relations firm in the City of London where she worked. At first it was more or less a hobby for her and she didn't do much for years because there wasn't much to do. Duffer's friends got him gigs or else he made contacts by word of mouth.

She never told her bosses about this extra-curricular work as she had some important corporate clients and she didn't want it to be known that she was also representing someone called Duffer. The fact that Duffer was her brother wouldn't make the arrangement seem better, as corporations are not known for their sentimentality.

Nevertheless, she made press releases about his forthcoming appearances and sent them out to local newspapers. Duffer was always listed as the contact if a reporter should call, which they never did. However, Duffer by now was writing a weekly column for the paper where he worked as well as performing other duties. These columns were his usual mixture of humour and insight and he was allowed to mention when and where he was next speaking in an italic footnote.

Margaret tried to get Duffer to expand his reach beyond the few pubs he was used to, urging him to let her try to get dates at clubs where comedians were welcome.

"The thing is, Margaret," he told her, "I don't think of myself as a stand-up comedian."

"Well, bring a chair for goodness sake," she said. "And what do you think of yourself as anyway?"

"I dunno, I just want to make people laugh and think."

"Well, lots of comedians do that. They take the stuff of life and make it funny. That is what comedy is all about. You'd be a big hit and you could make some real money. At least visit some more Rotary clubs and professional organizations like you did back in Australia."

Duffer wasn't going to tell Margaret that he considered himself a philosopher of sorts, because that was obviously pretentious. He might as well call himself a wanker and be done with it.

With an eye to the future, Margaret dutifully collected his newspaper columns, something that Duffer himself would never have remembered to do. But that future was a long time coming, or rather the age of the World Wide Web with all its potential took its own sweet time in coming. Once it came, with legions of pundits blogging from their homes and later working on full-time websites, everything changed.

But in the years before that, life served up a few calamitous disappointments for Duffer. He was the one who believed that life was the great teacher but at first he didn't take the lessons well. To be fair, few people do.

These events involved family, including his wife and his mother. Sheila was unhappy, that was obvious even to Duffer, who was wise in many ways but not in personal relationships, especially involving women.

Sheila, her patience exhausted with her hapless and unusual husband, was increasingly sparing with kind words in their marriage. She took to talking admiringly about a Dr. Burn, who worked in the casualty department with her at the hospital. Sometimes in unguarded moments she would call him Phillip, which suggested more than usual familiarity between doctors and nurses. He would hear her say to Dot or one of her other friends, "Well, Dr. Burn came to the rescue…" or, "So I told Phillip that the only thing that patient was suffering from was drunkenness."

Duffer didn't think much of this at first but clearly, she thought Dr. Burn was the ants-pants, as Duffer's mum would have said. Yet when Duffer met Dr. Burn at the hospital Christmas party, he couldn't imagine that Sheila would be enamored of him.

He was trim and well dressed, to be sure, but he was quite short and had a posh accent that would make the cows stampede and stop giving milk if ever he went to Mulgabimbi. No doubt Duffer's instincts were dulled by the fact that doctors with funny names such as Dr. Burn, or podiatrists called Dr. Foot or proctologists named Dr. Bumstead, were hard to take entirely seriously.

They had been in London five and a half years when Sheila told Duffer one night over dinner that it was time to go back to Australia for a holiday.

"We can't afford to do that," Duffer said.

"Not we, Duffer, me. We both can't afford to go but I could go and it would make me much happier. Besides, I am the one making most of the money in this marriage."

Duffer had no answer to that. He dearly wanted to go back to see his mum. He wrote to her every week and often called on the coin-operated telephone outside the flat, patiently dialing the long number for Brisbane on the rotary and sometimes getting a wrong number. He had never planned to be away this long.

But keeping his wife happy was in the job description of husband as far as he understood it. And she was right. They couldn't both afford it. So he said nothing more but sadly asked, "How long will you be away?"

"A month ought to do it."

"Fair enough. Will you go see Mum when you are there?"

"Of course. I'd like nothing better." Duffer wondered whether a faint note of sarcasm was in her reply but it seemed genuine.

She duly had a wonderful time back in Australia and Duffer kept his usual routine in England, only a bit lonelier with nobody to tell him what to do.

She was not home two weeks when a telegram came. Duffer opened it anxiously. It was from his brother George. "Mum died last night from a heart attack. Funeral pending. Sorry."

Duffer called his brother immediately. No, he couldn't come back for the funeral. Sheila's trip had drained their bank account, not completely but enough that it wouldn't stretch to an airfare. He broke down and cried as he explained these things, the first time he had shed tears since childhood. For her part, his sister Margaret did go back for the funeral, she could afford it but not enough that she could pay Duffer's way. She promised to convey his condolences.

Sheila reacted very sympathetically to Duffer in this sad situation. When he put down the phone, she encouraged him to rest his head on her shoulder. She told him how much she had enjoyed seeing his mother when she was back in Brisbane, how fondly his mother had spoken of him. Duffer thanked her for this and would always remember her kindness at that moment. It seemed like the tragedy, as awful as it was, had drawn them back together.

Three months later, Sheila came back from the hospital one night and said to him, "Duffer, we need to talk." How few words it takes to instill a sense of dread.

"We have grown apart," she said, settling on the sofa as if it were a judgment seat. "Our love life is non-existent. We have few common interests and we irritate the crap out of each other. I am sorry but I think we should think about getting a divorce so we can each start over."

Duffer nodded sadly. It was all true. He was acutely aware that their love life had disappeared. But the shock of this announcement finally made the coin drop for him. "Is there anyone else?" he stammered. "That guy at the hospital, Dr. Burn, is it? Are you and he…?"

"Dr. Burn," she corrected him. "And no, well, sort of. We do have feelings for each other."

There was a pause. She expected Duffer to get angry and to pre-empt that she said, "Nothing happened until I heard that you had an admirer too. That Gladys woman who stalks you at the pub."

He was dumbfounded. "Who told you that?"

"Wombat did. He says she kisses you all the time. He thinks it's a grand old joke."

"Sheila, I swear to you… nothing has ever happened with her and me. She is just a lonely lady who comes to the shows. And she does kiss me but I don't kiss her back. She reminds me of my mother and Mum kisses me too." As soon as he said this, he realized that his mum wasn't there anymore to kiss anyone.

Sheila saw his anguish and realized that he was telling the truth. "Well, it doesn't matter, all the rest of it is true. We are married in name only."

They both hugged and they both cried. Despite her sharp tongue, Sheila could be kind and she was genuinely sad. It didn't seem right that any love affair, no matter how ill-advised in the first place, should end like this.

She and Duffer parted amicably. She went to live in Dr. Burn's house in Chiswick. A few months after the divorce, she married him and they took a honeymoon to Australia. They even went to Mulgabimbi and the cows didn't stampede or go off their milk because of his accent. He liked the country so much that they eventually left England and went to live in Melbourne. But her good feelings about Duffer didn't stand the test of time. As Sheila aged, she kept thinking what an irritating and feckless clown he had been as a husband.

Duffer moved out too before their divorce, finding a little bedsit nearer his newspaper office. Although he liked Dot, he didn't want to stay at her house as part of an odd couple, she a cousin of his wife who had fled.

For the next year and a half, he didn't have any speaking engagements, although his fans sent him notes pleading with him to come back. He didn't go out much socially either, except to have an occasional dinner with Wombat and Malena. He never blamed Wombat for giving Sheila the wrong impression about Gladys; he knew his mate had meant well and the misunderstanding was a joke gone wrong.

He simply went about his business, doing his day job, thinking his night thoughts, quietly absorbing the lessons he had learned. He had been presented with a master class in death, desertion, and desolation. All the foundations of his philosophical education seemed now complete and it was no laughing matter, which is not a good place for a philosopher comedian to be in.

Chapter 29

Triumphant Return

"In choosing the great scourges of mankind, it is hard not to bet on the Four Horsemen of the Apocalypse, Conquest, War, Famine and Death, but my money goes on a rank outsider, Loneliness. Being lonely shrivels a person's soul. And no, lady in the front row, while I lately have been a candidate for Recluse of the Year, you don't have to buy me a beer." Duffer speaks at the Dying Swan, Richmond, 1988.

One day out of the blue of depression, Duffer called up Fred Boggs on a pay phone and asked him if he could make a presentation at his pub.

Could he ever! The joy in Richmond and Oxford when one funny philosopher came back to his senses was like the rejoicing in heaven when one sinner repents. The word spread quickly and his fans asked excitedly, "When? Where? What the heck?" It was terrific news to his small band of loyalists, starved as they were for entertainment and a sense of belonging to something bigger than themselves, and never mind how absurd.

Fred Boggs called his brother Walter in Oxford and told him of the imminent return of the prodigal pontificator. Fans in Oxford had somehow already got the word and were making inquiries.

"Hey, Walter, how are we going to coordinate this? Should he come to the Dying Swan first before he comes up to the Mermaid and Merkin? I have already heard from more likely attendees in London than we have seats in the pub to accommodate them."

"Maybe we should think bigger and look at another venue, a football club or something like that," Walter said.

"Wait on, Walter. We're publicans, not rock promoters. We need to sell beer and mixed drinks. How are we going to make any money?"

"Well, we can sell tickets. And then after the show, we can say that there's a 'welcome back Duffer' party back at the pub. And I reckon we should start in London first to see how it goes."

"Yeah, mate, that sounds like a good plan. Tickets, eh? The pricing has to be right. Not too expensive and not too cheap. I mean, the customers were used to seeing Duffer for free so that's a fine line there."

So it was agreed, at least among the Boggs brothers, as Duffer had yet to be consulted. A venue was duly found and tentatively booked. It was an old workingmen's club that was used for various civic and social events. It was called the Thameside Plumbers Lodge and Institute. As the locals joked with a little plumber humor, it was an old and cavernous hall and "not quite as good as it was cracked up to be."

Still, it would do. Licensed to sell alcohol, it was technically a competitor of the pub that was just a short walk away. But as Walter said, "Duffer's fans can lubricate their tonsils over there and then come back to your place for the party."

When Duffer was taken to check it out, the feel of the place reminded him of the Northern Suburbs Football Supporters Hall back in Brisbane, where his old high school teacher had once come to hear him speak, although that modern structure looked nothing like this ornate, Victorian building. Still, his lecture that night years ago had set him on a new path, and inspired by that memory, Duffer readily approved the plan. The admission price was set at seven quid after a little negotiation. The Boggs brothers wanted 10 pounds but Duffer, who wasn't in it for the money, felt uneasy about asking more than seven.

For Duffer, this would turn out to be the biggest opportunity of his curious life. The audience would be bigger, the enthusiasm would be higher and the expectations would be as lofty as the roof of the Plumbers Lodge. Usually, he was excited but unafraid before a speech. This time he was simply terrified and this anxiety showed a little when he announced the plan to Margaret.

By this time, Margaret had taken up with the love of her life, Colin Witherspoon, an actuary, whom she was eventually going to marry and take back to Australia. Over the course of his life, Colin had somehow avoided picking up the famed English sense of humor. His one contribution was when people would ask him what he did for a living, and he would reply, "I'm an actuary, actually." It wasn't much but it was something.

Margaret had invited Duffer to come for dinner at her flat in Hampstead, as she had done unsuccessfully for months in order to coax him out of his depression after the death of their mother and the departure of his wife. This time, to her great surprise, he accepted.

Although he presumably was starved for homemade meals during his social isolation, he didn't look any thinner. He did look more anxious, however.

"So, Duffer, what have you been doing?"

"Oh, you know, working and thinking."

"Given any thought to returning to your public speaking?"

"Yeah, next week."

"What?"

"Yes, next week. At the Plumbers Hall in Richmond. On Thursday night."

"Not the pub?"

"Not this time."

"How many people are coming?"

"The hall holds 350."

"What? Are you worried that just a few people will show up and you'll feel as lonely as the only naked person at a nudist camp on a winter's day?"

"Three hundred people have already bought tickets."

"What? There's tickets?"

"Yeah, seven quid each."

If Margaret were not so astounded, she might have realized that drawing this information out of the normally talkative Duffer was a sign of his foreboding.

But all she could think of was money. Her dreams of monetizing Duffer's eccentricity were apparently at last paying off. She was immediately back on the PR/promotion job, not that this latest event needed much promotion.

Prompted by an unaccustomed lack of confidence, Duffer decided to do something different. He would be creative and use props. As it happened, it was a good thing that he didn't warn the local fire brigade of his plans. There was probably a law against it.

When the big night arrived, he had Wombat and Malena stationed at the door to hand out candles to everybody as they came into the hall. When Duffer finally made his entrance, he too held a candle in his hand. The candles were long and white and were the sort that his mum sometimes bought at St. Ann's, her local parish church, to set up in the little shrine at the side to offer up prayers for loved ones in need of heavenly help, which probably included Duffer if the truth were known.

Duffer was greeted by his fans with great applause, proving once again that absence makes the heart grow fonder *and* there's no accounting for taste. When the shouts had subsided, he held up his candle and waved it around like a conductor's baton.

"Thank you, thank you, it's great to be back. You are probably wondering why I was away. Look, it's nothing any of you said. All I can say is I had a bit of trouble and now I am back after a mental rest.

"And why have I returned holding a candle? Did I resent the remark that I couldn't hold a candle to any other speaker? No, I got this idea when I visited my mum's church…"

Someone shouted, "Hey, Duffs, thinking is not allowed in church."

"They should have told Galileo that. He observed a swinging chandelier in Pisa Cathedral and figured out a great scientific principle concerning pendulums." That shut up the heckler for a while. Later, of course, the church did tell Galileo to lay off his thinking but fortunately for the cause of fewer interruptions the heckler did not know that.

"Now pick up your candles," Duffer told the audience. "I am going to light one then pass the flame on to my mate in the front, who will light the candle of the next bloke and so on."

When they did this at his mum's church long ago, at a Christmas Eve service to illustrate the light coming into the world, it was a very orderly and respectful operation and thus successful. Not so with Duffer's audience. They made it into something of a fiasco. This is the difference between a bunch of rowdy drinkers and a congregation of pious worshippers.

The first holder of the candle spilled some beer on the wick of the candle he was supposed to light. Then, after that person got a new candle, it kept blowing out due to the wind from everybody's shouted instructions. So the candle lighting proceeded fitfully and slowly. Then, after about five minutes, with only about a quarter of the audience with lit candles, someone dropped his lit candle on the wooden floor, where there happened to be a discarded racing form guide, and the paper caught fire. "Fire!" the cry went up. "Get a fire extinguisher!"

But by the time an extinguisher was found, some in the crowd had already poured beer on the paper to put the fire out. After the smoke had cleared and the shouting had died down and the people who had doused the fire went to replenish their drinks, Duffer resumed his presentation.

"OK, folks. Let's start again. Put your candles down. Feel free to keep them as souvenirs of a memorable night. I'll try to explain what I was trying to do, other than apparently burning the hall down."

To anyone else, this mishap would have been a disaster but when Duffer started his public speaking career a fight had broken out in the pub and everybody thoroughly enjoyed themselves. Duffer was encouraged by this memory. The fire was small, quickly extinguished and, with no damage done, everybody was happy except the club manager. He looked like he might have a stroke.

"If we had lit all our candles," Duffer continued, "you would have been part of a living metaphor. We would have passed the spark, one to the other, and each of us would have been illuminated."

"Aw, I really wanted to be part of a metaphor." The heckler was back.

"Well, mate," Duffer replied, "tonight you'll have to settle for being part of a simile."

He paused and waited for a second or two for laughter from those familiar with figures of speech but there didn't seem to be many in the crowd that night.

"See," Duffer said, "human wisdom is like that. All our ancestors and relatives lit our candles of understanding over many generations, and we continue to pass on our light to our children and friends. And every time we do it, it's like our collective light grows brighter. Each of us holds a part of the general understanding of who we are. Each of us has a part of the wisdom in the common consciousness."

"So what about Hitler? Did he have part of that wisdom?" the heckler said.

"Ah," Duffer replied. "A sensible question from the back of the hall, to the surprise of us all." The crowd laughed this time.

"When I say wisdom, I mean the collective consciousness which is made up of the good and bad but tends to the good as we human beings evolve according to nature's plan to what is best for the survival of our species. But there was a time when wisdom dictated we be in tribes because in a world with big and hairy Neanderthals it was helpful to have co-operative friends for mutual protection and support.

"But in our nuclear age, wisdom suggests that it isn't smart to treat everyone else as a Neanderthal, because tribalism is ultimately destructive to everyone. Love saves us, hate kills us.

"So, yes, Hitler was a bad man indeed. If he had any wisdom in the conventional sense, it was microscopic. But to believe that he had none is to believe he was an inhuman monster, which lets off humanity too easily. In truth, he probably didn't approve of people robbing banks, so while he had very little in common with the rest of us, he probably had some tiny little shriveled thing.

"But remember, as the metaphoric candle passes from one generation to the next, the people with the bad candles, the bad wisdom, ultimately don't succeed in passing their light along the line. And I am not saying that those of you who flubbed the candle test tonight are bad people, you are just momentarily incompetent." Some booed now but not loudly as Duffer obviously had a point.

Duffer went on to amuse and challenge the crowd talking about other subjects but that opening remark was more than it seemed then. Many philosophers, prophets, teachers and theorists can be summarized in a single sentence but Duffer was the man who memorably said, "We all have part of the wisdom."

Chapter 30

Uncle Frank's Last Kindness

"Most things in life are blessings and curses all at once. Religion is a comfort to many. Religion breeds fanatics. Beer makes us happy. Beer makes us idiots. And so on and so on." Duffer speaking to the Greater Metropolitan Train Spotters, London, 1996.

The irony of Duffer's unexpected return to public speaking was that it was triggered by another family tragedy. Duffer, who was always slightly superstitious, had secretly feared that more bad news was coming. He believed that life's misfortunes usually come in the traditional set of three. Duffer's mum had died, his wife had left him, so what else could possibly go wrong to complete the hat trick? It wasn't like he had a dog that could be run over by a bus.

Then another telegram arrived. Uncle Frank had died. His mum's gentle and kindly brother was gone. Uncle Frank, who always believed in him when his own father did not, who helped him after he returned from Vietnam, who let him stay and work at the farm at Mulgabimbi, who steered him to get the postman's job in Brisbane.

The death of Uncle Frank hit Duffer very hard. It turned out that Uncle Frank's passing and the subsequent funeral were unusual, to say the least. The problem was that he died not on the farm in Mulgabimbi but while taking a cruise to Fiji with old army mates from World War II.

As Duffer's Aunt Billie later described it in a letter, he just upped and died, a curious phrase when Duffer thought about it. Uncle Frank did not go up at all, he slumped down. He did it while on a park bench in Fiji. He probably was taking a solitary snooze after visiting a local pub, as tourists are sometimes known to do. The ship had left by the time his body was discovered and the Fijian authorities were not sure what to do with it, and, subsequently, nor did his family.

The funeral home in Suva could keep Uncle Frank's body in storage and put it on the next ship in a month's time to return it for a proper burial. That would cost a fortune. Or else, they could cremate the body and mail the ashes in a package to Australia, which would still be costly but not amount to an actual fortune.

The family spent a lot of time agonizing over this, because the Catholic Church had long frowned upon cremation. Although church policy was evolving, family members still clung to the old thinking. Eventually, frugality trumped theology. As one of his sisters put it, "The church doesn't have any problem saying Masses for people who are lost at sea. Frank was sort of lost at sea, wasn't he?"

Well, sort of. He was on a cruise and Fiji is in the middle of an ocean, and so Frank being lost at sea became the polite phrase used to justify cremation, but the explanation was not much spoken of, and certainly not at the service in the church a month later. Uncle Frank's ashes stayed home that day.

But there remained the question of what to do with them. At the family wake on the night after the service, the matter was much debated. "Why don't we just go and pour his ashes on his mum's grave?" Aunt Billie said.

"Actually, if you remember, he didn't get on with our mother very well. She wanted him to be a doctor and treat rich patients and he wanted to tend to poor cows," Uncle Bob, Billie's younger brother, said.

"Why not spread them on his farm?" Aunt Billie said.

"No, Billie, he worked hard on that farm. He wouldn't get any eternal rest there thinking about all the jobs that weren't getting done."

"As I understand it, when you're dead, you don't think much," Aunt Billie replied.

"That's just your theological opinion," Uncle Bob said.

Then, feeling a little guilty for his harsh tone, he added his own suggestion. "As a young man, I remember he loved going to the races and the football in Brisbane. Why not spread them at Eagle Farm Racecourse? Or at a stadium like Lang Park or the Gabba?"

"Wouldn't people notice and ask embarrassing questions?" Aunt Billie asked.

"Right," Uncle Bob said. "So, I could put them in my pocket and make a hole in it and walk around with his ashes coming out my trouser leg. I could rig a string to release them. Or you could come with me, Billie, and I could make a little trapdoor in your handbag and you could pour them out when no one was looking."

About this time even the dimmest members of the family realized that comedy and tragedy were now holding hands, alternately giggling and frowning at each other. Therefore, they accepted the shaky adage that when in doubt, people should do nothing in the hope the problem will go away. So they did, nothing, that is.

Duffer was never to know what became of Uncle Frank's ashes. Ashes to ashes, dust to dust, and then to a cupboard hidden away somewhere.

As Duffer read the letter Aunt Billie had sent him explaining all this, he surprised himself. As sad as he was, he started laughing. He laughed and laughed and whether the tears rolling down his cheeks were from sorrow or comedy, he himself could not have said.

He laughed because Uncle Frank would have thought it hilarious as well. There is nothing funny about death, except that part resembling a cosmic joke. Here was a family grieving their beloved brother but seriously wanting to lay him to rest with trapdoors in handbags and porous trousers at a racetrack or a footy stadium.

The more Duffer laughed, the more his own grief retreated. Uncle Frank, a good man, was dead, Duffer was alive and still capable of being a good man. To do that he must stop crying and start living again. Duffer said quietly, "Thank you, Uncle Frank, you have rendered your last service to me." But that turned out to be wrong.

A month later another letter arrived. It was from a law office. Uncle Frank, a life-long bachelor who had no children, had left his entire estate to Duffer, the last person in the family anybody expected. It basically amounted to the farm and about £250,000 in a savings account, the result of Uncle Frank's frugality over many years.

Duffer was astounded. The solicitor's letter asked him if he wanted to keep the farm. Not ready to be a farmer, he did not need the farm, so the solicitor then arranged for it to be sold at auction. As it happened, city dwellers were increasingly looking for country retreats, hobby farms, around that time and Uncle Frank's property sold for a tidy sum. While Duffer might not have been rich in the estimation of the really rich, he now had more money than he had ever dreamed of making himself.

And as his divorce was final, Duffer did not have to share it with Sheila, but, Duffer being useless in many things but kindly in all of them, he did give her a thousand pounds anyway, mostly for emotional reparations but also because he couldn't help himself. Sheila was once again thrown into conflicting thoughts concerning Duffer being so nice and a pain in the arse all in one awkward package.

Duffer also gave £200 to Margaret for PR services rendered, which was remarkably generous considering she hadn't done much rendering yet.

He did treat himself. For one thing, he decided to move to a better flat. The one he was in was of the traditional sort for someone of meagre means, being situated over a fish and chip shop. As usual in such circumstances, the smell of the frying oil permeated the whole building and the fish and chips were very tempting to him despite the odours emitted by their production. He feared that his beer belly was now mostly haddock and potatoes.

His new place was near a nice park in Willesden Green in northwest London and offered less immediate temptations in the way of saturated fats. For the higher rent, the furniture was not so worn, the paint not so flaky, the carpet not so dirty and altogether everything was nicer. It was bigger too, not just a bedsit as formerly, and it had a kitchen where perhaps proper meals could be conjured up if anyone other than Duffer was around to do the conjuring.

He also used some of the money to buy himself a car, not a new car, but a Morris Mini-Minor that was reliable despite the many miles on the odometer. By this stage, the old Kombi wagon was not his to use, having been bought by Wombat and Malena, who could use the sleeping space in the back to better advantage than Duffer or Sheila could.

The car really opened up possibilities. No longer limited by public transportation, as good as it was in London, Duffer could do his newspaper job better and reach more locations for his speaking engagements. These had grown steadily since returning to the public eye. He was not now confined to the pubs in Richmond and Oxford and was speaking in more clubs. Still, this process proceeded slowly.

He became friendlier with his American mate, John Foley, or simply Foley, as everybody called him except Duffer, who still called him Cowboy. Some months after Uncle Frank's money rescued his finances, he had Cowboy and his English wife Patricia over for dinner one night to celebrate his good fortune. Wombat and Malena were invited too.

Nobody who knew Duffer would have believed it. He had never hosted a dinner party in his whole life. Of course, when he was with Sheila, some mates sometimes came over and Duffer stuck meat on the barbecue to be grilled beyond recognition in a display more like cremation than cooking.

Wombat, being an old-school Australian who liked unrecognizable charred meat as much as the next person, assumed that he and Malena were in for the same.

He even asked Duffer, "So, mate, what are you grilling?"

"Not grilling, mate."

"Not grilling? How are you going to serve us a mouthful of ashes?"

"Not grilling. It'll be full-on gourmet all the way."

Wombat was shocked. He had heard the word gourmet but didn't really grasp the concept. "You mean, the blokes are not going out into the backyard to drink a few beers and play a game of guess-the-meat as you grill?"

"No grill, no backyard. My flat is on the second floor."

"How are you going to do it?" Wombat asked this question in wonder like a person asking a magician how come his top hat was full of rabbits.

"I have a helper. Her name is Victoria."

It was true. After months of social hibernation, Duffer had found a girlfriend. "She's an English lass," he explained. "Cooking is her hobby."

Wombat was dumbfounded. He could hardly wait to meet this mystery woman, Victoria, who was now apparently stirring the stew of Duffer's life.

When she appeared the night of the dinner party, wearing an apron with a spoon in her left hand, he couldn't believe what he saw.

He almost said in a stammer, "Sheila…?" But as he checked himself, she said, "Pleased to meet you, I'm Victoria." And she reached out with the hand not holding the spoon to shake his.

"I'm… William, er Wombat, they call me Wombat."

"Pleased to meet you, William."

She introduced herself to Malena, who also looked puzzled.

Victoria looked almost exactly like Sheila, they could have been taken as sisters. She had the same brown hair styled the same way, the same blue eyes, same nose and shapely figure and ample bosom. Even the cast of her face had the same no-nonsense aspect to it, enough to intimidate Wombat into calling himself William at first glance. Her English accent was educated but not posh, although she had a very formal manner.

Why she had become Duffer's girlfriend was anyone's guess. He was the human embodiment of informality. Even in his army uniform, he had looked like he had slept all night on the parade ground. Perhaps she saw him as a project for improvement, that doomed conceit of many women inclined to gravitate to men they see as having potential.

Why Duffer should like her was more easily explained, as Wombat explained later to Malena on the drive home.

"He's been lonely, of course. But there's another thing going on. Some men, and even some women but mostly men because they are more stupid, when they break up find a partner who looks very much like their old partner. It's like the perfect image of a partner is embedded in their brain, so they revert to form."

Malena said, "So, Womb Bat, did you ever have a girlfriend who looked like me and made an impression on your brain?"

"Of course not," Wombat said quickly. "You are my original lovable ideal of a woman." Then he remembered that the girlfriend he had briefly had on the good ship Patris, come to think of it, did bear a striking resemblance to Malena. He thought it best to keep this thought to himself.

They went on to talk about the dinner party in general. They agreed that Victoria's coq au vin was cordon bleu stuff, even after Wombat and Duffer put tomato sauce on it. They agreed that it was a jolly night, even if Duffer's girlfriend was from the same mold as Sheila.

Meanwhile, back in Duffer's new flat, Duffer was telling Victoria that Foley had given him some unwelcome news when they were talking in the kitchen.

"I am taking Patricia back with me to America," he had told Duffer.

"That's not fair," Duffer had said. "Just when I got to know you. So where are you moseying along to, Cowboy?"

"Pittsburgh, Pennsylvania," he said.

"Is there a need for rodeo clowns out there?"

"Well, no, but I am going to be a bigger clown. I am going to be an academic." It turned out that Foley's job in Britain really wasn't a paying job, he was studying for a Ph.D. at a local university. His thesis had been "The Prevailing Paradigm of the Mythic Cowboy as It Has Influenced American Mores."

"Crikey," Duffer said. "You managed to get paradigm, cowboy and mores in the same sentence. Surely a first?"

"Not even close," Foley said. "Not in the circles I move in."

"I will miss you," Duffer said.

"Me too, brother," and Foley gave Duffer a hug, which both found awkward, as Duffer was many things but huggable was not one of them.

Chapter 31

Two Friends an Ocean Apart

"Logically, the human mind is not like a radio receiver that receives and transmits signals from others. Yet somehow it does that. So many of our thoughts and emotions are contagious, even across great distances. And some of our thoughts seem to be continued by others when we are dead, after our radio brains are switched off." Duffer, speaking to the Guild of Bell Ringers, Canterbury, 1997.

Foley and his wife Patricia left England promptly. Foley went enthusiastically because he was returning to his home country, and Patricia reluctantly because she was leaving hers. This was the unfortunate part of matrimony that participants are warned about during the wedding service. For better or for worse.

As it turned out, it was for the better, and it was also for the richer, not for the poorer, the other part of the ever-chancy deal. Foley settled into the history department at the University of Pittsburgh quite well. While academics are known to snort and stamp their feet over comparatively minor issues, Foley remembered bulls doing that and was not overly intimidated, although it was a toss-up whether the bulls or the professors were more prone to crankiness.

215

Patricia, a commercial artist, found work easily and charmed her workmates with her accent and her manners. Both were paid well by their standards; more than she ever made in England and more than he could have expected if he had been lucky enough to get a job at an English college. Unexpectedly flush with cash, they rented an apartment in trendy Shadyside, just a short bus ride from the Pitt campus in the Oakland section of the city.

Foley missed his old drinking philosopher pal, and he and Duffer began writing letters to each other in what they did not know, then, was the last blush of personal correspondence with paper and pen. The art of letter writing, turned into an art form over hundreds of years, was soon to be made deceased by the Internet. Their letters did not live up to the majestic standards of old.

Hey Man,

How they hangin', dude? We arrived in Pittsburgh on Monday night. Some guy from Pitt picked us up from the airport and drove us into the city. He didn't warn us about the spectacular introduction to come that I have since heard amazes everybody who comes this way. You drive for about 15 miles through a nondescript landscape of towns and buildings, and then you suddenly shoot through a long tunnel, only to pop out onto a bridge and a completely different scene. The city is right there, three rivers, bridges, skyscrapers, all lit up. It's like being shot out of a cannon and tumbling into a big safety net before a large circus crowd. Or, more to our point, it resembles childbirth, being a newborn suddenly thrust into the light of a new life and slapped on the butt.

It's been two weeks now, and we are still fairly amazed. It's cold here, but unlike England, where it's cold and damp, here it's just plain freezing when it's not snowing. None of this is any problem for a cowboy from Iowa, but my English rose seems to have a touch of frost where the aphids usually roam and has taken to wearing thick woolen man-repellent stockings.

For their part, the locals have adopted a diet best suited to keeping them warm by making them large, as sea lions do by developing their blubber. They eat Polish sausages, Italian sausages, meatball sandwiches, pizza, and something called pierogis, which are like dough balls. They also have something called wedding soup, which also features little meatballs, but it's probably better than divorce soup, which I assume is bitter. Everything is washed down with Iron City beer, which may actually have a touch of iron in it, at least according to my taste. I keep forgetting to bring a magnet to the bar to test this theory.

They also have a thing about French fries. There's a famous place here that gives you the fries inside the bun of your steak sandwich, just in case you forget to order them. And they love fish sandwiches, which is strange because Pittsburgh is far away from the ocean, even at high tide.

By the way, I always thought you spoke funny, but this place has its own accent and even its own words. Lots of them say "yunz" instead of "you." The way they speak is not incomprehensible like your expressions, but you would have some competition if you came here.

How you doing? How is Victoria (the new girlfriend, not the old Queen Victoria)? Send a report please.

Yours not very sincerely,
Foley

A couple of weeks later came the reply, its letters formed carefully in a childish hand, as if Duffer was still at the Eagle Junction State School, writing on his slate with his tongue poking out:

Dear Cowboy,

We are doing OK, seeing that a great darkness has descended on the land since you left. Wait… it's England. That's just a rain cloud.

You ask about Victoria. Well, she is trying to make an English gentleman of me, which of course is a hopeless task. She increasingly does not approve of my speechifying. She wouldn't mind if I were speaking in the House of Commons, but she thinks that addressing drunks thirsting for philosophical knowledge is no better than being one of the fanatics who hold forth at Speaker's Corner in Hyde Park. This is a bit of a problem, seeing that this is my hobby/vocation/destiny?

However, she does approve of my latest achievement, such as it is. I have become a published author. Actually, this was the doing of Margaret, my sister, who has been nagging me to collect my speeches into a book of essays on various subjects. This was quite a lot of hard work because I don't usually write down my speeches; I just have a series of cue cards with single word prompts: Death, Love, the Almighty, Eternal life, Underpants… that sort of thing. So I have had to recreate my speeches into essays for the book, which is titled "The Joke Is on Us!" Subtitled: "The Meaning of Life Explained, Sort of." It is a self-help book for hopeless bastards with Common Sense Deficiency Syndrome, a not-uncommon complaint.

Now when I make my speeches, I sell the customers the book too. It costs 10 quid, and many of them buy it, themselves having less common sense than nudists have pockets for handkerchiefs, which is fortunate for me and my sales.

Of course, most of the literary reviewers for the big newspapers and magazines have ignored it, snotty as they are, but I have at least one great review, admittedly by Doris, the tea lady who doubles as our book reviewer at the weekly I still work for in London. She said, "It's a nice read for people hoping to kill some time waiting for the train."

I wish she had asked me to lend her some more descriptive adjectives, but it did the job. Margaret got the layout artist to put it on the cover as a promo: "A NICE READ!"

Margaret arranged a book signing and invited her professional contacts to one of the new wine bars in the renovated Covent Garden fruit and veg market. I didn't know anybody and felt totally out of place, shaking so many limp-fish hands that I thought I was in Billingsgate. Not one person in that well-shod crowd bought the book, but they looked very superior in averting their gaze from the stack of my unsigned books. All the while I was dying for a beer, which of course was unavailable.

Margaret declared it a great success. Victoria was very impressed too. When we go to parties at her fancy friends' houses now, she introduces me as Robert (she won't call me Duffer anymore, which she thought was funny at first). She says, "Fiona, my dear, I want to introduce you to my dear friend Robert. He is a writer, you know."

And Fiona says, "That's simply marvelous! You are a writer?" Fiona (or whoever) is always very thin; she needs to come to Pittsburgh to fatten up, and she is fashionably dressed, which is to say she is wearing an outfit that no sensible person would wear outside for fear of making dogs bark.

"Yes," I reply, "I write features for the Crouch End Crusader."

Then Victoria says with a forced smile, "Oh, Robert, you are such a wag. Stop being so modest and tell her about your amazing book."

At that same time, she delivers a death glare that misses me but threatens to set fire to the curtains.

So, what can I say? Life goes on, although I keep trying to drown my liver to make it stop. Wombat and Malena send their regards, ditto Gladys, the Boggs brothers, and Ernie, well, I think Ernie, but who knows what Ernie says.

I've got to go now. I am saving my hand for when I actually have to sign my book. I don't want to cramp up in the hour of my glory.

Your mate,
Duffer

This correspondence went on for years in the same superficial, casual, kidding terms that only vaguely flirted with whatever serious events were actually unfolding in their lives. Their letters were a free-flowing dialogue, more stream of unconsciousness than consciousness, as if dictated from the high vantage point of bar stools above the sawdust of life.

Foley gathered that Duffer was having a hard time trying to keep Victoria happy, but he couldn't judge whether this was a serious situation or not. It didn't take much to keep Duffer happy, and some women persist in a man-makeover project long after all hope is dead. Their letters got shorter as the years rolled by and less frequent, not for the fading of mutual friendship but for the lack of anything new to describe.

But then the World Wide Web came into everybody's lives. Foley asked in one of his letters if Duffer had an email address. He did. As soon as this letter was received, an email message came back via America Online.

The subject line was: Postmen and carrier pigeons be gone.

Hello, Duffs. Welcome to our new form of correspondence. This has the potential to change the world, make it a better place, bringing knowledge, goodwill, and friendship speeding across the globe at the tap of a keyboard. On the other hand, it may just drive everybody crazy. Who knows? All I know is that there's no ignoring it. We have to embrace it or else be condemned as hopelessly old-fashioned, which is probably true in both our cases. I do feel sorry for the letter carriers who appear to be screwed. If memory serves, you used to be a postman; you did well to leave that behind. First, they came for the carrier pigeons, then they came for the letter carriers. Fortunately for you, there will always be newspapers to work in as a base for your after-hours speechifying. But I reckon this is your chance. With the world in communications upheaval, what people need is a drinking philosopher. America is where it's all happening, buddy. I saw the other day that one of the local colleges (not mine) has this thing called Writer-in-Residence. I know a dean down there. What do you think? Like to come to America? Get paid for doing not a whole lot?

Your bud,
Foley.

Chapter 32

Duffer Has a Lucky Escape

"Celebrity is an addictive drug peddled by our hyped-up culture. The more you taste it, the more you crave it. Like all drugs, it makes you feel high, but it can also kill you. In the mass of people who may like you, one or two will hate you and want to see you dead." Duffer speaks at the Mermaid and Merkin, Oxford, 2003.

"You want to go where?" Victoria asked Duffer. "Pittsburgh, Noplacevania? It sounds absolutely dreadful."

"Foley says it's great."

"So you're taking advice from rodeo clowns now?"

"Former rodeo clown. He's a professor now."

"I don't care if he is the chancellor of a bloody university. That place has to be the pits. Why would I go to a city named for coal mines?"

"Actually, it was named for William Pitt the Elder, 1ˢᵗ Earl of Chatham, one of Britain's early prime ministers."

This shut up Victoria for a moment. "Oh!" she said, and pondered it a bit. "How in the world do you know these things, Robert?"

"I read a lot in a rundown Saigon hotel and on the back of a tank. You know what they say about war: Moments of terror interspersed with many hours of reading history books. Better than Oxford for an education, I reckon."

"Well," she said, "I am still not going to Pittsburgh."

"How about just a visit to see what it is like?"

"Not any time soon," she said. *Well,* thought Duffer, *that's good, she didn't rule it out completely.*

Indeed, while Duffer liked the idea of moving to America, it wasn't destined to happen anytime soon. The internet age had arrived with a new century. Soon legions of people in pajamas began to write for lots of other people in pajamas. Well, Duffer had a pair of pajamas and he had also had a sister, Margaret, who saw the potential of this new form of communication.

It was Margaret who made a blogger of Duffer, gave him his own professional-looking website, turned him into what would later be called an influencer, although what influence he had on society was anybody's guess. He was more an object of fascination for people. They came, they laughed, they thought, and in the process moved Duffer from being a minuscule celebrity to a minor celebrity, on the verge of medium.

While Margaret and others were still figuring out how to monetize free websites, his blogs attracted more people to Duffer's lectures, which led to more lectures, which led to more book sales and signings, where now even superior-looking people deigned to check out his wares. He published a new book, "An Eccentric Guide to England's Eccentrics," which did better than his first one. His feature writing job, as well as his own personality, made him an expert in eccentrics. All the characters who filled his column found their way back into his new book.

Duffer and Foley kept exchanging emails. His mate in America never stopped extolling the virtues of Pittsburgh and eventually, watered by the shower of steady enthusiasm, the seed sprouted years later. But why then?

Seeds keep their own sweet time and Duffer just thought it was time. He felt that he had achieved all he could achieve in England, but that was only part of it. He recognized that he did better in places where he did not really belong.

Britain had become very familiar to him. It had taken years, but the accents, the attitudes, the tastes, the landscape, even the bloody climate with its cold and drizzle, seemed more and more like home to him. As he said to Wombat once in a thoughtful moment, "Jeez, mate, I think I'm turning into an English person." Wombat said, "Oh the horror!"

If he went to America, he would be a stranger in a strange land again, with all his creative juices revived. But would Victoria come with him?

Maybe the idea of making a change would force some sort of decision about the future of their relationship. They had always kept separate flats, and while sometimes they stayed the night together in one or the other place after dinner or a party, neither of them wanted to move in together permanently. "I like my space," Victoria said.

"Well," Duffer said, "I like my ability to leave laundry in a pile wherever I want and put my underpants in the microwave if they don't dry completely in the wash."

Their romantic life was good enough for both parties, having low expectations that were easily satisfied. Victoria never read a magazine when they made love, but she only said she loved him when she was asked.

He would say, "How do you feel about me, Vic?"

"Oh, I dunno, you're OK, there's room for improvement, but you're not as bad as my last boyfriend."

"So do you love me, then?"

"Yeah, I love you. Do you love me?"

"Of course, I love you."

"Do you love me as much as you loved your mum?"

"Well ...."

"Do you love me as much as you love cricket?"

"Well, that's another hard one, Vic."

Another odd feature of their relationship was that for many years Duffer never met her parents. Sooner or later in a relationship, people feel they must introduce the new person in their lives to the old people in their lives.

As wise as he was in the ways of the world, the Great Observer had not thought too much about this. It was only because Victoria's parents came to London for a football match that he ended up participating in one of life's most frightening ordeals, meeting the partner's parents. They met in a café.

Peter and Poppy were from Birmingham. They turned out to be delightful people, but to Duffer's surprise they had working-class accents and sounded nothing like their daughter. He was a stonemason and she worked in a shop.

Victoria was obviously on affectionate terms with her parents, she wasn't embarrassed by them, but Duffer came to wonder whether their meeting was delayed because they contradicted the upper-class impression she tried to promote. Duffer didn't think any less of her for disguising her humble background. Everyone puts on a front, Duffer reckoned. Why, he got up on stage every week and pretended he was smart and wise.

No, he loved her all the more, that is, if he really loved her at all, which would be put to the test by his ambition to move to America. They hadn't mentioned it since the first time he raised the idea. Nor had they ever talked about getting married. Duffer assumed that this was because she was focused on her career at the bank, not that he was a distracted, divorced, disheveled no-hoper.

"So, Vic," he said one evening as they sat in a local Indian restaurant waiting for their curries to be served. "I have been thinking," Duffer said.

"Of course, you have," she said a little too flippantly.

"I have been thinking that it's time to make a break with our old routine," he said, snapping a papadum for emphasis, as you do. "We have been together for what is it now? Close to 15 years? I can't believe it's been that long. But we are apart more than we are together. We are a couple consisting of two singles.

"I am not saying we need to get married. I did that once and it seems like I wasn't very good at it. No, we could be domestic partners. We could share a flat together, have a joint bank account, get a dog."

"A dog?"

"Well, a cat, if you prefer. The point is that we should change things. We could go overseas."

"When you say 'overseas' you mean America, you mean go to that city where your cowboy mate lives, that Foley person."

"Yes, as a matter of fact. Pittsburgh, Pennsylvania. I haven't been anywhere since I went around Europe in a Kombi van years ago. I haven't even been back to Australia."

"What do you expect to find in America?"

"A new lease on life, I reckon. C'mon, Vic, let's go over on our holidays. We got a place to stay. We can check it out."

There was no "we" about it. Duffer went by himself to check it out and it was everything that Foley had said it was. After Duffer returned to London, he told Victoria this and once again she told him that she couldn't possibly live in Pittsburgh.

"Robert," she said (to the last she called him Robert). "I know it's a big corporate headquarters city, but the ethos is working class, just like Birmingham, which I have tried to forget."

It had come down to this. Duffer liked Pittsburgh for its working-class ambience and Victoria didn't like it for the same reason. They had irreconcilable geographical differences, with some sociological and romantic reservations thrown in.

So it was decided. There were no hard feelings on either part, only some sadness for what might have been, even if it was always improbable. She was not a bad person and she went on to better things.

While she knew Duffer much longer than the Long-Suffering Sheila, she did not suffer nearly as much and the same nickname never attached to her, and not because the name Victoria did not offer the same alliteration opportunity. She had been the mistress of her own fate. She made her own bed, she lay in it, and was sensible enough to get up out of it. She soon found a more mature man who was a well-off architect and did not need as much domestic training.

After they broke up, Duffer handed in his resignation at the weekly. His now large band of followers at pubs and clubs was very disappointed but promised to keep following him on his blog. The Boggs brothers scheduled a Saturday night public farewell for him at the Dying Swan, which was a great success, at least initially. Fans shed sincere tears, and prosthetic beer bellies shook with emotion, as he left the stage for the last time.

Just then, a hooded man somewhat spoiled the occasion. He rushed up brandishing a pistol, pointed it at Duffer's head, and yelled,

"You bastard! Think you can just walk away after what you said?" He pulled the trigger and a small cloud of smoke arose. But there was no loud report, more of a *pfft* sound, like a buggered bunger on Cracker Night.

The hooded bloke looked at the pistol, and seeing it had misfired, threw it at Duffer and hit him on the side of the head. It turned out to be an old flintlock pistol of the sort that the famous highwayman Dick Turpin might have used. Fortunately, it was good for only one shot, in fact, not good for any shot on this night.

There was pandemonium. The hooded man turned on his heels and tried to get through the scrum of shocked onlookers. He ran straight into Gladys, who hit him over the head with her large handbag. The man was momentarily stunned but lurched on toward the exit. Ernie yelled something, but nobody, as usual, could understand it. People were shrieking. Duffer, holding the side of his face, yelled, "What is it I said?" But his assailant was fleeing with no time for explanations.

A policeman appeared and gave chase. Duffer recognized the policeman. He was Constable Jones, now Sergeant Jones, the same copper that Duffer had helped in the fight outside the same pub years ago. Sergeant Jones called out, "Stop, police!" but the man escaped into the night.

Later, Sergeant Jones came back to interview Duffer and see if he was all right. He found him sitting on a bar stool, sipping a beer for medicinal purposes, and nursing his face with a handkerchief. He was OK, a bit battered and bloodied, but other than that just somewhat rattled.

"Sorry to meet you again like this, sir. Most unfortunate. We don't get many cases of people attacked with antique firearms, or any firearms for that matter. Do you have any idea who might have done this?"

Duffer had already considered this. Could it have been Bullah or Mr. Mitchell from his childhood? No, that was a crazy thought, both would be 100 years old. Could Malena's Norse Giant have come back after many years and confused him with Wombat? That was crazy too. "I really have no idea," Duffer said. "Maybe those lads that were in the fight with us way back when?"

"No, sir, I came to know them later and this was someone different. But I did hear the bloke say something about 'what you said' before he pulled the trigger. Right?"

Duffer nodded.

"That might be it. I know you write a blog. I enjoy it myself very much. But a lot of your followers are mean bastards, and I am afraid this internet thing, it encourages bad characters to say outrageous things anonymously. It is a forum for snakes in the grass who love nothing more than to hate. Maybe one got tired of hissing and decided to bite."

One week later, Duffer made a farewell visit to the Mermaid and Merkin in Oxford, where again he was feted by a large crowd, but this time no would-be highwayman appeared, whether because of the beefed-up security or the lack of another pistol.

Another week later, with the mystery unsolved and with a small Band-Aid still on his cheek, Duffer took up his new post as Writer in Residence at Three Rivers College in Pittsburgh, where a few months earlier he had prudently visited and charmed the administrators.

Chapter 33

Duffer in His New World

"I think the beliefs of many of our established religions pose logical problems, but in one respect they are right. People are more than their worldly circumstances – there is clearly a spiritual element in life and at least religious people seek to understand it."
The Society of Non-Belief in Religious Belief, London, 2004.

Duffer arrived in Pittsburgh the same day the snows did. The grand spectacle of coming through the Liberty Tunnels and seeing the city arrayed below was obscured by the squalls. It was late afternoon and the traffic moved slowly on the treacherous roads, headlights picking out the way in the feeble light. Duffer had the strange feeling that the outward scene reflected his inner life, everything unsettled, gloomy, foreign, cold, and a little frightening.

Foley picked him up and took him to their flat in Shadyside, which was on the top floor of a three-story building. As he slogged up the front steps through the snow in his soaked and frigid running shoes, he regretted giving his wellies to Wombat. Who knew he would end up in Siberia by the Three Rivers?

Leaving his shoes in a pile just inside the door, he padded up the apartment building's steep stairs in sodden socks and, after much puffing and a pantomime of chest grabbing, he found Patricia waiting for him with a cup of tea in her hand and her face lit up with a big welcoming smile. "There will be wine and beer later," she said, "but first you must return to room temperature."

"What! I have to wait a month to get a beer?"

"You'd better warm up now. It will be colder in a month."

As he drank his tea, he saw that the flat was small, just enough room for a lean cowboy and a petite woman, with visiting pub philosophers assigned to the couch. But on the stove was a big pot of steaming fish stew and a loaf of crusty bread to the side. A small radiator gallantly tried to raise the temperature and collective body heat did the rest for the cause of coziness. Duffer put on thick dry socks and the tea worked its magic.

"What were those black and yellow signs I saw everywhere coming in?"

"That's for the local football team, the Steelers. Their colors are considered to be black and gold, by the way, and there's a big game tomorrow. We can watch it on TV. The city lives or dies depending on whether they win or lose."

"Will they win tomorrow? I don't want to arrive just in time for a civic funeral."

"Of course, they will win tomorrow. On the other hand, if they should lose, mental health counselors will win because the demands for their services go way up after a defeat. Actually, I don't know if that's really true, but it could be."

"Maybe a pub philosopher might find his calling offering advice to those in pain at such times," Duffer offered.

"Oh, no, Duffer. There's nothing you can do for disappointed Steeler fans. Alcohol and bed rest are the only remedies. In fact, it's best if you avoid any subject touching upon football if they lose."

He slept well that night and arose refreshed the next morning to discover it was still snowing. After breakfast, Foley and Duffer went out to shovel the sidewalk. None of the other tenants in the building helped them because they were too old, pretending to be too old because they were too lazy, or, the charitable view, they had a medical condition.

Duffer wished he had an excuse. He hadn't done much hard manual work since helping on Uncle Frank's farm many years ago. Foley, who had tossed a hay bale or two back in his Iowa days and was still a runner in good shape, found it hard too.

"What do you think, Duffer?" Foley asked when they had cleared the frozen wasteland that had been the front path.

"I think snow is prettier than cow manure but no easier to handle. I think we should go upstairs and sit on our laurels in the hope they have been warmed up."

And up the many stairs they went and slumped down on Duffer's sleeping couch. It was 1 p.m., time for the game.

Duffer had seen American football only in American newsreels played at the Canberra Hotel in Saigon and he had found it quite exciting. But when he watched it now on live TV, he was surprised to see how stop-and-start it was, which to his mind spoiled the excitement. He saw that after someone was tackled but before the ball was put back in play, the players would hold what appeared to be a union meeting.

"That's called the huddle," Foley helpfully explained. "They discuss what they are going to do next. And each play is called a down and you have to go 10 yards to get another set of them."

Duffer soon figured out there were four downs, but if they hadn't got 10 yards after three downs, a smaller, more delicate-looking man who hadn't done anything up to that point except perhaps read a book of sonnets on the sideline ran on to the field and then punted the ball so the other team could have a go, then ran off, presumably back to his poetry.

"Why doesn't he stay on and play?" Duffer said.

"That's what he is paid to do and nothing else."

"Oh," said Duffer, the former rugby player trying to grasp the concept. He decided that it must be a cultural thing, because a nation's sport is likely to say something about the people who invented it.

"Is America a land of many meetings, specialization in jobs, and enticing people to buy things through incessant advertising?" he asked.

"As a matter of fact, it is. How did you figure that out so quickly?"

Then they both went back to watching the game with its many ads between the huddles.

Foley had muted the TV commentators in favor of the radio commentary, and apparently this was a common practice in Pittsburgh. Through Foley's transistor radio, a man named Myron, who had an excited, high-pitched voice and a strange accent, was going on at length about the play of the quarterback, which apparently was not up to his usual standards, although Myron used more colorful language to say this.

"Is the quarterback the most important player on the team?"

"Yes," said Foley.

"Then why is he the *quarter* back? Not first back or premier back or leading back? It sounds like he is outranked by the fullback. He is not even given the dignity of being a half back, like soccer and rugby. He's just a quarter."

"I never thought about it," Foley said. "It is another of life's mysteries."

So it remained a puzzle at odds with what Duffer understood to be the American penchant for using words to make things larger, more inflated, more swaggering, more immodest, as exemplified by the word

Super Bowl itself. No half measures for Americans, but apparently *quarterback* was all right.

Duffer decided that he had a lot to learn. The next day he took the Port Authority bus into town, following Patricia's written instructions. He got off the bus near Heinz Hall, the lavish concert hall decorated inside in ketchup red, and walked from the bus stop across Market Square and onto the Boulevard of the Allies, which Duffer thought was a nice name as Australia was one of the allies.

He was cold. Had somebody left the door open at the North Pole? The wind was howling down between the buildings on the boulevard as if it were a wind tunnel. He was nearly frozen by the time he arrived at the Three Rivers College building. After being greeted by department heads and new colleagues, he spent the morning filling out forms and being told what to expect. As he expected, academics have their huddles too.

Fortunately, the Steelers had won yesterday's game in a late rally, so he did not have to deal with a thick layer of civic funk, which probably would have penetrated even the corridors of higher learning.

At lunchtime, he went to Kaufmann's department store in order to get warmer clothes and drier boots for his new life. Students milled about on that first day, but he never met any.

The plan was that he would be the Writer in Residence and part-time lecturer in the Journalism Department for a year and then who knows where he would go and what he would do. But he did not make a great impression on his first day.

Gerald Barlow, the Dean of the Journalism Department, had been impressed by Duffer when he first met him in the fall. Now that Duffer had arrived at the college to teach, he didn't seem so impressive. As he said to his colleague Shirley Jones, "That guy is so ordinary as to be extraordinary. Do you think we have made the right decision?"

"Well, let's wait and see. He only just got here and must be feeling a little overwhelmed. But for my part, yes, I am officially underwhelmed," Professor Jones said.

So on his second day she sat in one of his first lectures, then a week later a second, then a third and fourth after that, just to make sure their first-day appraisal was correct. But what Professor Jones saw was what the kids saw. As crumpled and physically unimpressive as Duffer presented himself, and as unassuming as he was in first encounters one-on-one, he immediately transformed in front of a group.

Once again Duffer surfed people's low expectations. The Three Rivers kids witnessed the unremarkable guy with the strange accent disappear in front of their eyes, well, not the strange accent part. It was as if they were witnessing the human version of a chrysalis turning into a butterfly, but butterflies are usually beautiful and Duffer was a drab mothman, flitting furiously around and making his own light.

This, of course, was the routine that he had perfected in bars across two countries, and barrooms are a harder school than a real school, full as bars are of addled drunks and alcohol-fueled belligerents. But students, either in high school or college, pose their own challenges.

The students at Three Rivers College were mostly conventional blue-collar and lower middle-class kids typical of the socially conservative old mill towns, both in Pittsburgh and in the nearby communities along the rivers. They were polite kids, but many had not been challenged academically in high school.

Duffer was the unlikely man for the job. All those years of observing from the sidelines of life, the places he had visited, the characters he had met, the knowledge he had gained, filled every classroom he entered. His accent and his expressions baffled his students at first, but his enthusiasm was unmistakable. What he said and the way he said it were just another means to make the kids think.

His gift for public speaking wasn't the only quality that made his classes interesting. Duffer's columns for the Crouch End Crusader in England had won a number of prizes for feature writing. He had mastered the art of the interview and had honed the knack of turning anything into an interesting article, no matter how ridiculous the assignment. And when he looked at the students' writing assignments, he was never condescending, always helpful, unfailingly encouraging.

So after two months Professor Jones went back to Dean Barlow to report. "Remember when you said that O'Grady was extraordinarily ordinary? You got it half right. He is just extraordinary, but you have to see for yourself. I won't spoil it for you." The dean then went and audited the class. The two of them later conferred.

Duffer was then summoned to the dean's office and went apprehensively. While he felt good about his classes, after all, he could read a crowd and knew he was liked, observers see social clues that others miss and he had picked up on the doubt lurking in the dean's polite reaction to him when he met him again on his first day. He had also seen the dean at the back of his class with his best poker face on.

"Sit down, Robert. I have called this meeting to discuss your performance in your first weeks." Sitting beside the dean, to his left and looking very official, Professor Jones sat as if she were a witness about to be called for the prosecution. *Oh shit, Duffer thought. Here we go.*

"As you know, Professor Jones and I have sat in on your classes. And I must say I have rarely seen someone make such a connection with their students. You have a rare talent and I must say I learned things I did not know." And as he said this, he smiled, and Professor Jones smiled, and Duffer smiled, even though he was totally surprised and felt that his superpower of observation had for once failed him.

Sitting there flummoxed as he was, Duffer could not think of anything to say. Dean Jones went on, "Although it's early, Professor

Jones and I feel you should join our faculty permanently and that will probably entail a change in your visa status. We can help you with that if you become an associate professor."

"You want me to become an associate professor?"

"Yes, does that appeal to you?"

It appealed to Duffer so much he wanted to say yippee, yi, yah, as Cowboy probably did, but all he could manage was, "That's brilliant!"

"There's just one problem."

Ah, yes, Duffer thought, there's always one problem.

The problem was that Duffer did not have a degree. As he always told people, he had a Degree of Concussion from the University of Hard Knocks, which was apparently OK to teach as a Writer in Residence, but now he would have to work toward a bachelor's degree in his spare time and then a master's degree. The dean explained that he would be given credit for life experience and tuition would be included. The college was moving toward becoming a fully accredited university and the faculty had to be seen to be well qualified.

"Would there be any mathematics courses involved?" Duffer asked.

"We do have a core curriculum, but I think one introductory freshman math class would suffice and we can help you with that if math is not your strength."

Duffer was immediately mindful of what a turning point this represented in his life. He had unequivocally succeeded in something. His growing fame as a speaker and blogger aside, because that was still a work in progress, everything else he had done was barely up to par, student, sportsman, bank clerk, soldier, postman, bartender, writer, well, he had won a few prizes for his feature stories, so maybe exclude that one, husband, lover, all these things were stamped Mediocre in his own reckoning.

This was cause for celebration. By now, he had his own flat, more a hole in the wall than a flat but only a block or two from Foley and Patricia in Shadyside. He called them up and asked himself to dinner.

Duffer was gaining on every front. Only his social life gasped for breath. As he sadly told Wombat that night at his celebratory dinner, "I am as lonely as a beer bottle at a temperance picnic." Not for long.

Chapter 34

Kitty Makes Duffer Purr

"Falling in love is mostly the chemical attraction of two bodies. What follows is the period that allows the brain to consider any doubts about whether the chemicals got it right." Duffer speaks at the Kat Kit Club, Pittsburgh, 2004.

Just two weeks later, he met a woman named Kitty at the Kat Kit Club, where he had started doing his speaking routines.

Early in his first year in Pittsburgh, lonely and curious, he heard that an ex-TV talk show host named Jack MacIntosh, a funny, wild man, was hosting a gig at an old club on the South Side for wildly humorous people with something to say. It was called the Kat Kit Club because the club, like its name, was a little off. He went to hear the show as an audience member and ended up being one of the speakers or performers.

And there she was. Kitty Giordano was a performance artist, a term still relatively new then, although the way she performed probably resembled some of the more unusual vaudeville performances of an earlier time. Her act was not easily described. She danced, she sang, she played a ukulele, and sometimes used props. She did social commentary, complete with jokes, which were often raunchy, political, and shocking to those who cared to be shocked. That said, she had her work cut out for her trying to shock anyone at the Kat Kit Club.

She did all this with her clothes firmly on, which was more than you can say for some performers at the club. She wore long flowing black dresses, big black boots, black tights, and a black or navy blue blouse, depending on her mood. Her hair was black, a great wild mat of it, so that if she went out in the rain you feared that it might all tumble down over her eyes and turn her into a bedraggled goth sheepdog unable to see the flock. Fortunately, a black umbrella was one of her props, suitable for the stage or the weather.

Duffer was an unlikely candidate to be smitten by a very dramatic-looking, theatrical person, but when it came to Kitty, it was love at first performance. She was so striking, so funny, so interesting, and yet projected a light while dressed so dark.

The problem was that Duffer couldn't think of a proper way to introduce himself. He was mentally propelled back to high school, when apologetic stammering was the best a boy could manage in the presence of a cool girl. At the Kat Kit Club, he couldn't even raise a decent stammer.

When he did finally approach her one night two weeks later, as they waited in the wings for their turn while the talk show host guy got the show rolling, he couldn't think of a sensible thing to say, so he just stood there close by, going *ur, ur, ur* in his head, trying to start his voice box as if it were a cranky engine on a cold morning. Finally, she noticed him lurking and started doing the talking.

"Well, hello there, Duffer, how nice to meet you. I love your performances. I love your blog."

Duffer said in wonder, "You read my blog?"

"Yes, I love it. You write like you speak and I really love the way you speak. In fact, I have taken to reading your blog while imitating your Aussie accent. G'day. How was that?"

"Very good. I haven't mastered American as well."

"One thing I don't like is that Aussie expression you use sometimes, 'Stone the crows.' What have crows done to deserve a stoning? As a raven-haired person, that is not appealing. I say nevermore to that expression."

"Nevermore, it is, then, quoth the Duffer. But I don't think the expression is a call to throw stones at crows. It is just an exclamation of amazement or concern. It's like saying 'shit!' It's not a good image, but it can be a handy thing to say."

"Nevermore," she said.

"Nevermore," he said, and forevermore they were friends.

She went out and did her performance, which was, on this night, a medley of funny songs with ukulele accompaniment, and all the time she was staring at Duffer. The song that appealed to him most was "I've Got a Lovely Bunch of Coconuts," only this time she sang it as "You've Got a Lovely Bunch of Coconuts." Each man in the house, egotistical fools that men are, thought that the lyrics were all about him, but no one else saw that she was looking at Duffer.

And Duffer was very flattered. He had never thought he had a lovely bunch of coconuts, nor did he think that there they were, all standing in a row, but he certainly did think that this was an interesting way to start a relationship. He went out himself then and secretly dedicated his remarks to Kitty. While he did not dance or sing, which was a blessing to all, he was plainly a man inspired and he immediately got everybody's undivided attention.

Almost the moment after he had delivered his monologue, he couldn't remember a word of what he had said, which he attributed to Kitty's presence confusing his thoughts. He told Foley later that he thought the speech was something about the meaning of life.

"Aren't all your speeches ultimately about the meaning of life?" Foley had said.

"Well, yes," Duffer said.

All Duffer knew was that his remarks were met with great enthusiasm by the crowd, who began hooting and hollering, but the best part for him was to see Kitty smiling. He had really been speaking to a crowd of one and apparently his wit and wisdom were his lovely coconuts all in a row.

This was the start of Duffer and Kitty having a romance, but although Duffer loved her immediately, their relationship began so painfully slow that one might be tempted to believe it was a government project. Duffer had to get over his sense of wonderment and awe about her; Kitty had to overcome her better judgment.

Kitty was nothing like his previous loves in fond memory, the Long-Suffering Sheila and the Never-Suffering-Quite-Enough-to-Leave Victoria. Kitty was buxom, exotic-looking, and almost six-foot tall and her apparent profession was something not routinely mentioned by career counselors in schools. She was not a nurse (Sheila), she was not a bank employee (Victoria), and she was not a public relations consultant (Duffer's sister, Margaret).

At first, they didn't go out on dates, they just talked over a glass of wine when their performances at the Kat Kit Club were done. A long time elapsed before they actually went out to dinner and a movie. Their relationship developed like a parody of lovemaking, slow at first, then a little fast and eventually frantic.

On the way, practical details of their lives were portioned out one story at a time. Duffer told her of his hapless school days and unfortunate encounters with algebra, his unheroic service in Vietnam, his farm laboring in Mulgabimbi, his mail deliveries in fly-blown Brisbane suburbs, his writing of feature stories in London about bingo winners and sad clowns, and it all seemed to him insufficiently impressive to charm such a lively and sophisticated woman.

She told her stories too and the infatuated Duffer heard them as something out of One Thousand and One Arabian Nights, although in reality they were more commonplace than his stories. But they did answer some basic questions about her life.

Was she a native Pittsburgher? On football days at Three Rivers Stadium she wore a yellow (gold) scarf with her black ensemble and looked like a Steelers fan, but no, she came to the city from California to attend the drama school at Carnegie Mellon University and never left.

Was her name Kitty somehow related to her employment at the Kat Kit Club, a stage name perhaps? No, her real name was Katherine, which got shortened to Kat, which got lengthened to Kitty, as it purred off the tongue more readily. Duffer, whose real name was Robert, understood how these things happen.

How did she support herself, given that her gigs at the Kat Kit Club just earned her tips? She was a part-time actress, a part-time waitress, and a more than part-time receptionist at the Mattress Factory, a contemporary art museum on Pittsburgh's North Side famous for its installations, not usually featuring mattresses. Sometimes she performed there too.

She had one other occupation that surprised Duffer, the last big fact of her life that she was slow to announce, fearing that it might make Duffer run for the hills. She was a mother.

When she first told him, he said spontaneously with wide-eyed wonder, "Wow, my mum was a mother!" He meant this as the greatest compliment but it ranks as perhaps the stupidest thing he ever said. In retrospect, it is a wonder how their relationship continued after this.

Chapter 35

Duffer Becomes a Family Man

"When I was a kid, we sang Happy Birthday at parties and then followed it with the Aussie version: 'Why was he born so beautiful, why was he born at all? Because he had no say in it, no say in it at all.' True enough. So many people want to judge others because of their skin color, sexual preference, gender, class, physical or mental handicaps, etc. But why? All those people, they had no say in it, no say in it at all." Duffer speaks to the NAACP, Pittsburgh, 2005.

After their slow start, Kitty and Duffer reached a stage in their relationship where they were thinking of living together, although neither had spoken the idea out loud. Duffer finally brought up the subject one Saturday morning as they were having brunch at the Pink Rhinoceros on Walnut Street in Shadyside. "I reckon …," he said tentatively. Like all Australians, Duffer was always reckoning this or that, and Kitty paused in mid-bite with pancake on her fork to see what he was reckoning now.

"I reckon," he said more boldly, "that it makes sense if I move in with you."

There, he had said it, and it did make sense. Duffer was paying rent for a small apartment in Shadyside and Kitty owned a slightly more spacious house in the Mexican War Streets, a historic community on Pittsburgh's North Side.

The money Duffer saved in rent could buy a lot of groceries and pay for some much-needed repairs. And if they evolved into lifetime partners, he might chip in on the mortgage.

Besides, Duffer had bought a car, a VW Rabbit, which he was happy to share with her. The Mattress Factory was in the neighborhood, but other places they visited really required a car, the Kat Kit Club on the South Side among them. Love and practicality argued that they should share space, but he had yet to meet her son.

"I don't know, Duffer. It's a good plan, but ...."

"Come on. What's the reluctance?" He paused and added, "Do you have a ferocious dog that hates Australians and poos on the carpet?"

"No dog."

"Do you have a cat?"

"No cat."

"So what do you have that you think I might not like? Bad TV reception? A neighbor who plays the accordion? Odors from the Alcosan sewer plant down by the river?"

"I do have a neighbor who plays the accordion, this is Pittsburgh after all, but that's not it."

She paused now. It all came down to this: What sort of man was Duffer? Some men in a relationship can't bring themselves to accept someone else's child. Others have no problem. Would he accept her child?

He was just four years old and he talked a lot and got his little hands into things that he shouldn't, as little boys do. He had his mother's features and her olive skin, so he looked a bit like her, except his hair was light brown.

"You know I have a son at home," she said in an uncharacteristically small, uncertain voice. "His name is Benny."

"I know. So what? No worries!" Duffer said.

"Benny is a little kid. Really, no worries? You don't mind sharing a house with a four-year-old and his mom?"

"Of course not, provided he likes me. Why don't we drive the Rabbit over to your place and find out? Where is Benny at the moment anyway?"

Kitty explained that he had stayed the night with Kitty's Aunt Maris, who often did babysitting for her and would be dropping him off. Aunt Maris was the reason Kitty had come to Pittsburgh to attend school in the first place. Kitty's parents had been reassured that a relative lived in the city to help her if things ever got complicated. Twenty-five years later things were very complicated, but Aunt Maris was still on the job.

As they drove to the other side of town, Kitty told him a little more. "You are probably wondering about Benny's father."

"Yes," he said, "I didn't want to ask, and technically it may not be any of my business, but I am curious."

"Our affair was very short," she said. "Literally, a few days. He was a visiting actor and he said some lines that I wanted to hear at that time in my life. I knew it was love at first lust for him, but he was quite good looking and a girl gets lonely. What can I say? It was incredibly stupid of me."

"I am in no position to judge you," Duffer said. "Did you tell Romeo you were pregnant?"

"Yes, I knew where he was and I called him a month later. His idea of chivalry was to offer to help me pay for an abortion. I was always a big women's-right-to-choose gal and so I chose … I chose to keep the baby. I really surprised myself, but I realized this was my last chance at motherhood and he was at least smart, if not decent."

"What did he do?"

"He hung up on me. I think he was terrified. I think he joined the Witless Protection Program." She sighed. "Sadly, at least for Benny's sake, we have seen the last of him."

"Becoming a single mother was a brave and tough decision, I reckon," Duffer said.

"I am not sure about the brave part, but tough? Oh, yeah, tough all right."

Then she added anxiously, "Duffer, if you come to live with me, don't think you have to be Benny's dad. I hope you will be nice to him, but voluntary fatherhood is too much to ask of anyone."

"Well, let's see if he likes me first."

Duffer had not known many children in his life since he was one himself. The last baby he had held was in the orphanage in Saigon, where he learned how much babies crave love and attention. He was soon to be reminded that this wasn't just limited to babies. Everybody needs affection.

When they reached Kitty's house, Benny came roaring out when he heard his mom at the door and hugged her legs. When Aunt Maris went home after briefly meeting Duffer, Kitty introduced her little boy. "G'day, Benny," Duffer said. Benny looked at Duffer uncertainly for a moment, looked up at his mom for approval, and seeing it in her expression, rushed over and hugged his legs.

"You can call me Duffer, or Uncle Duffer, anything you like. Kitty, what can he call me?"

"I suppose Duffer," she said.

So Benny looked up and said, "Hello, Duffer. Do you want to see my trucks?"

"Oh, yeah," said Duffer, "I love trucks."

"I tried at first to give him nongender-specific toys," Kitty said wistfully, "but he always came back to wanting trucks."

So the two boys, the old one and the young one, went off to Benny's bedroom to see his trucks. He had two trucks and Duffer's first thought was the kid's fleet had to be expanded.

Benny never called him Duffer after their first meeting. He simply called him Duff. As Duffer later told Kitty, "I think the little guy has the makings of becoming an Australian. All words are reduced to the bare minimum in Australia so we can save our lip movement for eating meat pies and drinking beer."

Kitty didn't fully understand this remark, but she responded anyway, "Well, just don't start calling him Ben. The Steelers' new quarterback is Ben and I am a fan, but not to that extent."

So Benny and Duff, Duffer, became friends and Duffer did not mind. In fact, he quickly began to believe his life had suddenly and unexpectedly improved. It was never clear whether the boy needed the company of the man or whether the man needed the company of the boy.

Either way, they got on like a house on fire, and, as it happened, Duffer's first present to Benny was a toy firetruck. Both of them liked red fire trucks as siren noises could be made while playing with them.

Two weeks after he moved in, Duffer and Kitty were eating breakfast in the kitchen at the back, overlooking a small garden where Kitty grew her herbs. Benny had already finished his bowl of cereal and was navigating his fire truck around the Weetabix box. "Whoo, whoo!" he said.

Kitty said, "Eat your fruit, Benny, before it catches fire." He obediently took some slices of apple and, when he was done, Kitty said, "Now take that fire truck to the living room and play on the floor so you don't knock over the milk."

When Benny was settled and putting out fires in a safer sector, Kitty turned to Duffer and remarked, "Duffer, I have only known you for a few months, but I have never seen you happier."

"Yes, I think you can blame Benny. I like the little guy's company. He seems to like mine, which prompts a cheeky request."

"And what would that be?"

"Remember when we were talking about me moving in with you. You said that I don't have to be Benny's dad. No one should be forced to volunteer for that duty, you told me. Well, I am not being forced and I would like to volunteer for the job. Obviously, I can't really be his father, I'd be battling biology on that, but I can be a father figure."

Kitty replied slowly and spoke sadly, "Oh, Duffer, you are a nice, kind man, but modern relationships are fragile. I hate to say no to you, but I wonder if it's best that you and Benny don't get too close. What if we split up? It happens. It happened to you, what, twice? It has happened to me, not since Benny was born but before that."

"Do you want me to leave?" Duffer asked haltingly, fearing the answer.

"No, heaven forbid. It has worked out great. But what if the worst happens? Benny would be heartbroken."

"But what if the best happens? I have spent my whole life wanting my father to acknowledge me, to love me. Benny doesn't even have a father at home. How much harder will it be for him? And if I stay here, I think our relationship will evolve to become closer anyway. I don't think there's anything we can do to avoid it. And maybe he won't grow up so conflicted inside that he is driven to become a pub philosopher."

"Yes," said Kitty, "maybe he can grow up better adjusted and become a truck driver and the only sadness in his life will be the country and western songs on the radio."

They both laughed. "Carry on, Duffer, it seems inevitable. And thank you. But if you leave, I will kill you."

By Christmas, Benny was no longer calling Duffer Duff. He was calling him Dad. No one told him to, it was just the natural progression of things, just a few letters difference, but all the difference in the world.

Only one regret intruded on these productive and carefree years. Foley and Patricia moved to California not long after Kitty and Duffer met. A new university was being established in Monterey, the same place where coincidentally Aunt Maris was originally from. The new California State University, Monterey Bay, was situated on land that had only recently been decommissioned as an army base.

For Foley it made some professional sense, his field was Western Studies and this was the West, and indeed the county seat hosted the California Rodeo every year. Or as Duffer said, "Well, if it doesn't work out for you on the faculty, you can always be a rodeo clown."

"You have to come to visit!" Foley said to Duffer at the inevitable farewell bash. He had said that once before to Duffer and Duffer had come. He would again, but not just yet.

Chapter 36

Duffer and the Old Language

"Americans are a people who are practical, talented, idealistic, creative, hard-working, but often literal-minded, and this makes America the land that irony forgot." Duffer in his blog, 2006.

In the chapters of Duffer's and Kitty's lives, these were some of their happiest times. With the encouragement of Kitty, Duffer's fame grew as he increasingly spoke before other groups, not just in bars and clubs. All the while he wrote his blog, with the help of Margaret in England.

Students loved his courses at the college and his own studies earned him a bachelor's degree and a master's in quicker time than he thought possible. As he explained later, "To my surprise, I found that a library is a better place to study than the top of a tank. Unlike library card holders, the people who shoot at you in a war are not easily shushed."

But his greatest distinction was a typically American one. He earned the most respected title available to anyone in this wide and boisterous land. Not President. Not Senator. Not Governor. Not Mayor.

Coach.

Duffer became Coach Duffer for the North Side Hornets, Benny's Under-6 soccer team, who wore black and gold jerseys, which reminded onlookers of the Steelers, except that it was a different football and the kids did not know what they were doing but did it very cutely.

Every Saturday morning, Duffer would be out there urging on the boys and a few girls to pass the ball, run to the ball, dribble the ball, spread out to receive the ball, try to get the ball from the other team, run the right way with the ball, shoot the ball, and, well, not score necessarily, that was hoping for a bit much, just do something, anything, with the ball. Duffer knew next to nothing about soccer. He had always played rugby.

However, he had an accent and the parents didn't know any better. In the land of the blind, the man with one eye is king. In the land of soccer-blind America at that time, the person with an accent could be coach.

Coach Duffer, remembering his own humiliations as an often left-out kid, was scrupulously fair in giving each kid a fair chance, or a fair go, as they say in Australia. Even the most hapless kid was encouraged. Some might say that, unfortunately, Benny was the most hapless kid. But Duffer didn't think less of the kid for that. He knew that kid because he had been that kid.

In one game, Duffer put in Benny at fullback. The other fullback was a little girl named Jenny. Both of them stood together in the back of the field near the goalie waiting for something to happen that might require their attention. They were all by themselves because it was the rare occasion when most of the Hornets were swarming around the opposing team's goal for a while, trying to manage a shot.

When the opposing team cleared the ball, as usual, Duffer looked back and there were his little fullbacks, Benny and Jenny, holding hands together. And for once Coach Duffer did not shout out any instructions. The scene was too perfect.

Living in Kitty's cozy little North Side cottage, Duffer found the ability to put aside his usual anxieties and a sort of mental clarity settled upon him. Perhaps the cause of his enhanced understanding of life was just advancing age, a time often said to promote greater reflection, just as youth breeds stupidity in teenagers, a source of joy for them and vexation for everyone else.

When he spoke in public now, his thoughts were sharper and more inspired. And with the flowering of the World Wide Web, Duffer was able to better express his thoughts to a larger audience, including the central idea that had long intrigued him, each of us carries a part of mankind's collective wisdom.

Among the first dividends of Duffer's insight came at a meeting he addressed of the Allegheny County Atheists Association. Duffer's range of venues had expanded beyond bars and clubs, but this event was still among the more unusual. It was a lunchtime meeting, with the 30 or so attendees.

The chairman of the group was the well-named Ernest Philpot, who was indeed earnest. His enthusiasm for the boring business of chairmanship was put to the test by frequent interruptions from the members. Duffer thought that Ernest would be better served by saying, "For Christ's sake, you people, let's get on with it." But, of course, the remedy of invoking the name of You Know Who was too illogical for the chief atheist.

In their general comments before the meeting, some in the small crowd made it plain that they considered belief in God to be the scourge of mankind, an illogical force at odds with plain reason, the instiller of guilt and shame, and, they might be tempted to say, an evil, notwithstanding that concept is firmly rooted in traditional theology.

As Duffer later explained on the phone to Foley, now in California, "They were nice people but I found myself in a weird place, atheists who assert their atheism in a fundamentalist sort of way. And like the fundamentalist Christians, they think they are absolutely right and the other side are completely wrong and harming society to boot. They are two peas in a pod. And the ironic thing is that they won't know who is right until they die. But even then, only the Christians will be able to say 'I told you so.' They will have their heaven but the poor old atheists, who might be right, will only have oblivion, not a good place to say 'I told you so.'"

"No doubt atheists have a hard time of it," Foley said, "but are they all fundamentalist atheists? What about the agnostics, the ones who aren't quite sure one way or the other?"

"Yes, that's a sound position and there must have been agnostics in the crowd, but why go to lunch with people who are very sure of what they don't believe when you are not very sure of what you believe?"

"Maybe the chance of a good lunch with a bit of different conversation?" Foley asked.

"Well, you might have a point there, mate," said Duffer, who himself liked a good lunch and out-of-the-ordinary conversation.

Possibly the godless members of the ACAA had invited Duffer to speak on the assumption that he was one of their own. He was known as being rational, commonsensical, straightforward, even if his sense of humor was a bit weird, so surely, they may have thought, such a person would be led naturally by logic to put aside religious superstition.

Actually, Duffer said a quiet prayer for the repose of his mum's soul every night before he went to bed, and he added a good word for Uncle Frank while he was at it.

As far as he was concerned, the brain had its thinking work to do, the heart had its feeling work to do, and he would somehow synthesize all suggestions. He remembered the example of Socrates, the Greek philosopher, not the bouncer from long ago in the Mulgabimbi pub, who believed in a deity even as he questioned everything in Grecian life. So he started his speech like this:

"I wish I could be an atheist like you. I would not be constrained in anything I did. No heaven, no hell, no moral responsibilities. I might walk out one day and decide not to wear pants. I might tell my boss that he is a jerk. I might throw custard pies at passing pedestrians for a laugh.

"But you don't do any of those things, do you? You aren't constrained by fear that a vengeful god will judge you harshly. You can do anything you like but I am guessing most of you don't. Just because you don't believe in God doesn't make you behave like a jerk. On the contrary, I am sure that many of you live more upright lives than people who go to church regularly. Religion can certainly bring out the inner jerk in people, as it did in the Inquisition, and in the case of the Ku Klux Klan with the burning crosses.

"On the other hand, religion also brings out the good in people too. Those people are sometimes not so obvious because their goodness is of the more humble variety, expressed in quiet, daily kindnesses to their fellow human sufferers.

"But, as it is on Earth, how is it in heaven? Is there a God up there? Is there a heaven for Him to sit in? I don't know. The one thing that is certain is that nobody knows. Oh, religious people feel they know, but that is called faith. The atheist community thinks it knows too, but that is non-faith, which is just the opposite side of the same coin and can be just as powerful.

"Ah, some of you atheists will say, but we have logic and rationality on our side. Perhaps, but that doesn't explain how we got here in the first place, how we, our world, and all the planets and stars came to be created.

"As for the certainty of the faithful, they can quote the Bible or the Quran as their absolute authority, but a church or mosque up the road could be at that very moment quoting the exact same text but with a different interpretation of it.

"We need to tread carefully in matters that we assume to be settled and unarguable. How do we proceed? With a little kindness for those who don't agree with us, a little understanding for the perils of certainty.

"Which brings me to the one fact that I think is obvious. The human race did not evolve into a powerful presence in the world without cooperation. We act as a group. We love heroes, because the group needs encouragement, but the strength of the group is the group.

"From the earliest times, when we lived in caves and were hunting wild beasts, they could only be killed with a concerted effort. Brawn had to be beaten by brain, and we had then only little brains for the job. We needed to put our little brains together to make a big collective brain. But to do that we needed to communicate with each other, and we surely managed this before enough words had been invented. We couldn't say, 'Hey, Uggh, stand on top of this rock, mate, and wave your hands about when you see the beast, distract him a bit so that we can sneak up behind and throw a spear up his keister.'

"I propose that there was a time, even before words, that we could speak to each other just by thinking. It was a survival instinct that we developed after a lot of trial and error, no doubt involving guys standing on rocks to distract beasts and then being eaten, but eventually came some success.

"We are not alone in speech beyond words. Many animals communicate with reflex, instinct, intuition, and a spirit of mutual understanding. Schools of fish seem to move as one to avoid predators and nobody gurgles, 'This way, Mac.' Flocks of birds, swallows, homing pigeons, for example, expand and contract like accordions in the air, and the sergeant bird doesn't say 'Number from the left,' as would happen in the army. Many sorts of birds fly great distances between continents, sometimes in formation, and while they may honk and chirp a bit, it is unlikely they are asking each other for directions.

"You can see a vestige of our lost animal language in our species. Married couples after many years come to think the same thoughts at exactly the same time, although I must confess I never reached that level of understanding with my ex-wife. Body language, social clues, ESP, call it what you will, the combining thread, the primeval pulse of the world, the language without words, the shared consciousness. I think old Shakespeare had a more poetic way of putting it, as he had a habit of doing, 'There is a tide in the affairs of men …'

'If we only had a tide chart.' But this I think we know: The movement of each bird in the soaring flock, each fish in the diving and twisting school, somehow affects the whole. I reckon that is how the shared understanding operates. So it is with mankind.

"We see it in history. Ideas arising around the same time in different parts of the world far from each other. We see it with the recent invention of the World Wide Web. Millions of individuals making the tide of opinion turn this way and that, no central authority, none actually connected to each other but each adding his or her little bit of wisdom or folly. We see it in the operation of free markets. Prices go up and down, but eventually they find the right level as if they were water.

"Our genes help by carrying what we have learned from one generation unto the next. It does not matter that our tribes look different or have different customs; what matters is that they in turn are members of the same tribe with the same common ancestor, heirs to the ancient pre-verbal language.

"A mass of individuals make up humanity, each of us adding something to the store of knowledge. Everybody has a piece of the wisdom. This may be God's plan or maybe the plan is the result of random nature. We don't know for sure.

"So, if you die, is that the end? Not if you have left a good thought to the world, not if you have passed on some good physical trait, or a talent for kindness perhaps, an ability to love. That's what I reckon anyway. Living a good life is the best bet in the eternity sweepstakes. What's good? What's bad? Ah, just listen to what your senses tell you in the lost language, the one we still know intuitively if we only stop to listen."

There wasn't much in this speech for the atheists to laugh at and moreover they didn't understand what the hell he was talking about. Later, groups of Christians would confess to the same befuddlement.

Chapter 37

Life Is a Roller Coaster

"Because America is irony free, it is a natural soil for fundamentalist religious movements whose members support the death penalty, even though Jesus Christ provides history's most glaring example of the injustice and cruelty of the death penalty."
Duffer in his blog, 2010.

Life was good. Duffer did well in his lectures and his blog, Duffer Daze, garnered numerous hits, not as much as blogs and videos featuring dancing kittens, or singing dogs, or webcams of young ladies entertaining spotty boyfriends in bed, but relatively good numbers of hits considering his unpromising subject matter concerning the meaning of life with a few jokes thrown in. His sister Margaret had finally married Colin Witherspoon and taken him back to Australia to live in Melbourne, where she continued to manage the blog.

Duffer now had speaking gigs almost every week, just about every single service club in the tri-state area invited him to speak, plus Young Republicans, old Republicans, ditto Young and old Democrats with a few Libertarians in the mix, church groups, at least one confused garden club, and book clubs. Duffer now had three books to his name, the latest titled "The Immoral Majority: Should I Join Them?"

But one of the most memorable appearances came about simply by having lunch at Froggy's, a popular restaurant that was a short walk from the college on the Boulevard of the Allies. Duffer went there with Dean Barlow to discuss journalism courses.

Froggy's was mostly a lunch place, popular with business people from the offices in the Golden Triangle, plus lawyers and politicians who frequented the courts and government offices on Grant Street and journalists from the Post-Gazette at the end of the boulevard. Some of the same people reappeared at the bar in the evening to pour drinks on the expired expectations of their day.

They were all greeted personally by Froggy himself, who had the squat, ample build of a frog but was more walrus thanks to a drooping mustache. He seemed to know everybody and, even if he didn't, he made everybody feel like he was his friend. Once Froggy had croaked his warm welcome, a waitress in a light blue button-down shirt and a neat gray skirt escorted Duffer and the dean through the large dining room to a corner table. The tables were quite close together and soon enough the dean, with a flourish of a bread roll, was making a point about enrollment being up and down like a roller coaster.

"Did you say roller coaster?" said a man at the next table excitedly. He had previously just seemed a serious character having a quiet lunch, perhaps a lawyer with a case not going well in nearby Common Pleas Court, but suddenly he shed his years and in a moment had transformed himself into an exuberant twelve-year-old boy. To him, roller coasters were the elixir of youth.

It turned out that he was Jerry "the Rocket" Roddey, president of the Classic Coaster Riders of America. He had come to Pittsburgh to scout out one of its holy of holies, Kennywood Park, which holds a legendary importance in the ways of the city.

When it opened in 1899, Kennywood Park was an entertainment destination at the end of a trolley line in the borough of West Mifflin, a few miles from Downtown beside the Monongahela River.

The name of this grand old amusement park has been immortalized in Pittsburghese, the colorful language of the region. A woman, often a woman being of the gender more concerned about such things, will tell her husband or boyfriend, "Pssst, Joe, Kennywood is open." This is the universally understood code for absent-minded Joe to do up his fly and close the fun park.

Kennywood is a mecca for roller coaster lovers everywhere. They are especially drawn by the park's vintage wooden coasters, the Thunderbolt, the Jack Rabbit, and the Racer, hence the presence in town of Mr. Rocket Roddey. His members would be coming to Pittsburgh in a few months for their annual convention.

Duffer and the dean did not want to be rude and tried to humor their unexpected lunch partner, so Duffer told the man the only roller coaster story he knew.

The last time Duffer had been on a roller coaster was half a century ago when his family took a trip south to Sydney and visited Luna Park under the Harbour Bridge, on which occasion Duffer had chundered on his older brother George. Though this caused a big family row, Duffer remembered the episode fondly, not the roller coaster part but the projectile vomiting part.

Although this story might not have been a winner with some people, the roller coaster president was charmed. The upshot was that Duffer was invited to be the keynote speaker at the association's convention at Kennywood. Dean Barlow, barely concealing his laughter, heaped praise on Duffer as a spell-binding speaker and the matter was settled. The lunch ended with no further mention of college enrollment.

As it happened, the best part was that Benny got to come to Kennywood for the occasion. The Classic Coaster Riders had no clue who Duffer was but were in a mood to have fun. Benny particularly liked the dinner, which was not the usual fare, instead consisting of corn dogs and cotton candy for dessert.

Duffer's regular routine was not suitable for this occasion. He offered no deep philosophical insights, but the topic of roller coasters did lend itself to some easy observations. What is life but a series of ups and downs? And when you finally come down, it's natural to marvel at the ride. For roller coasters, as in life, the experience is fleeting and one should feel exhilarated.

And the coaster enthusiasts did laugh heartily at his Luna Park story. It brought back their own happy memories of throwing up after a corn dog or two in the days before they developed their ride legs.

After it was done, Duffer and Benny went out and enjoyed the rides. Someone told Duffer that kids had to be as tall as a wooden rabbit next to the entry gate to be allowed to board some of the rides, but that wasn't an issue as Benny had recently grown taller. Together they had a wonderful time and no corn dogs were lost to motion sickness.

Unfortunately, life is indeed a roller coaster and now it was time for it to come down.

After years of residence, Aunt Maris had left Pittsburgh. She went back to California, to care for her ancient mother, Kitty's grandmother, in Monterey, which she did for only two months. The old lady reached 100 and then died. By then, there was no going back for Aunt Maris and she soon got sick and needed help herself.

Kitty explained the situation to Duffer the morning after she found out. But first she had to wake Duffer up, which she did using her usual method.

She would quietly climb out of bed and start changing into her day clothes. After taking off her nightie in the dressing room just around the corner from the bedroom, she would stand in the open doorway, topless, and throw her nightie over Duffer's slumbering head about 10 feet away.

If Duffer awoke fast enough during this routine, he would have glimpsed the goddess in her natural state. He seldom managed it. Usually, the missile nightgown, black, of course, folded over Duffer's head like a parachute canopy. But the mere chance always woke him up. This striptease doubtless kept interest in their relationship alive and ladies would be well advised to practice strategic nightgown throwing at home. If only the Australian Women's Weekly magazine had carried a feature on the benefits of this dance of the one veil, Duffer might still have been married to Sheila. It was probably just as well that he wasn't.

"Now that I have your full attention, Duff," Kitty said on this fateful morning, "I have some bad news." All frivolity aside, she explained that Aunt Maris was now seriously ailing.

"I don't know what to do. Aunt Maris has been here for me almost every year of my life. She acted as my surrogate mother when I first came to Pittsburgh years ago. She helped me through childbirth and then later as a babysitter. I have to go to her."

"Of course, you do," he said.

"But what about us? I'd have to leave you."

"Certainly not forever," Duffer said. "Where you go, I go. I'll look after Benny for a few weeks and you go visit Aunt Maris and see how that goes. Benny is a big boy now, almost in the fourth grade, and we'll have a blast together, he and I. And you'll come up with a plan for the longer term."

So she left Duffer and Benny together and went off to care for Aunt Maris. "Now don't be going to the ice cream store," Kitty had said to

Duffer as she said her goodbyes at the airport. Duffer only remembered that when he and Benny were sitting on the high stools at the ice cream parlor hooking into large vanilla sundaes with sprinkles on top.

Mostly, though, Duffer followed Kitty's instructions with only occasional lapses concerning temptations that no jury would have condemned him. He made regular meals, he made sure Benny didn't watch too much TV, and he took him for outings, such as visits to the aviary and zoo. It helped that the summer had begun and classes at both the college and grade school were no longer in session.

But clearly things were not going well in Monterey. Aunt Maris was now using a walker and having trouble breathing and it seemed very unlikely she was going to get any better. Night after night, Kitty would call up tearfully with a voice trembling with anxiety. "I miss you and Benny so much," she would say, "I just don't know what to do."

One night, after one of her most painful calls and a month into their separation, Duffer had an idea. The next day he went to see Dean Barlow and asked if he could take a sabbatical. He had been at the university for ten years and never taken one before, being a stranger to the whole concept. Duffer explained his difficulty and, although it was short notice, a sabbatical was granted for one year.

He never went back. He left his professorship, made a farewell appearance at the Kat Kit Club, and said goodbye to all his friends and fans. A little while later, when it was clear that Pittsburgh now firmly belonged to a previous chapter of their lives, Kitty arranged for her house in the Mexican War Streets to be sold.

It seemed like an unfortunate move. But from the moment Duffer and Benny got off the plane at Monterey's little airport, they felt confident that everything was going to work out. The only disappointment was that Foley and Patricia were no longer in Monterey; they had just moved to Arizona, where Foley had been offered a new professorship.

Chapter 38

Down in Monterey

"Some people never change their minds or their underwear. The results are similar." Duffer speaking at the Pink Otter Cocktail Lounge, Monterey, 2014.

In 1770, the English explorer Captain James Cook sailed up the east coast of Australia on his famous voyage of discovery. Not long after, far across at the other end of the Pacific, Spanish colonizers founded the picturesque port of Monterey.

That history, bitter for indigenous peoples and sweet for others in the cruel way of the world, nevertheless made historical twins of California and Australia. Parts of them even look alike, a resemblance made stronger when a century or so later Australian gum trees, eucalyptus trees, were imported from Down Under as unsatisfactory lumber and became ideal fuel for the forest fires up over.

Duffer's arrival in Monterey had the shared elements of mixed blessings too. In England, he had felt like a distant relative returning to the ancestral hearth only to find it changed from what he had imagined, a feeling that dissipated over the years thanks to the kindness of new friends like the Boggs brothers and, of course, his fans.

In Pittsburgh, the working-class spirit of America seemed very much like that of Australia and the people were as friendly too, but still Duffer was to find that California was the best fit yet.

With a Mediterranean climate, Monterey had more agreeable weather and the people were casual in attitudes and dress. California has long been the epicenter of Bohemian and alternative lifestyles and Monterey, the old garrison town with its respectable early-to-bed habits, wore a gentle paint stroke of liberality. And with its old adobes and meandering streets, reminders were around every corner that the flags of Spain and Mexico had once flown over the town.

Duffer, his modest fame preceding him, found audiences again, mostly at the Pink Otter Cocktail Lounge near Cannery Row. We all have part of the wisdom, he told his newfound fans, whether we are black people, white people, Asian people, Latino people, gay people, and as many people in the crowd fit part of the description in diverse California, everybody thought his words were very wise.

For her part, Kitty, although busy with her duties in looking after Aunt Maris, was happy to have her family with her again. She found that caregiving was more fulfilling now that anxiety had retreated. As a signifier of her new mood, she no longer wore exclusively black.

Kitty kept up her performances but when not playing the ukulele she indulged a long-held interest of hers, which was to invent things. Most of her inventions never got off the drawing board but they were all creative and unusual. She had an idea for reading glass frames that flashed location alerts whenever they were taken off the bridge of the wearer's nose. This was inspired by Duffer's story that his dad was always losing his glasses and, after a search of the house, they were always found sitting on the end of his nose.

Kitty envisaged that, when someone was not reading, they could rest the glasses on a fake nose holder so the location finder would not flash. This was one of the items that never proceeded to manufacture. That's because Duffer, who often helped Kitty think up ideas for inventions and then discouraged them, asked a question. "Kitty, someone always losing their glasses and forgetting they were on their nose would not see the location-finding flashing lights because they would be inactive on their nose."

"Yes," Kitty said, "that is a problem." So her idea to help short-sighted mankind remained just that, an idea. Today chips might be installed in a frame to locate glasses on a cell phone but once again Kitty was perhaps ahead of her time.

Her most successful invention was the Yuletide Kissomatic. This was a festive red frame worn around the head. It had a rod positioned at the top, curved outward like a fishing pole with a piece of fake mistletoe dangling on a string in front of the wearer's face at about lip level. Jolly people wishing to be kissed at Christmas parties could put on the Kissomatic and dangle their lure for passers-by. This became a big novelty seller at stores dedicated to celebrating Christmas all year round.

Kitty bought Benny many treats with the proceeds from the Kissomatic. In the move to Monterey, Benny, of course, was Kitty's and Duffer's biggest worry. But Benny demonstrated once again how flexible kids can be. He fit right into his new school, made friends quickly, and began playing soccer again, although this time Duffer did not coach him. One of the dads had a Mexican accent, so obviously he was a much better choice for coach.

As close as they were, as much a family as they were, Kitty and Duffer did not marry. Kitty didn't believe in it and Duffer thought he was a proven failure at it. Nevertheless, they considered themselves an inseparable couple, so why bother with the bureaucratic details?

At first, one possible reason to marry was Duffer's immigration status. He had a green card but he began to worry about what he saw as rising anti-immigration sentiment in America. So eventually he applied for and received American citizenship and with that another reason to get married disappeared. He was able to hang on to his Australian citizenship and thereafter was the proud owner of a hyphen.

They decided to get a dog as the final proof of their domestic stability. Benny was delighted and named the dog Dropbear in honor of the mythical animal Down Under that his good-as-a-father Duffer had told him about. Dropbears, Duffer said, were notorious for dropping out of trees on hikers passing below.

One day, Duffer told his good-as-a-wife partner, "It's time for me to go home for a visit." Kitty thought this was long overdue and she wanted to come, but between looking after Aunt Maris and Benny, that would have to wait for another time. So Duffer booked his flight to Australia for two months hence.

A week later, his phone rang. Duffer's brother George was calling from Australia. It was 11 a.m. Tuesday back in Brisbane but 6 p.m. Monday in Monterey, and Duffer's urgent questions and shocked tone told Kitty that tomorrow was already delivering bad news to today. Duffer was asking, "When, where? ... Not on the golf course?" Kitty understood even before the last detail was told. His father had died overnight in his sleep.

Chapter 39

Duffer's Belated Homecoming

"To be an expatriate is to be doomed to remember people and things that are gone or changed back home, even the way of speaking about them, while not really understanding this has happened." Duffer in his blog, Monterey, 2014.

Duffer had put off his return to Australia too late, decades too late. He should have gone when Mum died, but he didn't have the money back then and later inertia had done its delaying work. Now he could go and had all the reason to go. Qantas kindly obliged by advancing his booking so that he could leave the next day.

As arranged, Duffer's older brother George picked him up at the airport and it did not take long for him to have an expatriate moment, his old memories shoved aside by the new sights he was seeing.

Brisbane Airport, now Brisbane International Airport, was no longer a few sheds and hangars that as a kid Duffer had pedaled his bike to from Eagle Junction to watch the propeller-driven planes and have a Cottee's Passiona soft drink for 20 cents out of a cooler in the waiting area. It was huge terminals surrounded by big circular roads and the din of screaming jets.

Outside, the weather was as hot and as sticky as ever and the people of Brisbane appeared to have taken the hint and become troglodytes, or at least their cars had.

Before disappearing into an underground freeway, Duffer had a quick glimpse of the Brisbane skyline. *Bloody hell,* he thought, *skyscrapers everywhere, the place has turned into Los Angeles!* He asked his brother whether they could stop at the funeral home before they went to meet the rest of the family.

This request bewildered George.

"Why do you want to go there?" he asked. "Robert, Dad is dead, it's not like you can sit down and have a chat with him. The funeral is tomorrow." Duffer silently noted that his brother still insisted on using his given name.

"Well, you never know, he might be in a coma or maybe just having a bit of a nap," Duffer said. "No harm in checking."

"A nap? A bloody nap?" said his brother.

Duffer knew it sounded ridiculous, but he needed an excuse. They weren't much for viewing dead people in Brisbane before their funerals. Open caskets just weren't the culture. Maybe it was because the city has a sub-tropical climate and, in the summer heat, eggs could easily fry on the pavement, assuming wandering hens were short-sighted and nested there, so perhaps people feared dead bodies might sweat in their caskets, not a good look for the deceased and an unwelcome sight for the living. Maybe they thought that the body of their loved one would smell like a bag of lamb chops left in the back of the truck on a hot day while the driver drank his lunch in the pub.

But having lived in Pittsburgh, Pennsylvania, where the call of the old country was still heeded, Duffer liked the idea of a good viewing, and besides he wanted to see his dad one last time, albeit not as animated as he was when living, particularly on the subject of his youngest son being a useless bludger who couldn't hold down a decent job if he threw a net over it.

Actually, Duffer wasn't a bludger in the usual meaning of the classic Aussie term for a lazy slug. Duffer had become a professor and his public speaking had made him quite famous, but the old man showed no sign of being impressed. Duffer assumed that "useless bludger" might have been his father's actual last words if he had chanced to remember Duffer at that hour.

"OK, Robert, I'll drive you, but I think the undertaker will think you're weird."

No doubt the formal gentleman who met them at the funeral home door did think Duffer was weird but not because of his request to see his dad lying in what passed as state. While most grieving souls in this part of the world thought a closed casket was a relief, a few did ask to spend some moments alone with the body of the departed.

Undertakers see it all in their job, so when a weirdly disheveled character like Duffer came to the door, his shirt open over his beer gut and flapping as much as humidity would allow, looking like the Peanuts cartoon character Pigpen grown to manhood, it seemed perfectly natural that he would want to see his father in the flesh and say a little prayer. Duffer's request was a bit unusual but not really rare.

"Come this way, sir, into the little chapel here. I will wheel your father in on the trolley and open the coffin up so you can pay your respects. No rush, take all the time you need."

"Robert, I'll wait in the car. Give us a shout if he wakes from his nap."

So Duffer sat down and made himself comfortable, as comfortable as a man can be sitting in a chair preparing to stare at the earthly remains of his father. Duffer thought wistfully of his ancestors long ago in Ireland holding a wake, as he understood it, a sort of party, everybody chatting and drinking and eating cake beside the dead person in the corner.

He didn't look straight at his dad immediately. Instead, he closed his eyes and mumbled something like a prayer, if only in the sense that some supernatural transmission had to occur for anyone dead or living to hear it in this empty parlor with its desolate drapes and depressing furniture.

"Hi, Dad, hope you are doing well in the circumstances, wherever you may be. I just wanted to let you know that I thought enough of you to come see you off. And I want to say I am really sorry that you thought I was a useless bugger, a hopeless bastard, a drunk, a wanker, a waster and a bludger. I am not saying I wasn't any of those things at times, I am just sorry I gave you the wrong impression or maybe the right impression but overstated.

"See, Dad, what I have learned in America is that being a useless bugger and all the rest can be monetized. That is the greatness of the States. You can be a hopeless bastard but still have hope if you become a pundit or commentator in the nattering trades and thereby win the respect of lots of people who identify with you. What's more, you can make a fair income doing it.

"It is truly the land of opportunity. I wish you could have seen how I took the many obnoxious attributes you think I had and made myself into a product brand, not that I was ever very comfortable with that. Of course, the marketing part was mostly the doing of my sister, your daughter, Margaret, but she had to have just the right sort of hopeless bastard to work with and there I was.

"So, Dad, I just want you to know that I bear you no grudges. I won't be standing up on Judgment Day and saying, 'He took my cricket bat away because I hit the ball through the window and shattered the glass.' No, I wish you well and pray you are in a better place, with cold beer eternally on tap. By the way, if you see Mum and Uncle Frank, give them my best."

He then choked back a sob, more for Mum and Uncle Frank but his dad was part of it too.

Duffer opened his eyes and saw it then. To understand this moment you have to know that Duffer's dad had a memorably big hooter of a nose, a hooked nose in the impolite description, a Roman nose in the more polite version. Duffer himself had a little stubby nose more typical of people with Irish forebears but somehow his dad's family, the O'Gradys, must have got out a bit more than his mother's side of the family. While nose sizes rarely matter, as the mothers of Jimmy Durante and Charles de Gaulle often told them, this time was the exception.

Duffer had a sideways view of the coffin straight ahead. He did not see his dad in full figure. He only saw his nose rising from the foothills of his face and peeping over the lid of the coffin. "Crikey," Duffer said to himself, "his nose looks like the fin of a shark patrolling the reef." He had a strong urge to alert nearby surfers.

Out in the brilliant sunshine again, absurdity having put grief to flight with his dad managing the incredible feat of looking comically dead, Duffer found his brother with his car running and the air-conditioning roaring.

Then it was on to The Gap. Their father had long ago left the old family home in Eagle Junction after Mum had died and had bought a house in the more prosperous suburb in the forested foothills of Mt. Coot-tha.

"So how is your partner Kitty? I am sorry that she didn't come. I would have loved to have met her," George asked as he drove.

"I am sorry, too. I would have liked to show her the old place and introduce the family, but she has to look after her aunt who is ailing and her son, my son now, Benny who is going to a local school in Monterey. For all the uprooting from Pittsburgh, we are all doing well."

"What about your job at the university?"

"Well, I'll have to wait and see. I am officially on sabbatical but it is very nice on the Monterey Peninsula and maybe it's time to take a break."

Soon they arrived at his dad's new house. "Crikey," he said, "it's bloody big. Is the whole of Brisbane on some sort of architectural steroids now? Why did Dad need a big house like this? There was only him and his golf clubs, which I grant you probably fill several rooms."

"Do you need any golf clubs, Robert?"

"No, thanks, I long ago decided to waste my time in other areas."

"Dad wanted you to have his best set."

"He did?"

"He did. He told me personally. Made a point of it."

"Did he leave a will?"

"There's a will alright. Dad saw the house as a great investment and now we, his offspring, will enjoy the benefit. We'll sell it and share in a tidy sum." Duffer thought to himself: *Great, but I would have settled for a kind word when he was still alive.*

Margaret came out to greet him on the front verandah, the builders' unconvincing take on the classic Queenslander house with wide verandahs, unconvincing because those houses were old and this house was plainly modern and its verandah too perfect to be perfect.

Husband Colin was there too, looking absent-mindedly at the hills while at the same time greeting the prodigal brother of the family. Margaret and Colin were staying in the house with Duffer and would stay on for a few days after the funeral to take care of the loose ends.

That night George got Chinese take-out for them and stayed around to talk a little about things, his career being the biggest thing, but it was a friendly, pleasant evening.

The next day they went to the funeral service at St. Ann's, the Catholic Church in Kalinga. George did the eulogy; Duffer, the great speaker in the family, served only as a pallbearer, but he was content with that. He had made his speech to Dad back at the funeral home and nobody else needed to hear it.

After the service was done, nobody went to the cemetery for the burial except Duffer, who called for a cab to follow the hearse. His father would not have wanted this, "Too bloody depressing," he would have said, but Dad was to be buried next to Mum, and he had never visited her grave to pay his respects.

After that, he got the cab directly to the wake at the Indooroopilly Golf Club, where his dad had always been a member. It was a long way across town, so he arrived late to the eating and drinking. The place was packed, unlike the service which had attracted a sparse gathering of family and friends. *Ah, the power of free drinks and hors d'oeuvres to make anyone suddenly popular,* Duffer thought.

Duffer met relatives he had never met, including George's two boys, graduates of the Brisbane Boys Academy and now studying at the University of Queensland. They had their father's looks and his manner, *poor buggers,* but were polite enough without being much interested in a visiting uncle. He met his dad's friends, whose tongues being loosened by wine and beer, made thoughtless observations: "His youngest son, eh? He never mentioned you at all. I guess George was his favorite. Did you ever play football? No? Oh well."

It went well enough. They couldn't tell him anything he didn't already know. He was at peace with Dad now.

Next day Duffer rented a car and by himself went north up to Noosa and the national park, which used to be his favorite place to surf.

In Brisbane, he found the right highway hole to disappear into to find the exit for the northern suburbs. He found that the Eagle Junction State School had little changed and the girls were still sitting out front waiting for boys to pedal up the hill, slip and bust their balls on the bike bar. His old house on Lewis Street was no longer there; someone had erected two little houses on the same lot. He did see a train go by, an electric train with no steam to put soot on the laundry. *Oh Mum,* he thought, *would that you were still alive at this hour.*

When it was his time to return to America, Margaret decided to accompany him to the airport to help return his rental car so that they could have a nice chat together, then she took a train back to the city to meet Colin for lunch.

"Stay in touch," she said as they parted. "Don't you go and die on me either!"

"I wouldn't think of it," he said. "And if they say I'm dead, don't believe it. Visit the funeral home to make sure I am not having a nap or something."

Chapter 40

There Comes a Time …

"What is wisdom? What is good or evil? They are hard to define but easy to recognize. As U.S. Supreme Court Justice Potter Stewart once said in trying to come up with a definition of pornography, 'I know it when I see it,' and, no, I don't have any examples with me today to illustrate the point." Duffer speaking at the Pink Otter Cocktail Lounge, Monterey, 2015.

To his surprise, Duffer returned to America feeling differently about his life. He didn't think that going back to Australia would change anything. He thought he was just reacquainting himself with a country he knew well and still loved. But now he knew his home was in the north, not the nostalgic lost land of his imagination in the south. Kitty and Benny met him at the Monterey Airport, and after all the hugs and kisses had made him realize that he was missed more than he had ever imagined, he delivered the blow-by-blow account of his trip.

When Benny finally went to bed that night, wearing a Queensland rugby jersey that Duffer bought for him, in the shade of maroon that colored his boyhood dreams, he and Kitty retreated from the patio into the living room because the old Monterey fog was on its rounds, bringing a creeping chill street by street. "So, Duff, what did you learn?

Beyond that there are new buildings and highways there after forty years."

He pondered that for a few moments, slowly taking a sip of the red wine she had poured just a minute or two ago.

"I learned … that I don't speak the bloody language anymore."

"You don't? Has English gone out of favor Down Under?"

"I think it's always been out of favor. I mean that the expressions that we invented to make English more interesting, more authentically Aussie, they don't say them like they did anymore, or not much, and the younger blokes anyway have expressions I don't understand. They still call their mates 'mates,' of course, but they don't call them their Chinas, in rhyming slang, China plates, mates, and they never call them cobbers, as they used to call their friends in the really olden days. I suppose there are ancient fellas using the old expressions but I didn't talk to many of them.

"The younger generation has its own lingo. George's boys, Tyler and Kyle, names, by the way, that not a single kid at the Eagle Junction State School had back in the day, were perfect examples.

"At one point, one of them said something that sounded like it was total BS, so I said, as you do, or as you did, 'Don't come the raw prawn with me,' and the kid looked at me as if I were a drongo.

"He understood, I think, but then he started to smirk, and I thought he was about to use his cell phone to call the museum and tell them one of the figures from the Neanderthal exhibit had come to life and was causing a problem."

" 'Strewth,' " I said, because I realized then that I was a stranger in a strange land speaking an antique tongue."

"OK, Duff," Kitty said, "slang changes and goes out of fashion. What about sympathy for the underdog? You always told me that was a traditional Australian value."

"I reckon the underdog is well and truly rooted by the over-dog these days. Where would an underdog live anymore? In the big cities, especially Sydney, but Brisbane too, even a shed can cost an arm and a leg, and not even a nice-looking shed."

"Well," Kitty said, "I suppose the meat pies you love are all gone, the surf is always flat, the temperature of the water in summer is cold now, not lovely and hot, nobody plays or watches cricket, the parrots are not in the trees and the kookaburras forget to laugh and Vegemite is considered as horrible as Americans think it is."

"You make a sensible point, Kitty, as usual. Of course, it's the same old story. A kiss is just a kiss, a sigh is just a sigh, no less in Australia than in Casablanca."

"Yes," she said, "and it sounds like you had a wonderful time even in the absence of raw prawns coming your way. It also sounds like there is plenty of grist now for your philosophical mill. Your fans anxiously await you."

"They may have to wait a bit longer."

"How come?"

"Ah, here is the biggest change in my thinking since the trip. All of a sudden, I don't feel the need to speak in public anymore. I don't want to blog anymore. I think I have said everything I needed to say."

"What?"

"Yes, I have lost the desire. I don't know exactly why. As much as I like doing it, maybe I did it to prove my father wrong. Now Dad is gone, I reckon there's no sport left in it. And, let's face it, while people have enjoyed my little gigs, what good have they done? Judging by the growing idiocy epidemic, nothing I have said has made any difference."

"No finale at the Pink Otter Cocktail Lounge?"

"No, I think I am done. I don't know what I'll do now but it's not that. My only worry is this: Will you still love me?"

"Of course, I will always love you, and as long as you tell me your thoughts, I will be your audience."

"To our private future!" Duffer raised his glass and she raised hers and with the clink of glass all second thoughts were banished, except one.

"It's sad, though," she said, "you were so good, so funny and wise. But the timing is good."

"How so?"

"There's something I haven't told you. I didn't want to tell you immediately."

"What is it?"

"Well, when you were away a man came to the Pink Otter Lounge, the night of my performance. He was creepy. He wore a dark hoodie. Middle-aged guy with an accent. I thought it was an Aussie accent at first but then I thought it was more English. He asked where you were. I said in Australia. He asked when you were coming back. I said you would come back when you come back. Not soon, I said.

"He muttered and walked off. I guess he didn't believe me because he turned up at this address two nights ago."

"What? The bastard. What does he want?"

"Not sure. I asked him but he never said. I told him to bugger off and if he didn't I'd set our dog on him."

"Kitty, our dog is a labradoodle."

"He didn't know that. He didn't see Dropbear. Besides, being savaged by a labradoodle can be quite upsetting to a man's self-esteem."

"Are you OK, Kitty?"

"I am fine, but the worst of it was that Benny opened the door when he knocked and he scared the daylights out of the kid."

"He seems OK now."

"Yes, he is feeling safe because you're back home. I do too. Who is this guy anyway? Do you know him?"

"I don't think so, or at least I can't remember meeting him. But clearly something I have said or done has pissed him off. This may be the same guy that stalked me back in England for a while. He even tried to take a shot at me once with an antique flintlock pistol."

"Oh great, I'd forgotten that. How could I forget that? Maybe because it was too stupid to be taken seriously. Now I don't feel so fine. I think we should call the police."

"Not to worry," Duffer said. "A man borrowing a highwayman's pistol and botching the job is not James Bond. The guy is clearly an idiot."

"An idiot who comes to America with a grievance can easily get a better gun over here," she said. "Unfortunately, Americans are very helpful in that regard."

"I think he just wants to scare me into silence. What he doesn't know is that being silent is what I now plan to be anyway. I will go onto my blog one last time and say my farewells. My guess is that our hooded visitor is one of those who regularly seethes on the blog. He will probably go home when he reads that."

"There's people who really hate you on your blog?" Kitty knew he had his critics but she always thought they were mostly harmless idiots who needed a hobby now that stamp collecting was in decline.

"Yes, in the modern world, that's what some people do for entertainment. There's about three or four of them who viciously tear into me at every opportunity. They are all anonymous commentators, of course. I think this guy might be someone who calls himself Muscle Man, which, by the way, makes me think he is a little insecure."

"Well, Duff, telling everybody the blog is closing and you are giving up philosophizing is a good first step, but for the sake of Benny's safety and peace of mind, not to mention ours, I think we need to do something else. And I have a plan that just occurred to me."

Chapter 41

Duffer Becomes a Farmer

"Everybody should love somebody, and not just themselves."
Duffer speaking at the Pink Otter Cocktail Lounge,
Monterey, 2015.

The gist of Kitty's plan was suggested by Aunt Maris. It turned out that Maris's mother had bequeathed her the family farm where she had grown up in Sonoma County north of San Francisco. Kitty was told about this the day before but she had forgotten to tell Duffer in the excitement of his return.

"I have always liked Monterey," Maris had said, "but I have dreamed of going back to our farm on Poppy Hill. I didn't think there was any way that could happen but my mother's old friends, the people who have been renting it for years, called to say they can't manage the work anymore and are planning to move into a retirement home."

"Do you think you can take me up there to live for a little while? I know I am not going to last much longer and I want to begin my last journey surrounded by my happy childhood memories. The area is even more beautiful than Monterey. I know your partner husband is between jobs but it would be an ideal place for him to think his big thoughts. And didn't you say he once worked on a farm in Australia?"

"Yes," Kitty said, wondering to herself if Duff really knew one end of a cow from the other. "But what about your medical treatments?"

"As rustic and quiet as it is, there is a town with a hospital not very far away. Besides, there's not much they can do for me at this stage anyway. I'll be fine up there."

Kitty thought that it would be hard to refuse any request made by Aunt Maris in her present dire situation. At the same time, she shrank at the idea that they would have to move again, especially for the sake of Benny who had made a good adjustment to his new school in Monterey.

But that was before Muscle Man, if that was his name, had arrived menacingly on their doorstep. As Duffer said when she explained Aunt Maris's last wish, "He'll never find us up there and if he does, he'll stand out like a ham sandwich at a vegetarian picnic."

"But what will you do, Duff? How will you keep occupied?"

"I'll do the farm work," he said. "I will become my old Uncle Frank. I will get physically fit and, as I toss the hay and manure into the air, I will think my thoughts. And in the evening, I will sit out on the porch and watch the last sunbeams reflect off a tall bottle of beer."

So it was decided. Duffer's announcement that he was quitting the philosophy business actually made the local newspaper, the Monterey Herald, as one of the reporters was a regular at the Pink Otter Cocktail Lounge and was an admirer of his performances. She interviewed him in the bar one afternoon before the crowd arrived.

"Are your critics on the internet forcing you to quit?"

"No, I wouldn't give them the satisfaction. I just got tired and decided that I had said what I wanted to say."

"So what do you think of them?"

"Most of the people who follow me are great, such literary taste. But then there are the cranky ones. They are only a few but they come in various flavors of vile. Everyone who puts themselves out there these days attracts the venomously insecure, the moronically immature, the incorrigibly incoherent, and the verbally incontinent. I view them all as fleas and, being an old dog, I have attracted my share. Most of them are not worth the trouble of scratching."

The young reporter struggled to take down this long gem of a quote, the sort reporters dream of. "Did you say 'verbally incontinent'?" she asked at last, hoping that all the adjectives had not busted her tape recorder so she could check her notes later.

"I certainly did," said Duffer. *Take that, Muscle Man!*

"What do you think you achieved?" the reporter asked. "I mean, all this talk of a lost ancestral language. What was the point?"

"I remember once as a kid. I was really little, maybe two, and I didn't know any words except Mum, Dad, dog, and cat. We took the train from Eagle Junction into the city and at the end of the trip I jumped up and ran toward the wrong side of the carriage and Mum and Dad opened the door on the other side to get out onto the platform, and suddenly I thought I was going to be left on the train and lost forever, and all this I knew without knowing a single word to describe my terror. It was all pure consciousness.

"That is the forgotten language and that is what I think we carry on generation unto generation, a communication beyond words, the eternal consciousness through the ages. That is the nature of immortality to me. I don't know whether I am right or wrong. The old philosophers had some wacky theories themselves, but I know that the quest to understand the greater purpose of our lives inclines us to appreciate humanity and to love and be loved."

"Crikey," Duffer said to the reporter. "You got me talking. Where was I? You asked whether I achieved anything? I don't know. That's another of life's mysteries to be piled on top of all the rest."

He paused for a moment and added wistfully, "I had a few laughs along the way, though."

Kitty and Duffer, with Benny in tow, lost no time in leaving town and they did not tell the world. People knew only that Duffer's public speaking days were at an end. Nobody knew where they were going except their good friend, Joanna Bishop, the owner of the Pink Otter Cocktail Lounge. "Can't I tell Margaret I am moving? Or Wombat or Foley?" Duffer asked.

"No," said Kitty. "You can send Margaret, Wombat, and Foley Christmas cards without an address. You can tell them all about it later after we have settled, maybe a year down the road."

They left like the Anzac troops at Gallipoli in World War I, undetected, in the middle of the night, without a word, without a casualty.

Once they arrived at Poppy Hill, they kept a low profile. As they settled in, they found little need to go into town much, except for shopping and Aunt Maris's medical visits. The farm work consumed Duffer's waking hours. They had cows, sheep, and chickens and after school Benny would help Duffer with the chores. Duffer could not help himself and always called the chickens chooks, as they did in Australia, and he taught Benny to call them chooks too.

Kitty herself did her puzzles and invented things for which the world was not prepared. Her latest was an egg beater that played a musical tune when you beat it, and that would have been a great novelty if only people still used hand-held beaters and not electric ones.

Kitty felt a great contentment in the little farm on Poppy Hill. Aunt Maris was happy too and, just as she predicted, she was peacefully taken away in her dreams about two months after they arrived. After a quiet service in a church, sparsely attended because they still hardly knew anyone, they came back to the farm and spread Aunt Maris's ashes around the rose garden at the back of the barn. Then they raised a glass of Sonoma Chardonnay to her memory.

Five months later there was another death, the last of this story, but this time they did not know the deceased who nevertheless did them a favor by dying in a helpful manner. His name happened, coincidentally, to be Robert O'Grady, which, of course, was Duffer's name, even if the full name was rarely spoken of except by his brother George.

Details of his life and death were sketchy. He seemed to have no family. Only this was known: this Robert O'Grady, not the live Duffer, was visiting Sonoma County from Salinas, of all places, just fifteen miles up the highway from Monterey, and he was said to be a retired history professor. He was also sixty years old, roughly the same age as Duffer.

He was fishing on the rocky shore of the ocean when a big wave came along when he wasn't looking, or when he was looking with just enough time perhaps to utter his unfortunate last words, "Oh shit!" But that is conjecture.

The one certain fact concerning this other O'Grady was that he was swept away and was missing, presumed dead. The local weekly paper reported his disappearance in a brief story on the front page, and there Kitty spotted it as she waited in line to pay at the grocery store, "Prof. Swept Away in Seaside Tragedy."

Kitty added the free paper to her groceries bag and went back to tell Duffer the news. "Duff," she said, "you are not dead, are you?"

"Not that I know," he said.

"And you haven't been fishing?"

"I like to wet the worm as much as the next person, but no, not lately."

"Well, look at this."

Duffer took the paper and read the brief story, wondering whether this was tragedy or more comedy in action, although he couldn't imagine anybody who would laugh except the local fish.

"Another O'Grady bites the dust, or the water, in this case. I am not sure we are related, but 'say not for whom the bell tolls,' eh? This is a bit close to home. If any of my fans read this, they might suppose it was me."

"Yes," she said.

A week later she went to the grocery store again and picked up the latest edition of the paper. She quickly turned the pages to see if it included any follow-up story. Had Mr. O'Grady's body been discovered after a search? Were there any details about his family or the funeral arrangements?

Nothing. The news had moved on. The front story was about teen vandals in pick-up trucks smashing rural mailboxes with baseball bats, a story so traditional in some parts of rural America that Kitty wondered why it was news. *Maybe next week they will have an exposé on cow tipping.*

That evening, as she and Duffer drank their chardonnay on the patio with the sun setting over the hills, she proposed a new plan.

"Duffer," she said, "do you think we have seen the last of Muscle Man?"

She tried very hard not to laugh while saying the pathetic name.

"Who knows? It wouldn't take Sherlock Holmes very long to find us, and I don't think that bloke is Sherlock, nor even his arch enemy Moriarty. I think Muscle Man is just another wanker with a mad obsession."

"Which means that he might possibly hire a real detective to find you, if his sleuthing was not up to his wanking."

"I suppose. Are you still worried?"

"Not particularly. But I am worried that Benny might be worried. He seems to have settled in well here but he has had a few nightmares, as you know, and it's not clear why."

"So what to do? We can't move again."

"Well, I was struck by what you said about that other O'Grady man, the fisherman who was knocked off the rocks, never to be seen again. You said, 'If any of my fans see this, they might think it was me.' I think you were right about that and, moreover, I think any fanatic fool who saw that might also be confused."

"What are you saying, Kitty?"

"I am saying that you are as good as publicly dead anyway, no blog, no gigs, so we might as well make it appear official. With the evidence of the newspaper story in hand, we can put it about that you had gone fishing and the final score was Duffer zero, fish ten thousand. Because nobody is available to appear for the viewing, we have the perfect excuse to have a Celebration of Life, without the presence of the deceased."

"Isn't that dishonest?"

"Nah, it's for a good cause and I think we should consider it as performance art. It will be the final proof that comedy and tragedy are playing the same game and the joke is on humanity."

"Where would this event be held?"

"The Pink Otter Cocktail Lounge in Monterey, of course. Our friend Joanna will be the Mistress of Ceremonies. I will wear black again for the one day. While I have enjoyed wearing bright-colored dresses out here in California, I still have quite a few widow outfits to choose from."

"Who will know that it's not real?"

"Nobody. Well, Joanna will have to know, but I wouldn't even tell Benny what's going on. We will leave him with a babysitter."

Duffer thought about this. "We should wait maybe two months and do an internet search to make sure an obit doesn't appear in the Salinas or Monterey papers or anywhere else with details contradicting our story."

Kitty knitted her brow as one last anxious thought came to mind. "What if Muscle Man attends the Celebration of Life?"

"All the better, I reckon," Duffer said. "But let's make it a cash bar. I don't want that bastard raising a free drink to my non-health."

Chapter 42

The Last Insights

"Time does not flow evenly. When I was a kid back in Eagle Junction, the hot sultry days in school seemed a sort of purgatory, with time almost at a standstill. Now in the late afternoon of my life, I find that the river of time has sped up. I had expected a gentle, meandering progression along the lazy current of hours, with a nice nap, a read of the paper, a chat with mates, lunch, another nap ... No, instead it's whoosh, here we go over the waterfall." Duffer's last gig at the Pink Otter Cocktail Lounge, Monterey, 2015.

As time passed on the farm at Poppy Hill, Duffer forgot that he was supposed to be dead. While he made no public appearances and his blog and his website were discontinued, he did not do much to hide his identity. He hid in plain sight, as the saying goes, although most of the time he was out of sight working on the farm.

More and more, the shadow of the sinister man in the hoodie no longer darkened anybody's consciousness. He and Kitty figured that he had bought the ruse and had gone away to detest someone else, because a hater who has no one to hate might have to hate himself, and that would never do.

Once a week, Duffer went into town to do whatever business needed to be done. He wore no disguise. He appeared more or less as he always did, except he was a bit older and grayer and his signature beer belly was now flattened by farm work.

He made one concession to the stealthy life: If he needed to give his name to anyone, he used his real first name, Robert, although he felt he had to abbreviate it or else give his brother George a moral victory. So to the world, he was now Bob. He slightly amended his family name too. The O' was dropped. As he said to Kitty: "If the Opossums can do it, so can I." Nothing changed officially, his driver's license still read O'Grady, but these slight changes were enough to make him seem like a new man free of his past.

Which is why he should have reacted with more surprise when a man in a hoodie called out to him as he carried a case of beer out of the grog shop one Saturday afternoon. He did not see the man at first, he was behind him as he came out of the building, and paranoia had retreated sufficiently that someone calling out his name seemed as natural as it was once before.

Then, out of the corner of his eye, he saw the man in the hoodie and his mind instantly sounded the alarm. *Bloody hell, this bloke is going to shoot me and I'm going to drop the beer.*

Then, just as quick, he got a proper look at the guy and the fear of a double tragedy in the making was instantly gone.

"Well, hello, Wombat, what are you doing here?"

"Looking for you, of course. We heard you were dead."

"Dead, me? I have always tried to avoid it. I hear there's no beer in heaven and the beer in hell is warm."

"Mate, this is good news. Have you said hello to Foley?"

Duffer's brain, taken by surprise once, was now overwhelmed by the sight of "Cowboy" Foley ambling toward him. He had been waiting in the car.

"What? Where did you guys come from?"

"I came from Arizona," said Cowboy Foley, who now gave Duffer a sincere but awkward hug. "Your mate Wombat called me from Australia to ask if you were still in the land of the living. I didn't know anything about it. He was coming over to America to look for you, so I volunteered to come back to California to help him in the search."

"How did you know where I live?"

"We didn't really," Wombat said. "After we convinced the lady at the Pink Otter Lounge in Monterey that we were mates, she told us that you were living around here but she had no street address, just a postbox. That's why we were hanging around outside the booze shop. We figured you would have to turn up here sooner or later on a Saturday afternoon."

"Follow my truck, boys. We are going back to Poppy Hill."

Although as gracious as ever, Kitty was taken aback by the arrival of Duffer's unexpected friends, their first visitors at Poppy Hill, and her surprise had a tinge of fear. How the heck had they found them? If they could find them, who else could?

But when they all sat down that evening on the patio under the ancient oak tree to have a few pre-dinner drinks, beer for the boys, Chardonnay for the presiding woman, anxiety faded into the blue of the distant river.

"We met in San Francisco and drove down to Monterey and found the Pink Otter Lounge, where the paper said your Celebration of Life was held," Wombat said.

"Hold on. What paper?"

"The Courier-Mail in Brisbane. They carried an obit on you that your brother George saw and he contacted your sister Margaret and she even contacted the Long-Suffering Sheila. They were all very concerned, except Sheila, I think, and anyway she asked me if I knew anything about it, and I didn't, so I called Foley here, and he didn't know anything either, so at Margaret's urging we decided to get to the bottom of it."

Just then, Benny came around from the back of the barn: "Dad, I fed the chooks!"

"Good boy, Benny, you can go and watch TV now until dinner if you like." Benny ran back to the house, which was good, because Duffer didn't want Benny to hear this conversation about his recent death.

"Benny speaks Australian?"

"Yes, his instruction is coming along quite well."

Foley, who didn't speak Australian and didn't know a chook from a bald eagle, took up the interrogation:

"What the heck is going on?" Foley said. "Did you finally rob a bank and have to go into hiding?"

So he told them about the hooded guy who had come to his house in Monterey while he was away and made it clear to Kitty that he wasn't from the Welcome Wagon.

"I remember that the guy who took a potshot at you in London with a flintlock pistol wore a hood too," Wombat said.

"Yeah, I remember once in Pittsburgh you saw some sinister character at the Kat Kit Club checking you out," Foley said. "Do you think some thug is stalking you across continents?"

"I don't know," Duffer said. "And I don't know why anyone would bother either. What have I ever done except make a few comments about life and crack a few jokes?"

"There's none so bitter and humiliated as the man who doesn't get the joke," Wombat said.

"That sounds familiar. Who said that?" Duffer said.

"You did, mate, in one of your speeches."

"Oh!"

"So," Foley said, "you came up with quite an elaborate plan to get away from this bastard."

"No, we just buggered off and buggering off is very simple. We didn't have to leave, but Kitty and Benny were a bit nervous and Kitty's aunt had just inherited this farm. I felt my job as a philosopher of the people was done and it was easy for me to pretend I had bought the farm. For everything there is a season, a time to laugh, a time to weep and a time to leave. So we left."

"It wasn't as simple as that," Foley said, "you had a Celebration of Life and you didn't even ask your mates to celebrate. I mean, I pick up my phone one day and Wombat announces you died without my permission."

"Sorry, but that was Kitty's brilliant idea, it was performance art, mate, and it's not good form to be offended, it makes you look like a Philistine. Besides, I was supposed to be dead and dead people don't go around asking their loud-mouthed friends to come over for a party."

"Did Kitty say it went well?"

"Kitty did say it went well. I thought so too."

"What? You were there?" Wombat interjected.

"Of course, I was there. I wouldn't miss my own funeral for anything."

"Didn't anybody recognize you?"

"Of course not, I was in disguise. I was dressed as an older woman. I had a brown frock, a big handbag and a gray wig with a little hat with mosquito netting on it. Besides, the last time anybody saw me I was a fat guy. I modeled my outfit after Gladys, that lady who used to come to my gigs at the Mermaid and Merkin. Kitty told me that nobody looks at older women and she was absolutely right."

"Did anybody talk to you?" Foley said.

"Yes, not only that, but I talked to them. I got up and made a few remarks about what a good bloke Duffer O'Grady was."

"Crikey," said Wombat, "but what about your voice?"

"I did a bit of a falsetto, which wasn't hard as I used to sing Bee Gees songs a lot when I was younger, and if anybody thought I was a man dressed as a woman, well, mate, this is California. Where's the news?"

"Was anybody in a hoodie there?" Foley asked.

"Yes, a fella named Fred. I know him quite well. He worked as a mechanic down the road. A nice bloke. Just because a fella wears a hoodie does not make him sinister. Some people just like keeping their ears warm."

"Kitty said you are now calling yourself Robert Grady, is that right?"

"Actually Bob, but for a while some people called me a duffer out at the golf club."

This was the most shocking revelation of all.

"You have taken up golf?" Wombat and Foley said this in amazed unison.

"Yes, Dad used to play, and because he did, I wasn't interested. Well, after he went to the Great Green in the Sky, he bequeathed me his clubs and they were darn good ones too, so good I figured I'd take them back here and sell them. But one day I gave it a burl and it turned out I had a talent for the game. I am better with the hitting than the scoring. It makes a nice break from the farm."

Duffer left out one detail. When he finally decided he was going to play golf and picked up his dad's prized clubs, he found a handwritten note in one of the compartments. It read:

Dear Robert,

If you are reading this, I have finally handed in my scorecard. A lot of bogeys on it, I reckon. When you get on a bit in years, you start looking back and making an audit of your life, what you got right and wrong. So I reckon I owe you an apology. As you didn't fit my idea of an ideal son, I was tough on you when I shouldn't have been. You did very well in your own way and I wish I had shown you the love you deserved when you needed it. Please forgive me because I don't want to be sent to the other eternal course, the one with the impossibly hot sand traps.

Love to you, Duffer.
Dad xxxx

PS. Keep your head down when you swing.

But this night held another huge surprise. Wombat suddenly said: "I almost forgot," and he took a crumpled letter from his coat pocket. "The lady who owned the bar in Monterey gave me this for you. She received it a day or two after you left but forgot to send it on, thinking it was just another fan letter. Hey, it may be the last fan letter you ever get."

Duffer took the letter and saw it had British stamps. A spidery hand had written the address: Duffer O'Grady c/- Pink Otter Lounge, Monterey, California, USA.

More curious now, he opened the envelope. It was from Gladys, his old admirer, the old gal who Sheila had once mistakenly thought was having an affair with him. He read it slowly as the writing was hard to decipher. It seemed that she did not know he was supposed to be dead.

Dear Duffer,

My Dear Boy, I am so sorry to have to contact you like this but my son Harry said he had been over to America. I asked him if he had tried to contact you and by the look on his face, I knew he had. Well, I got it all out of him and I am really ashamed. It's enough he tried to shoot you back at the Dying Swan in Richmond but I thought when I hit him over the head with my handbag, he would have learned his lesson. No such luck. I'm afraid he takes after my late husband, Bert, mad as a hatter Bert was. Apparently, he thinks I love you and you were leading me on with your words and of course I do love you but you were always the proper gentleman.

Anyways, I set Harry straight and he will never bother you again, because I said to him, No more Sunday dinners for you, sonny, if you bother Mr. Duffer again, and you can forget getting your laundry done. Hope this finds you well.

Love always, but not that sort,
Your forever friend Gladys.

Shocked and astounded are too mild to serve as a description of Duffer at that moment as he slowly put down Gladys' letter and looked off into the far hills.

Crikey, he said to himself, *Mr. Muscles was not to blame for the stalking! Gladys once had a husband and she has a son! And the son had the same misunderstanding of my relationship with Gladys as Sheila did! This is too crazy!*

For the first time in months, Duffer felt the stirring of an urge to tell drinkers in pubs how truly random and strange life was. But he put this temptation aside and told Wombat and Cowboy instead.

Duffer and his mates talked into the night and then resolved to meet again in the future, in whatever place might be most convenient. As soon as they left, all sworn to continued secrecy, Duffer called his sister Margaret, as he had promised his friends, and apologized for seeming to be so dead. "I did send you a Christmas card," he said in his defense. "And the last thing I said to you when we parted in Brisbane, if you remember, was to verify that there's a body before assuming that I am deceased."

Margaret was mad and glad to receive this belated call and she in turn called George, who was equally amazed to hear his brother was alive, playing golf and now using the name Robert, Bob, to his new friends.

"I think I'll start calling him Duffer," George said.

"No, you won't," Margaret said sternly, "because we need to keep up the fiction that he is dead." The fiction remained and no hooded man came by who wasn't just keeping his ears warm.

In the years to follow, Benny grew up to be a good man, his talented mother and her philosophizing mate setting a kind and hard-working example. Duffer, reborn as Bob in his well-deserved obscurity, formed his last insights concerning what is obvious: There's more to this life than our surface impressions, fame is nothing and family and friends are everything, just as the lost language has been telling us in its wisdom. But whether life is a tragedy or a comedy remains one of life's mysteries, although it makes sense to laugh as much as you can while you can.

<h1 style="text-align:center">Acknowledgments</h1>

This novel could not have been completed without the encouragement and help of a small group of family and friends in Australia and the United States. Their assistance ranged from literary suggestions and proofreading to computer know-how.

My Australian helpers were old mates Gary Fites, the first reader of the manuscript, and Doug Kelly, my sister-in-law Caroline Henry, army mates Don Campbell and John Fairley, as well as Toni Smart and Rosyln Smart. In the United States, I am indebted to Marcy Alancraig, Linda Bell, Collin MacLeod, Rich MacLeod, John Kurzava, Alice Knapp, Gail and Mike English, my son Jim Henry, and Helen Mackinlay, an expatriate New Zealander. Thank you all.

My greatest gratitude goes to my wife Priscilla Henry, a.k.a. the Lovely Priscilla. Having a writer working on a long project is like having a grumpy bear resident in the house. Sorry, thank you, and love always.

www.ingramcontent.com/pod-product-compliance
Lightning Source LLC
Chambersburg PA
CBHW061334160726
47995CB00001B/25